American Jewish Loss
after the Holocaust

American Jewish Loss
after the Holocaust

Laura Levitt

NEW YORK UNIVERSITY PRESS
New York and London

NEW YORK UNIVERSITY PRESS
New York and London
www.nyupress.org

Frontispiece: Portrait Mary Chirlin Levitt. From the Levitt
family collection.

Library of Congress Cataloging-in-Publication Data
Levitt, Laura, 1960–
American Jewish loss after the Holocaust / Laura Levitt.
p. cm.
Includes bibliographical references and index.
ISBN-13: 978-0-8147-5217-3 (cloth : alk. paper)
ISBN-10: 0-8147-5217-9 (cloth : alk. paper)
1. Jews—United States—Identity. 2. Holocaust, Jewish
(1939–1945)—Influence. 3. Holocaust, Jewish (1939–1945),
and the arts. 4. Levitt, Laura, 1960– I. Title.
E184.36.E84L48 2007
305.892'4073—dc22   2007023052

New York University Press books are printed on acid-free paper,
and their binding materials are chosen for strength and durability.

Manufactured in the United States of America
10 9 8 7 6 5 4 3 2 1

For my father and his two mothers
Irving Levitt, Lena Levitt, and Mary Levitt

Contents

Acknowledgments

First and foremost, I thank my parents, Irving and Phyllis Levitt, for everything, especially my father for what cannot be articulated. I am grateful to my cousin Phil Pearl, who I regret is not here to read this book, but to Jeanette and Ira Rosen, who are; I am grateful to them for bringing me into their lives. I am indebted to Frances Levitt for her love, her honesty, and her willingness to open up to a distant relative and bring our various families' pasts closer, and to Muriel Wilson and Phil Kartzman for always believing in me and, early on, for taking my father and me back to the graves of several relatives, especially those of my grandmothers. I also appreciate their taking us to the various homes that Muriel and my father shared as they were growing up. I am grateful to Paula Mishkin for being there with both my father and his siblings and for sharing the letters my father sent her during the war. And I am grateful to my brother, David, for understanding my obsession. I thank David Watt for listening over and over again to the various arguments that are this book, for being there for me throughout this entire process, and for making a real space for writing in our lives. And, finally, I thank my family in Alabama, especially Elise Watt, who brought me into this extended family and made the South a place of grace.

I am profoundly grateful to Catherine Staples for reading everything many times over with insight and inspiration, and for her extraordinary editorial eye. I am indebted to Ruth Ost for her brilliant interventions at just the right moments, and to Susan Shapiro for believing in the project and, always, for believing in me. I am also greatly indebted to Tania Oldenhage, Michelle Friedman, Marian Ronan, Deborah Glanzberg-Krainin, Liora Gubkin, and Amy Weigand—the girls—the most wonderful once and current graduate students, now colleagues, for their brilliance and their ongoing engagement with this project. Many of these women were there since the beginning. I thank Cecelia Cancellaro for believing in this book, for her edits and suggestions, and especially for helping me find a home for it. And I thank Deborah Lamb for teaching me more than I can say. This book would not have been possible without her.

I am grateful to Abraham Ravett for his ongoing engagement with and support of my work but mostly for the brilliance of his vision and the power of his films. I am also indebted to the artistic, poetic, and scholarly works of Irena Klepfisz, Marianne Hirsch, Leo Spitzer, Adrienne Rich, Art Spiegelman, Michelle Citron, Larry Sultan, Mary Gordon, Susan Suleiman, Joanne Leonard, Lori Novak, James Young, Barbara Kirshenblatt-Gimblett, Muriel Hasbun, Helène Aylon, Michael André Bernstein, and Roger Simon.

I thank Janet Jakobsen for inviting me to edit "Changing Focus: Family Photography and American Jewish Identity," a special issue of *The Scholar & The Feminist Online,* www.barnard.edu/sfonline, and the amazing staff at the Center for Research on Women at Barnard for making that multimedia project fly. I am grateful to Larry Silberstein and Shelley Hornstein for teaching me so much as we worked together on *Impossible Images: Contemporary Art after the Holocaust* (2001); this book carries the traces of that collaboration. I am also grateful to Larry Silberstein, Zak Braiterman, Larry Roth, George Diamond, and Josh Perlman for their critical reading of earlier versions of the preface and introduction to this book at Lehigh during the summer of 2006 at the Judaism Postmodernism seminar. Their insights were crucial in helping me rewrite these opening chapters. I also want to thank the following readers who offered important and critical insights into the manuscript as a whole: James Young, Oren Stier, and David Shneer. One could not wish for more generous and insightful readers. At NYU, I am extremely grateful to my editor, Jennifer Hammer.

At Williams College I am grateful to my dear friend Olga Shevchenko for discussing many parts of this project with me on our daily dog walks. I am also grateful to Carol Ockman, Wayne Meeks, Bill Darrow, Richard Fox, Jude Fox, Dara Goldstein, and Maria Stehle; Rebecca Ohm, librarian extraordinaire; media folks Phil Remillard and Sharron Macklin; my students, especially Meg Bossong and Emily Gorin, who all made my time at Williams amazingly productive.

At my home institution, Temple University, I am grateful to my extraordinary colleague and chair, Rebecca Alpert; no one could ask for a better colleague and friend. I am also grateful to my various deans in the College of Liberal Arts: Dean Susan Herbst and Acting Deans Morris Vogel, Phil Alperson, and Carolyn Adams, as well as the various administrators and staff members in the college who helped me complete this book while working on many other things: Tom Hecker, Heidi Grunwald, and Kim Riley; Nadia Kravchencho, administrator for Jewish Studies; and Linda Jenkins in the Department of Religion. I am grateful to the Study Leave Committee of the College of Liberal Arts for granting me a study leave during the fall of 2005, and to the Provost's Office for granting me a leave without pay to go to Williams College during the spring of 2005. I am indebted to Deborah Glanzberg-Krainin for running Jewish Studies while I was away; there are few graduate students as talented and gracious. I am grateful to many of my wonderful Temple students over the years, including Erin Schmidt, Inbar Gilboa, April Rosenblum, Terra Steele, and Marisa Coyne. I am especially grateful to Inbar for teaching me most of what I know about images, and about the pleasures of technology. I look forward to seeing her name up in lights.

I am grateful to some extraordinary friends and colleagues who have always supported my work, especially Miriam Peskowitz, Susan Shapiro, Janet Jakobsen, Ann Pellegrini, Ruth Ost, Larry Silberstein, Shelley Hornstein, Lori Lefkovitz, Andrea Lieber, Rachel Havrelock, Rebecca Alpert, Rachel DuPlessis, Christina Crosby, Matthew Krauss, Aaron Taub, Tim Spears, Elizabeth Castelli, Rob Baird, Carol Zemel, Patricia Melzer, the Creoles—Tracy Fessenden, Liza McAlister, Jennifer Rycenga, Deborah Dash Moore, Ava Chamberlain, Kate Joyce, and the always inspiring Leonard Primiano; also my new colleagues at Temple —Beth Bailey, Kathy Biddick, and Hana Iverson. I am inspired by the example of their work. I am grateful to the Photo Archive at the United States Holocaust Memorial Museum (USHMM) in Washington, D.C., and especially to Teresa Pollin for sharing her encyclopedic knowledge of Holocaust images. I also thank the USHMM for granting me permission to reproduce images from the Tower of Faces and the Rosalind L. Fund for Family Photography for helping cover the cost of publishing many of the images in this book.

I want to thank the places that housed me while I wrote: Infusions Coffee Shop in Mount Airy, Philadelphia, and Tunnel City Coffee in Williamstown; and, for inspiration, Moses and Walden and all of our pals at the dog park, especially Tim Sedmak, who just got it.

I am grateful to the various audiences that heard and read pieces of what has become this book and those who invited me. These presentations included: "Ordinary Jews, Unraveling and/or Another Way In," at the Judaism Postmodernism Conference, Lehigh University, Bethlehem, Pennsylvania, May 2006; "Telling Stories Otherwise (or Revisiting My Father's Visual Archive)," Distinguished Lecture, The Center for Religion and Media, New York University, New York, March 2006; Guest Lecture, "Keeper of Accounts, Mary, Irena and Me," Performance Studies; "Getting Schooled: Performance, Politics, Pedagogy," Graduate Seminar; Ann Pellegrini, New York University, New York, March 2006; " 'Haptic Viewing' and Abraham Ravett's experimental film *Half-Sister*,' " Judaism Postmodernism Conference, Lehigh University, Bethlehem, Pennsylvania, June 2005; "Peering Out from under a Long Shadow: Remembering Ordinary Jewish Loss," University of Massachusetts, Amherst, Massachusetts, November 2003; "Secret Stashes: The Recovery of Family Photographs and American Jewish Identity," conference on "The Faded Image: Visual Culture and the Transformation of Memory," Centre for the Study of Historical Consciousness, University of British Columbia, BC, Canada, May 2003; "Images and Intimacies: American Jews, Family Photographs and the Longing for Connection," luncheon seminar, Institute for the Advanced Study of Religion, Yale University, New Haven, Connecticut, November 2001; "Jews and Feminism: The Turn to the Personal," SUNY Albany, Albany, New York, October 1998.

And, finally, for their early inspiration I thank the following people: Daniel Boyarin for encouraging me to call this book "Ordinary Jews"; Susan Levasseur, graduate assistant extraordinaire, for her help doing preliminary research toward this project; and both Deborah Malmud, then at Princeton University Press, and Alan Thomas at the University of Chicago Press for thinking with me about what this book might become.

The lines from "Transcendental Etude," from *The Dream of a Common Language: Poems 1974–1977* by Adrienne Rich. Copyright © 1978 by W. W. Norton & Company, Inc. Used by permission of the author and W. W. Norton & Company, Inc.

I thank Irena Klepfisz and Eighth Mountain Press for allowing me to cite from *A Few Words in the Mother Tongue: Poems Selected and New (1971–1990)* by Irena Klepfisz. Copyright © 1990 by Eighth Mountain Press.

Preface

Unraveling, a Personal Story

> . . . nobody's life is a mere embodiment of American good fortune.
> Even the inhabitants of a culture of plenty can be intimately ac-
> quainted with loss.
> —Jonathan Rosen, *The Talmud and the Internet*, 125

No event informs the narrative of 20th-century Jewish history more than the Holocaust. Against this backdrop of traumatic loss,
the lives of ordinary American Jews who have grown up in "a culture of
plenty" are seemingly immune to such devastation, and their lives and
losses are somehow less consequential. What does it mean to explore
the provocative and uneasy tension between this traumatic narrative of
Jewish history and the more ordinary narratives of loss that have
shaped the lives of contemporary American Jews? What happens when
we[1] focus on ordinary losses as they animate our engagements with this
larger legacy of Jewish loss? Can we do this without having to bind the
everyday stories to, or contain them within, the larger Holocaust narrative? What happens when we take the time to explore the complicated
and messy strands within these quotidian legacies of loss and dwell on
them? What do they tell us about ourselves, and what do they tell us
about the Holocaust?

In an effort to address these questions, this book moves between an
intimate tale of loss from my own family, a series of intertwining stories
about my father and his two mothers, and pieces of that larger history
as depicted in contemporary works of Holocaust commemoration.
Making associations and distinctions, I use intimacy as a way of making
connections between these different legacies of loss.

My father's mother, Lena Levitt, died in 1936, at the age of thirty-
seven. She left behind three children and her husband, my grandfather.

My father was ten years old at the time. Even now no one in the family knows for sure the cause of her death. This was not a topic ever discussed in my father's extended family. Three years after Lena's death, in the midst of the Depression, my grandfather remarried. Mary Levitt became my father's mother and the woman I would come to know as my paternal grandmother. Perhaps our relatives never told us about my father's first mother out of a deep love and respect for Mary, but this was never articulated. They seem to have had a desire to smooth over those parts of this family's story that did not fit together neatly. Not only was Lena's memory buried, but no one ever talked about Mary's story—her late entry into this family and her inability to bear children of her own.

For much of my life I did not know that my father had had another mother aside from Mary. Although I had been named in memory of Lena,[2] I did not learn that she had existed until my early teens. And it was only after Mary died that I can remember having had any open discussions about Lena in my extended family.

This family secret, this silence, speaks to a larger feeling of brokenness within my father's family. The various relationships within this blended and extended family have always been mysterious. I was often confused about which relatives were related to one another. At times, family members joked that some relatives could actually marry each other, but none of this was ever explained. It was all somehow understood. Even now, after years of searching, critical pieces of my father's and grandmothers' lives remain elusive. And I remain haunted by these missing pieces. In fact, it was almost fifty years after Lena's death that a picture of her first came to light.

These hauntings, which have profoundly shaped my relationship with my father, allow me to see how everyday legacies of Jewish loss inform our critical engagements with notions of Jewish history and memory and make tangible that which was lost in the Holocaust, the everyday lives of countless European Jews. Through a series of close readings that move between my family stories and Holocaust texts, I will argue that this strategy can open up the compelling possibility of thinking about community, family, and identity in the present. Such intimate and critical engagement, the crafting of texts and stories from our own families' pasts in relation to works by contemporary poets, writers, filmmakers, and scholars, can become the basis for building other kinds of intimacy. One need not be a family member, or even Jewish, to make these connections. By taking seriously ordinary and intimate stories of loss and bringing them to bear more explicitly in my critical writing, I hope to invite others to look again at their own family stories. As we share what was once private with others outside our families and communities, I believe that we will be able to build new kinds of alliances and connections.

Unraveling

> I think of the preciousness of ordinary life and of the strange, hard truth that outside fiction, some stories never end.
>
> —Jane Lazarre, *Wet Earth and Dreams*, 122

> Far from being faraway, ancient times, people and places are made familiar and close at hand by the telling of stories. But in the process of storytelling, what cultural work is done? In making the past familiar and usable, what complexities are flattened and effaced? Whose past does it become? We create our pasts, in various ways and with various texts and artifacts. Despite the habit of wrapping history in objectivity and stability, our pasts are pliable.
>
> —Miriam Peskowitz, *Spinning Fantasies, Rabbis,*
> *Gender and History*, 1

To unravel is to undo, to separate tangled threads or clarify the elements of something mysterious or baffling. It is to solve a mystery by taking apart its component pieces or its various threads. One can literally unravel a knitted fabric and reuse its threads, or one can, more figuratively, untie the pieces of an intricate tale and, in a similar manner, put these pieces together again to form new stories.[3] That is one way of imagining what comes from unraveling.

One can also simply live with the various loose threads. For me it has been helpful to think about my efforts to untangle the story of my father and his two mothers as a kind of unraveling. The challenge has been trying to figure out how these narratives do and do not come together to form any single story. Like the ancient tale of Penelope, whose own story of spinning and unraveling is a complicated story of fidelity and arrogance, purity and deception,[4] I, too, can neither spin together nor fully unravel the stories I have to tell. And like Jane Lazarre's narratives of the preciousness of ordinary life that do not end, the stories at the heart of this book also have no endings. Caught in the contradiction between the interplay of creating and then destroying that which I have created, I begin by simply appreciating the unfinished character of ordinary life. It is this "strange, hard truth," in Lazarre's words, that connects me to Penelope; my loyalty is about both putting together and taking apart my beloved family stories. I may not be waiting for an explicit return of those who are now gone, as Penelope waited for her husband, but I am attempting to make sense of these stories by putting together some of the pieces and challenging others. And so, it is in these ways that, as with Penelope, my fidelity to my family stories is necessarily ambivalent. Both my efforts to weave these stories together and my insistence on pulling them apart are signs of my loyalty to these same legacies. This book is about these double and contradictory impulses. Oddly, they reflect a tension built into the word "ravel" itself, which means both to tangle and complicate as well as to separate and clarify. Even when the prefix "un" is attached, the word continues to have these contradictory meanings.

Of course these efforts are not as simple or as innocent as they might seem. There is an urgency to these engagements. The all-too-familiar landscape of the grand narrative looms large. That familiar tale provides the context for these stories and it is, after all, a story of Holocaust and Redemption, the destruction of eastern European Jewish life and the rebirth of the Jewish people in their ancient homeland. This overwhelming legacy demands our urgent attention. And yet, even as I say this, I am keenly aware of the fact that there are other stories, more immediate, more intimate tales of loss that remain open-ended and that also somehow demand our attention. The narratives of the so-called lucky ones, my own immediate ancestors, the segment of eastern European Jewry who made it to America well before the Holocaust, those who came to the United States in the vast migration of eastern European Jews at the beginning of the 20th century, need to be studied. And yet in the face of the Shoah,[5] the destruction of the worlds, the lives, and the communities many of our families came from, how can we possibly address these "lucky" American stories? But, how can we not? This is the challenge at the heart of this book.

In order to appreciate the intimacies that link contemporary American Jews to these pasts, I argue that we must explore the legacies of those closest to home. By raveling and unraveling these embodied and intimate tales, like the story of my father and his two mothers, we can begin to imagine other Jewish futures after the Holocaust.

And so I begin at home with the family stories that tie me to a specific eastern European Jewish immigrant past. And because endings are often beginnings, I need to turn to the death of Mary Levitt, the grandmother I knew, as it marks another beginning of the tale I will unravel.

My Grandmother's Death

During the summer of 1979, my paternal grandmother, Mary Levitt, died. Her death was not unexpected. It was the culmination of many years of illness and physical ailment. For as long as I had known her, my grandmother had been frail; her health had always been vulnerable. My grandmother was a tiny person, considerably shorter than five feet tall. I was told that this was the result of some kind of congenital condition. Even still it puzzled me as a child because her sisters towered over her—at least that is how I remember it. The sister to whom she was closest, Rose, was around five feet eight inches tall, and Rose's son was well over six feet tall and played basketball.

Aside from being small, Mary had thin hair and a chronic case of eczema. She was blind in one eye, and as she got older, she began to lose her hearing. She also developed heart disease. As a child I worried about her health and often felt helpless. I felt protective and, not knowing what else to do, I turned to God. I wondered why God seemed to pick on my grandmother. I wanted to know why he did this to her and demanded that he stop it. In this way, Mary brought me to God. This was my first serious engagement with God, my prelude to years of theological study and a PhD in Religion. But God never seemed to heed my calls. While I knew her, Mary was never granted even a brief reprieve from all of her physical ailments.

A few years before Mary died, her poor health was exacerbated by a terrible car accident. Neither of my grandparents had ever learned to drive so they had to rely on a friend who was driving them to an event when he had a heart attack and died at the wheel. It was a cold winter night. They were on the New York Thruway when their friend lost consciousness. The car swerved off the road into a huge snow bank that stopped the car, preventing them from plunging down a large embankment. Perhaps it was at this moment that my prayers were finally answered, but only partially. My grandparents were saved but not unscathed, at least not my grandmother. My grandfather left the scene of the accident perfectly fine, not a scratch, but Mary was never quite the same. The impact of the car hitting the snow bank permanently damaged her balance. She now had trouble walking. In the end, it was her heart that finally failed her during the summer of 1979. She was seventy-two years old.

The summer Mary died, I was nineteen years old. It was the summer after my freshman year in college. I was in Washington, D.C., working as an intern for Senator Bill Roth from Delaware. It was my first time living away from home in a real apartment. I was sharing this space with my college roommate and some law students. I was even being paid for my labors and felt very grown up paying my share of the rent. When I got the call that Mary had died, I quickly made arrangements to fly to Albany, New York, for the funeral. My parents and my brother would drive up from Delaware and I would meet them there. What this meant was that I ended up arriving well before my parents. This was actually the first time I had spent time with any of my paternal relatives outside of the company of my parents.

Although Mary had been ill for many years, I was not ready for her death or the death of anyone I was close to. The only other relative whose death I had lived through was my mother's father, but I was only four when he had died. Mary's was the first funeral I attended as an adult. It would also become the first of many funerals I would attend in Albany over the next number of years.[6] And it was on these occasions that I would continue to learn more about my father's family.

When I was with my extended family at my aunt's home waiting for my parents to arrive, the rabbi came to talk to the family about what he should say about Mary in his eulogy. Although there were lots of people in the house, the rabbi sat down in the kitchen with a much smaller contingent—my grandfather, two of Mary's sisters, and Mary's children: my aunt, my uncle, and me; I was there in my father's place.[7]

As the conversation began, the rabbi asked us all to tell him about Mary—about her life. The things my relatives had to say were all true. Mary was a wonderful wife and mother. She was a lovely person, good natured, caring, and kind. And yet I was disturbed by this conversation, by what was not being said or acknowledged. I do not know why I chose to speak up, but somehow I could not help myself. I just had to say something about what made Mary unique. I felt I owed it to her to say out loud what everyone knew but what no one was prepared to say, and that was that Mary was an unusual mother. When I realized that there was a real chance that none of these things would ever be said unless I said them to the rabbi in the presence of my relatives, I spoke up.[8] What made Mary special, I volunteered, was that she was really good at mothering in spite of the fact that she had never been able to give birth to children of her own. And she mothered many. Not only did she become mother to my father, his sister, and his brother after their mother died, but she also mothered her youngest sister when their own mother died after giving birth to this daughter. As the eldest daughter, Mary took on the role of mother in her childhood home, and she continued to take on this role throughout her life; she was a devoted aunt and grandmother who helped care for some of her sisters' children as well as many of her grandchildren.

After I finished speaking there was a long pause. There was no rebuke, no anger, but everyone seemed to be stunned. They did not know what to say. And although I now no longer remember if the rabbi ever addressed any of these things specifically in his eulogy, I do remember that I felt that I had somehow done Mary justice. I had said these things out loud to her loved ones in front of the rabbi, who made it all somehow official. I had recognized and honored my grandmother's virtually invisible labors of love and devotion within her family. Now, these many years later, I realize that there is more to say. There is more to Mary's story than I had thought. There are things I have only come to know well after her death, things that have complicated my own neat depiction of her.

I have chosen a formal portrait of a young Mary as the frontispiece for this book. Like all portraits, this is an idealized image. Its rich sepia tones smooth out the contours of her young face. She glows. I do not know much about this picture. I suspect it was her high school graduation portrait. Part of what I like about this picture of Mary is its plentitude and promise. This is a young Mary with full ruddy cheeks. She is not the gaunt older woman I remember. Instead, here Mary is young, pretty, and full of life. There is something perky, even a bit impish, about her smile. No one can tell how small she is by looking at this image. Here she easily conforms to the cultural norms that dictate what such portraits should look like. She is wonderfully ordinary. For me this is a dream image. It is Mary as I now imagine she would like to be seen.

She is normal, happy, healthy, and hopeful. She is so many of the things I always wanted her to be and feared she never had been.

This picture speaks to a truth I did not know as the child who feared for her fragile grandmother. It captures Mary's optimism, her hopefulness. When she died, I did not know this part of Mary's personality. But a few years ago, my mother shared with me some letters that Mary had sent to her after my parents announced their engagement. I had heard many stories about this time, about the clash between my mother's parents and my parents, tensions around class and my maternal grandparents' disappointment that my mother was not marrying a doctor or a man from a solidly middle class Jewish family. I knew that my maternal grandmother was scornful of my father's parents and was not very discrete about her displeasure. What I had never known before was how Mary responded to any of this. I only knew what my mother had told me about her own parents. I knew about how ashamed and embarrassed she was about the way her mother had treated my father's parents.

Mary's letters were revelatory. For the first time I heard Mary's own voice, strong and confident. These were joyous letters. Unlike my other grandmother, Mary enthusiastically welcomed my mother into her family.[9] In these letters, Mary expressed how happy she was that her oldest son had finally found someone with whom he could share his life and start a family of his own. This was especially meaningful to Mary because my father was already in his thirties at the time of my parents' engagement. She had been afraid that he might never marry, and she had not wanted him to be alone.[10]

By the time I knew Mary, her health was already compromised. The vigor of this image, the strength echoed in the letters she sent to my mother, was not familiar to me as a child. These are parts of Mary that I could not have spoken about at the time of her funeral. It is only now that I have been able to catch a glimpse of this Mary, a strong and generous woman with plenty of love and energy to go around. The story of Mary did not end with her death.

Jerusalem 1983: In Search of Authenticity

After graduating from college, I spent the 1982–83 academic year in Israel. I was enrolled in an intensive Jewish texts program sponsored by the Jewish Theological Seminary (JTS). I went to Israel to learn about my Jewish heritage. I was going to make up for all that I had not learned growing up in my parents' liberal Jewish house—Talmud, Mishnah, Midrash, and codes. I was not only going to learn to read Talmud, but I was also going to learn how to live a "real" Jewish life. In Israel that year I took on Jewish dietary practices and I also became Sabbath observant. For that entire year I neither wrote nor drove on the Sabbath.

In all of these ways I worked on becoming an educated, observant Jew in what I imagined to be the center of the Jewish world, Jerusalem. This Jerusalem was not only the capital of the modern Jewish nation-state but it was also at the center of an ancient and indeed sacred Jewish longing for authenticity and home. It was Zion, the land of promise if not the Promised Land. In Jerusalem I lived in the midst of many other observant Jews. I spoke Hebrew and studied Jewish texts. I was trying to place myself within what I wanted to believe to be a timeless, eternal Jewish tradition. Unfortunately, my efforts to take on this identity were more difficult than I had imagined they would be. While in the eternal city studying Torah, I often found myself distracted by more everyday things. My efforts to place myself in a more ethereal other-worldly realm were regularly interrupted and complicated by other Jewish legacies, practices, and traditions—the things I thought I was trying to overcome or perhaps escape: politics, gender, history, and memory.

Although I longed for a purer, more authentic version of Jewishness and turned to traditional Jewish study in Jerusalem to find it, my efforts came up short. I could not avoid the contingencies of my position. It was the late 20th century, and I was an American Jewish woman, a granddaughter of eastern European immigrants. I came to Jerusalem with little Jewish education and a degree in Religious Studies from Brown. I was trying to become a rabbinic Jew for the first time in my early twenties.

Within the confines of my yeshiva program, I found myself explicitly struggling for the first time with issues of gender. It was not so easy to find my place within rabbinic Judaism as a Jewish woman. On a regular basis I was confronted by gender inequities in a system I was committed to learning and enacting on its own terms. Thus, even as it excluded me from key aspects of its practice time and time again, I struggled to keep these realities from interrupting my studies. Even as I came to Israel to find a new, more authentic Jewish identity, I struggled to figure out how to reconcile this version of Judaism with the liberal American Jewish identity I already had, my family's less observant version of Judaism. I worried about how I would translate my life in Israel as an observant Jew into something that I could perform in my family's home in America. How could I continue to honor my parents and grandparents if I rejected their Judaism? Was I going to stop eating in their homes? Was I going to continue to participate in their more liberal Jewish rituals?

All of these struggles posed challenges to my studies and efforts to reform myself into what I hoped would be a more "authentic" Jew. These are not things I could have articulated then, but over time, in different ways, they have contributed to my subsequent efforts to find other ways of claiming a less coherent, more contradictory Jewish identity.

I did not go to Israel to study in a yeshiva. I was on an academic program sponsored by the liberal Jewish Theological Seminary (JTS), the academic arm of the Conservative movement, the movement in which I was raised. I had just graduated from Brown, and it had not occurred to me that there would be limits on my studies because I was a woman. But even in this liberal academic environment, I was confronted with gender inequities that made my learning and my observance different from and less significant than the learning and observance of my male peers. Although JTS and the Conservative movement, the sponsors of my study program, believed that women could and should study Talmud, they were not yet convinced that women could be rabbis or that observant Conservative Jews should even participate in egalitarian forms of communal worship. These policies were something I had not anticipated. So while I became kosher and Sabbath observant, as a woman I did not learn how to pray or how to read Torah.

Although the women in my program were at least as highly educated and dedicated to our studies as the men, because we were not obligated to do these things as women we were not taught how to do them. Being exempt from these obligations according to Jewish law meant that there were no structural mechanisms in place to teach us to lead services or to read Torah, and, as a result, few of us learned to do these things. To do so would have required studying outside of the contours of the regular curriculum. Just to participate in an egalitarian worship service once a month took great effort on the part of many men and women in the program.[11]

I spent that year trying hard not to pay attention to the gender inequities that were shaping my Jewish education. I was enamored of the tradition, and I was determined to keep my focus on traditional Jewish learning. Despite this, I now realize that the inequities in my program profoundly shaped my efforts to become a traditional Jew and helped shape the Jewish feminist position I eventually embraced.

I ended my year of study in late May 1983. My parents asked me to plan on returning in time to attend my first cousin's bat mitzvah and, just after that, my brother's graduation from Dickinson College. Although these plans had been decided upon before I left for Israel, somehow the reality of leaving Israel and immediately jumping into my family's American Jewish versions of ritual observance haunted me. To attend these events, I would need to drive on Shabbat; this was not an issue in my extended family, but it was a newly acquired issue for me.

As I became increasingly more observant, I struggled to consider the implications of my new commitments as they differed from the forms of Jewish observance I had known growing up. Was it more important for me to remain involved in my family and its Jewish and familial practices, or was it better that I let go of these attachments in order to more authentically practice Jewish law? Before I went to Israel, I had known other young people who had become observant and had often been taken aback by the way many of them had distanced themselves from their families as they became more observant. I remember a couple in New York who refused to go to a seder at their parents' homes, believing that their parents' level of kashrut was not strict enough. Even then I found this decision painful.

I was never interested in alienating myself from my parents. I wanted to be able to continue to eat in their home and celebrate Jewish holidays and family celebrations with them. Even in my classes on Jewish practice I asked questions about the relative importance of the commandment to honor one's parents as opposed to keeping kosher, or not driving on Shabbat. For me these were always vital questions that remained unanswered. I knew what I wanted to do, but I had few role models for how to do this; no one in my extended family was observant, and all of these practices were foreign to my family. I struggled with how the new form of Jewishness I was taking on, however ancient and authoritative it might be, could take the place of the no less real Jewish way of life in which I had been raised.

Portrait Lena and Sol Levitt. From the Levitt family collection.

Revelation

A revelation is a disclosure. It is often dramatic. Theologically it is considered a manifestation of divine will or truth.[12] During the spring of
1983, while I was studying in Israel, I received a photocopy of a portrait of my paternal grandparents. It was the first image I had ever seen
of my father's mother, the woman I was named for, Lena Levitt. The receipt of this portrait of my long-lost grandmother was a revelation. It
was just not the kind of revelation I thought I had gone to Israel to find.

Although I taped the copy of the photograph of my grandparents up
over my bed in my dorm room along with art postcards and snapshots
of friends and family, I did not really consider the implications of this
discovery. I was too busy searching for other forms of Jewish revelation
and enlightenment. Like so many other American Jews of my generation, I had gone to Israel to try to take on what I thought would be a
more "authentic" version of Jewishness, yet my efforts to place myself

squarely within an authorized version of rabbinic Judaism did not work. All these years later, I realize how much this more humble revelation that came to me unexpectedly in Israel has taught me about my Jewish identity. The portrait offered me an early first clue into the very different version of Jewish identity that would eventually shape my work in the field of Jewish Studies. At the time, I did not yet know that mine would be a messier, more partial familial and feminist Jewish position.

During the winter of 1983 George Leavitt,[13] an estranged relative from Florida, my father's first cousin, had put the sepia-toned studio portrait of my father's parents into an envelope with a note to my father and sent it to him in Delaware.[14] I learned about this photograph from my father. It was something he excitedly described to me during one of our weekly overseas phone calls. A few weeks later I received my photocopy of the picture. My father was eager for me to see it for myself even through the distortions of a photocopy.[15] As I have already explained, this was the first image I had ever seen of my father's mother, the woman who had given birth to him and to his siblings. Until that moment, Lena had been a faceless specter. She had been a woman I barely knew existed. Seeing this photograph and thinking about the other grandmother I had known and lost marked the beginning of my efforts to unravel the tale of my father and his two mothers, my twenty-five-year fascination with Lena Levitt, and my growing need to reconcile her story with that of my other grandmother, Mary Levitt. In my urgent desire to piece together the story of Lena, I did not want to lose sight of Mary. I did not want to substitute the legacy of one of these grandmothers for the other. I needed to find a way to honor them both.

No one in my father's family remembered having ever seen the portrait of my grandparents. My father and his brother and sister insist that before this picture surfaced, they had not even known that any images of their mother existed. Because of this, the portrait became a kind of revelation. An image of my father's long-dead mother had come to light, and in coming to light, it revived her, forcing her to become a part of the family's memory once again. It was miraculous.

With the receipt of this image, my father began to talk about his mother. Having not seen her for so long, he had forgotten what she had looked like. The picture brought her back to him.

Almost fifty years after her death, what seemed to fascinate my father most was the resemblance between his long-lost mother and me, his daughter. This is the first thing my father told me about the photograph.

For him, it was thrilling to see the resemblance across a generation. This was part of why he was so eager to share her image with me in whatever form he could. When I finally received my copy of the portrait, I got to share in the revelation.[16]

What strikes me even now as I remember first seeing the copy of the photograph is the resemblance between my father and his mother. I did not see myself as much as I saw my father in this woman's face. Oddly, given my obsession with Lena, I have often forgotten that my grandfather was also in the portrait, that he, too, links all of us together. Nevertheless, for all of us, the salient figure in the picture was Lena.

For my father, the photograph was a crucial link between us. He saw me and he saw his mother. And although he did not see himself in her face, he made the connection to her through me. Perhaps it was easier for him to link his mother to me than to focus on his own resemblance to her. In a similar way, my own desire to see him in his mother's likeness has made it hard for me to appreciate how much I look like Lena. And yet, all of these resemblances are not only apparent in the photograph, but they are also clearly a part of how we have all come to live with this image and what it has revealed to us about Lena.

As I write these words and retell this story, a seemingly obvious point, a point that I had somehow missed at the time, comes to mind. When the portrait arrived in my father's hands, now over twenty years ago, my grandfather was still alive, and yet I do not recall any of us discussing or looking at the photograph with him. I remember asking him to tell me stories about his first wife, but not in relation to the picture. I no longer recall when I had these conversations with him. What I do remember is a romantic tale, a narrative about a beautiful woman, a shared ice cream, and falling in love. But in truth, I am no longer sure about where any of these stories actually came from. They are stories I have already come to embellish and remake into tales of my own; I can no longer remember who first told them to me. I find myself thwarted and frustrated by my own inability to remember. This is a humbling experience, a reminder of how much harder all of this must be for my father, the little boy who lost his mother.

Part of what I have come to understand over these many years is that instead of finding an affirming story, a rich and whole tradition to fit myself into, my efforts to come to terms with my various Jewish identities since that year in Israel have been anything but neat, clean, and simple. My experiences in Israel and since then have been marked by a different kind of reckoning. Sometimes this has been disappointing and frustrating. But it has also been satisfying in other ways. I have discovered time and time again that for me, the Jewish past, present, and future are all marked by contradictions and discontinuities—losses large and small. And yet these same contradictions have offered me room to grow and explore other ways of claiming my Jewishness in its complexity. The closer I get to my family's stories, the more I have come to appreciate the tensions between very different kinds of Jewish narratives—stories from home and grand Jewish historical narratives—not only how these stories coexist, but also how they touch one another.

These are elusive engagements. Our reckonings are always partial and incomplete. Even so, I hope to show how this kind of emotional and intellectual labor is both relevant and important, how the personal is critical, and how the critical can be personally meaningful. Through close and compassionate readings of family stories alongside artistic and literary works about aspects of a more recent Jewish past, I want to show what a new kind of intimate writerly and engaged scholarship can look like.

Making Connections

In what follows, I attend to the story of my two grandmothers, an ordinary tale of loss within my own American Jewish family as it has come back to me in the context of facing the legacy of the Holocaust. By engaging with works that address this more authorized legacy of Jewish loss, commemoration and memory alongside my more ordinary story, I have been able to see some of the more subtle and elusive ways these narratives are connected. Although there are no simple ways of bringing together the everyday and the extraordinary, the ordinary and the grand, thinking about these legacies next to each other allows us to see our place in the broad span of Jewish history, however discontinuous that might be.

For me, family stories have most immediately informed my connection to a Jewish past. That said, I have rarely experienced these connections outside my work with other Jewish texts and practices, works that initially seemed quite distant from my family. The story of my father and his two mothers in some ways haunted my efforts to claim the legacy of the Rabbis that year in Israel even though they appeared to have little to do with each other. It has also continued to shape the contours of my scholarship, especially my desires to claim a feminist and an American Jewish position. As I will demonstrate in the pages that follow, I am increasingly convinced that attending to those ghosts closest to home is essential to understanding what it means to identify as a Jew in the present and lay claim to various Jewish pasts.

It seems to me that for a long time, many American Jews like me have failed to reflect upon, or even value, our ordinary family stories. In the face of either the promise of an ancient and enduring Jewish tradition, or absorption with a more recent history—the urgency of the Holocaust and with it, a redemptive faith in the establishment of a Jewish nation-state in Israel—many of us have let go of these more intimate tales of specific Jewish pasts and the losses that mark us so profoundly. The need to affirm and secure Jewish life in larger-than-life terms seems to have taken precedence as a way of addressing an uncertain future. But part of what I have come to learn in raveling and unraveling my family story in relation to these larger Jewish histories is that this uncertain future has often been an excuse not to attend to the seemingly mundane and ordinary legacies closest to home.

The relative smallness of these tales, especially the tales of ordinary losses, have all too often been overshadowed and rendered inconsequential in the face of the Holocaust or in our focusing on timeless forms of Jewish practice. Family stories of intimate loss have appeared trivial and somehow unworthy of our best critical thinking. After all, there is so much important work that has yet to be done in Holocaust studies. In this respect, my efforts might appear to be counterintuitive, but I believe that if we take everyday stories of loss more seriously and if we pay attention to how they brush up against and interact with these larger Holocaust narratives, we might be better able to understand the past and imagine a different future.

Although I generally follow the practice in feminist and critical studies that resists using the "we" in scholarly work because of how it has been used to force the reader into a grand collective, in this case I am making an exception. The "we" in this book is decidedly not grand. It is offered as a gesture of inclusion allowing me to connect to my readers, especially those I do not know but who will learn a great deal about me in these pages. This "we"—and sometimes "you"—is an experimental pact between me and my readers; it is a way of acknowledging the intimacy of this scholarly treatment of loss.

Introduction
Indirection and Ordinary Jews

In his analysis of Alain Resnais' film *Hiroshima Mon Amour* (1959), cultural critic Michael S. Roth explains why the filmmaker could not directly address the legacy of the dropping of the atomic bomb on Hiroshima, why he could not offer viewers another version of *Night and Fog*, his acclaimed documentary film about the legacy of the Holocaust.[1] As Roth explains, for Resnais, *Night and Fog* had already "explored why documentary knowledge was impossible. Film offered the temptation to . . . provide a representation of the past *as it really was,* Resnais had already refused (and illuminated) that temptation" (93). Given that such a use of film was not possible, in *Hiroshima* Resnais offered a fictional narrative. He created a seemingly mundane encounter between strangers to explore "what other kinds of connections to the past could be established and maintained in both the most extreme and the most ordinary conditions" (93).

In this film, two strangers, a man and a woman, spend a single night together in a hotel room in Hiroshima.[2] The woman is French and the man is Japanese. Both are young. She is an actress who has come to Hiroshima to shoot a film about peace, he is an architect. They communicate with each other in French. In this banal setting, watching newsreel footage of the horrors that took place in this very city twelve years earlier, the two strangers discuss what it means to know this past. She claims to have seen Hiroshima while he claims that knowing Hiroshima is impossible. They disagree. The film suggests that both are right. The woman's position, although she claims a kind of knowledge, is more complicated. As Roth explains, the woman knows that "recollection is about the confrontation with absence and forgetting, and that is what she has seen in Hiroshima and everywhere else" (93–94). Remembering her forgetting, the woman does not deny the necessity of memory. In this strange and haunted city she finds herself able to tell a stranger about her own wartime experience, a story she has kept to herself for the past twelve years. She tells of her love affair with a German soldier who was eventually shot and killed by snipers as the Germans fled France (95).

I am drawn to this woman because, as the film unfolds, we come to see her investment in not telling this story. We learn about the allures of keeping this story secret and about how, in not telling, she has been able to keep the memory of her lover alive. This dynamic reminds me of my father and his secrets. It helps me think about what it has meant for him not to talk about his mother, Lena Levitt. But it also helps me think about what it means to look at my father's loss in the broader context of 20th-century Jewish history. To claim my father's story as Jewish, I am ever mindful of the interplay between traumatic losses in everyday Jewish life and the extraordinary losses of the Holocaust and how, in trying to tell any of these stories, we risk losing our loved ones all over again.

Resnais explicitly juxtaposes very different experiences of loss in *Hiroshima Mon Amour,* and he makes no attempt to depict these experiences as somehow equivalent. Instead, he shows how being in the presence of the trauma of others can trigger memories of our own. The French woman's being in Hiroshima triggers her own memory; her proximity to the pain of others enables her to gain some awareness of her own trauma. In this way, the film shows how memory works in relation to trauma and loss. It shows how there is a movement between very different experiences of loss; the encounter with one triggers the recognition of others. It is important to see these stories side by side, not to make one into a version of the other, but to see what happens when we allow them to touch, to stand alongside each other in our imaginations and in our efforts to consider different kinds of losses, both grand and small.

What interests me most about the French woman is her silence, the twelve years in which she has never spoken of her loss. I am drawn to how this act of not speaking gets figured in the film in terms of a kind of fidelity. This notion of fidelity or loyalty as an intimate and internal experience resonates with how I have come to understand my father's silence around his mother's death.[3] For twelve years the story has been her preoccupation. It has floated through her consciousness as if of its own volition. By never telling her story, the woman has protected herself from the distortions of narrative and the problem of forgetting.[4]

Her precious memory is intact. What the film suggests is that she has done all this at a cost. In giving herself over to this memory, she has not been able to fully live in the present. As she has held on to the past in this way, the memory has remained vivid and independent, completely out of her control. It has taken over her life at various intervals as flashbacks and hallucinations. Again and again it has interrupted her present. But through this lack of control, the woman has been able to experience her dead past as somehow still alive.[5] When she finally tells the story, her love story, in Hiroshima twelve years later, she gives up this intimate and animated relationship to that past, at least in part. She lets go of the overwhelming otherness, the seeming independence of the past, and begins to live again in the present. In other words, in Hiroshima she begins to learn the necessity of forgetting.

Forgetting and Remembering

As I write about this French woman, I am also flooded with other traumatic examples of this dynamic; I think about poet and child survivor of the Holocaust, Irena Klepfisz, and more specifically her prose poem *Bashert*.[6] Through the voice of the narrator of this poem, Klepfisz explores what it means for a child survivor of the Holocaust to struggle with issues of fidelity both to the obligation of remembering the past and to the present necessity of forgetting. Like the woman in *Hiroshima Mon Amour*, the narrator in *Bashert* has moments when she does let go of the hauntings that have prevented her from living in the present, but there are other moments when she has no control. For her, the struggle to live in the present is never simply resolved. Despite being able to make distinctions between past and present, there are times when she quite self-consciously allows herself to be taken over by the past. This is most clearly articulated in the final section of the poem, "Cherry Plain 1981: I have become a Keeper of Accounts."[7] Despite everything that has happened since 1945, this woman cannot escape the lingering hatred that is the ongoing legacy of the Holocaust. She literally gives herself over to Jewish ghosts whenever she is confronted with horrible stereotypes of Jews in the present.

Unlike the French woman in *Hiroshima Mon Amour*, the narrator in *Bashert* succumbs to these ghosts deliberately, calling upon "the ancient myths again and again,"[8] inviting them all to live through her, to inhabit her body. In this way she surrenders herself to become a "keeper of accounts."

> At those moments I teeter shed my present self and all
> time merges and like rage like pride like acceptance like
> the refusal to deny I answer
> Yes. It is true. I am a keeper of accounts.[9]

For Klepfisz's narrator, this refusal to deny becomes the ultimate act of loyalty and self-sacrifice.[10] For her, in contrast to the woman in Resnais' film, the external repetitions of the trauma that continue to shape her present life trigger this loss of self. She embraces this identification repeatedly. In this way her refusal to forget is made visceral, demanding that she succumb. Thus, despite or perhaps because of the narrator's ability to make distinctions between past and present, she knowingly blurs the boundaries between "then" and "now" in order to give herself over to these ghosts.[11] For her there is no final reckoning, these enactments are ongoing.

In *Bashert* the past can and does interrupt the present. Fidelity is not about holding on; rather, it is about being confronted again and again with still living versions of antisemitism. It is manifest in both minor slights and larger stereotypes. For this narrator, surrendering to these Jewish ghosts is an act of defiance and resistance in the present. For her, the trauma continues.

In part this poem suggests that there is perhaps no simple reckoning with the past for any of us. Even as we learn to make distinctions, the past can and does return to us, often in unexpected ways. And because of this, we cannot allow ourselves simply to move on. There are things we may come to learn about our dead even well after they are gone. And more than that, we have no control over these moments of recognition in the present.

I think about my father. I think about my grandmother Mary Levitt and her sisters. I think about the relatives who sat with me as I told the rabbi who would conduct her funeral something about the specifics of Mary's life, some of the story that had not been spoken in my father's family. Although I am keenly aware of the differences among Klepfisz's narrator, a Jewish survivor, the French woman in Resnais' film, my father, and myself, I also see connections. The loyalty Roth attributes to the woman in *Hiroshima Mon Amour* and my father's resistance to talking about the death of his mother Lena Levitt and how her death lead to Mary Levitt's entry into our family are not identical to the kinds of haunting Klepfisz describes.[12] But they all share certain formal characteristics.[13] In all of these cases there is a loss of self, a giving over of self, and a lack of control. There are also differences of degree and kind. In the film, in my father's case, and in my own, a kind of magical logic is often at work. By not pinning down what we experience, by not committing these losses to words, we allow them a certain autonomy.[14] They remain in a nebulous state of potential; they swirl around as if they are alive and separate from us. Unlike Klepfisz's narrator, we operate on a different register; we seem to be more in control, freer to allow this process to happen. For Klepfisz's narrator there is seemingly no choice. Ironically, a kind of inevitability to this process is echoed in the title of the poem as a whole, *bashert*—the Yiddish term for that which is fated, predetermined, inevitable for better and for worse.[15] By choosing to embrace that which she does not control, she finds some measure of agency. But this does not mean that she is freed from these hauntings.

I suspect that for my father, the fear of letting go, of telling, is that he might lose both of his mothers all over again, especially Lena, the mother he has come to know in his own imagination since childhood. In his private imagination she is still somehow alive; if he lets out his secrets, she can no longer live there. There is a fear as well as a delight in this unspoken haunting; he is haunted in some of the ways I have attributed to the woman in the film. I suspect that my father has been able to believe that his mother is still somehow alive. And in a sense she has been. She has been his, and his alone, for all these years. And at the same time, while having this first mother, he has been able to protect his second mother, Mary. There has been no competition.

Hiroshima Mon Amour reproduces some of these sensations, the intermingling of different losses. In the film, indirection functions as both a strategy for getting closer to these elusive legacies and as a way to reproduce the distance that always marks these engagements with the past. Both Klepfisz's poem and Resnais' film offer enactments of how memory works as a kind of unraveling. In each, the haunting presence of loss is a part of everyday life. Neither Klepfisz's poem nor Resnais' film allows narration to conquer forgetting. These works acknowledge how traumatic memories linger and how they help form the texture of everyday life. This is also true of the legacy of my father's childhood. It, too, has left traces that have shaped not only his life, but also my own.

Iterations, Reverberation: This Book

> The urge to find a new way to tell our stories is not due to any faddish longing after novelty, or to a careless dismissal of the masterpieces of the past, but rather to an urgent need to find a narrative strategy that adequately expresses the full range of intellectual premises of our own epoch as persuasively as earlier stories corresponded to, or self-consciously challenged the basic convictions and assumptions of their times.[16]

In order to show how different legacies of loss move in and out of each other, I have had to find an alternative to standard academic writing. I take readers into my critical practice. I invite readers, both lay and academic, into a space where critical texts and complicated works of art and commemoration intermingle with ordinary stories of loss from my own family. By taking seriously the ways that these "texts," for lack of a better term,[17] engage with issues of loss, I explore how different memories of loss become a part of our everyday lives. I call attention to formal and thematic connections, to the overlap between these characteristics in very different kinds of narratives, and to the ways these narratives can illuminate one another. In order to show what this process looks like, much less what it feels like, this book offers an innovative hybrid form of academic writing. On the one hand it is intimate, almost as if a memoir. On the other hand, it is academic, relying on scholarly discourse and methodologies.

I offer an experiment in both form and content in this book. What I am trying to come up with is a way to illuminate how academic work matters and a way to bring both the broader reading public and academics into this process. I also want to make clearer the intimate stakes that animate most academic work.

This means that I share with all kinds of readers the interplay between close readings of difficult texts and how they link up with and inform how I think about my own family stories. I show how I deal with the ways those ordinary tales of loss can make more sense when seen alongside some of these seemingly more difficult works. In all of these instances I take seriously the ways narratives of loss are always partial and incomplete and then ask what we can learn from reckoning with this most basic truth. This takes time. Readers will come upon long, complex engagements with difficult or allusive works, multilayered readings. I do these readings because, as I have experienced it, these complicated texts can make visible heretofore invisible dimensions of how we deal with loss. They can help us to see more familiar processes in new and often unexpected and illuminating ways.

Throughout this book, I show what happens when public and private losses are seen next to each other, what happens when difficult works of art or commemoration are seen alongside ordinary family stories about more intimate losses. For some this will be uncomfortable. This effort risks what might be dismissed too quickly as a form of sentimentality.[18] We cannot censor the kinds of memories that are triggered in a space of commemoration or in critical engagement with books or films about the Holocaust—or, for that matter, in any encounter with another person and his or her life stories. Narratives resonate with one another in the space of imagination and memory whether invited or not. Whether welcomed or not, I am interested in exploring these resonances critically, in seeing what they might teach us about more intimate engagements. This is about allowing different stories of loss to touch one another and seeing what happens in these encounters.

There is a compelling need to make space for individual narratives of loss and mourning within Holocaust commemoration and in this way to appreciate anew the open-ended nature of Holocaust memory. What I offer is a more individualized, less totalizing notion of Holocaust commemoration. At the same time, I argue that, in making these connections, we may be able to appreciate more fully the other more intimate losses that haunt so many of our engagements with the Holocaust in the first place.

Touching

This book moves back and forth between my own family's story and specific works of art, commemoration, and writing that address the legacy of the Holocaust. It examines these disparate tales in relation to one another. Like Resnais in *Hiroshima Mon Amour*, I am interested in the interplay between these losses. By taking the unusual step in academic work of emphasizing my family's story, I hope to invert the all-too-pervasive logic of Jewish memory that insists that the Holocaust must always come first. In so doing, I hope to show how legacies of ordinary Jewish loss need not displace the Holocaust but, instead, how attending to ordinary stories might help many of us better appreciate the human dimensions of the Holocaust. And from the other direction, just as Resnais' film and Klepfisz's poem have worked in this introduction as another way into my family stories, engagement with Holocaust commemoration can help some of us who have no intimate connections to the Holocaust better appreciate some of the various legacies of loss closest to our own homes.

In order to more fully explore these kinds of interactions I have organized this book into four interlocking sections. Each section offers a demonstration of how these interactions work and brings together a different aspect of my father's story and particular esthetic works of Holocaust memory and commemoration. Each of the works I have chosen resonates formally and thematically with some of the dynamics that haunt my own family story.

1. Looking Out from under a Long Shadow

In the first chapter, I explicitly address the allure of family photographs in the context of Holocaust commemoration in late 20th-century America. I use my own response to the images that make up Yaffa Eliach's Tower of Faces in the United States Holocaust Memorial Museum in Washington, D.C., and my desire to see my family pictures somehow on display in public as a way of complicating the notion of identification. I bring together this monumental album and my own family pictures through a close reading of the Tower and the way that it functions within the museum. In the process, I reread cultural critic Marianne Hirsch's notion of "postmemory" and the question of identification and offer another way of understanding what happens when visitors enter spaces like the Tower of Faces. I show how other losses and ghosts enter these places and animate many visitors' engagements with Holocaust commemoration, and I explore some of the productive possibilities these interactions may provide. In this way, as I recount my own journey from the Tower into the haunted terrain of ordinary losses and their relationship to the Holocaust, I show how the Tower offers yet another way in, a more formal introduction to this book.

2. Postmarked Pictures

In this chapter, I offer a close reading of experimental filmmaker Abraham Ravett's 1985 film *Half-Sister*, a nonnarrative film about Ravett's belated discovery of the existence of his mother's first child, his half sister, who was murdered by the Nazis. The film offers a visual meditation on a single photograph that brings the loss of his half sister back to life in the present. Through my reading of this twenty-two-minute film, I show how Ravett uses film to engage his own ambivalent desires to learn more about his half sister and this part of his mother's life. By focusing on Ravett's literal attempts to "reanimate" the single photographic image of this child, a photograph that was returned to him belatedly through the mail, we can see how Ravett shows us both the impossibility and the urgency of this quest. This film about a family photograph belatedly returned offers a formal connection to my story about the photograph of Lena Levitt that was belatedly returned to my father. It affords a way into the fractured tale of my father's mother's life and death which is not that easy to grasp, that is itself elusive. In moving back and forth between my family story and Ravett's film, I add something important to the way future viewers might appreciate this film. I remember the intimacy of losses like Ravett's that, although very much a part of the Holocaust, need also to be recognized as intimate and familiar.

3. Secret Stashes

In this chapter I begin by taking seriously the frailty of memory. Instead of beginning with a Holocaust text, this time I turn to my father's story first. By discussing my father's fractured memory and the desires that have animated his efforts to both hide and forget so many of his own most precious objects and stories from his own past, I reflect again on what it means to redeem the past, not only in relation to the legacy of the Holocaust. I open with a more general account of my father's predilection for hiding things, and then I discuss a particular stash of family photographs my father had kept hidden for almost fifty years, a stash he only revealed to me after the publication of my first book.[19] This set of pictures reveals a more intimate vision of the family he lost after his mother's death. These are images of his entire family together. They are the only pictures I have ever seen of my father with his mother, father, and siblings. They may be the only pictures that were ever taken of his family in this configuration. I then turn to Ann Weiss's *The Last Album: Eyes from the Ashes of Auschwitz-Birkenau*[20] and then *Before They Perished . . .*[21] to consider what happened when another stash of hidden family photographs was brought to light. I read Weiss's account against the account offered by the museum. I then relate these narratives of recovery back to my father and all that he has hidden, especially his stash of photographs.

By juxtaposing these very different recovered narratives and images, I challenge the fantasy that by bringing any of these pictures to light we can redeem the past. We can neither fully realize why they were hidden in the first place nor what they might have meant to those to whom they once belonged. Instead, I argue that these acts of recovery are elusive, especially to those of us who come to them belatedly. In all of these ways, I resist the notion that salvage is an act of redemption. Instead, I try to respect the elusive tangle of desires that led those at Auschwitz-Birkenau to risk their lives to hide what were once simply personally precious images and what made it possible for these images to come to light and become public, not only in these volumes but also in a new permanent exhibit at the State Museum at Auschwitz-Birkenau.[22] I use my father's forgetting, his act of hiding, and his slow and only partial memory about why he hid his secret stash to complicate any simple redemptive reading of the recovery of the 2,400 family photographs from Auschwitz-Birkenau.

4. Mary, Irena, and Me: Keepers of Accounts

In this final chapter, I return to my grandmother Mary Levitt and to poet Irena Klepfisz, and I ask what it means to pass on legacies and not to have children of one's own to bequeath them to. Instead of looking at excess as a symptom of loss, in this chapter I turn more directly to a different kind of engagement with the question of children and issues of loss. To get at these issues, I offer another reading of the final section of Klepfisz's poem *Bashert,* this time alongside her 1977 essay, "Women without Children/Women without Families/Women Alone." Through these texts I reconsider not only what it means to be a "keeper of accounts," but also what it means to "mother" and to be a woman without children. I bring together the speaker in Klepfisz's poem and the first person voice of her essay in order to offer a different take on my grandmother Mary Levitt and her legacy to me as a woman without children. And to clarify what is at stake in the gendering of these discussions, I contrast these texts and stories with those of two contemporary writers, both men of my generation, and their efforts to grapple with these issues in writing. I offer readings of Jonathan Rosen's *The Talmud and the Internet: A Journey between Worlds* and Daniel Mendelsohn's *The Elusive Embrace: Desire and the Riddle of Identity.*[23]

Returning to my family in order to get at these issues in a more intimate way, I use a few different images of Mary, a snapshot taken in the summer of 1939 at her wedding to my grandfather and another taken with her first grandchild. I look at these images in relation to the photographs described by Klepfisz in her poem in order to discuss Mary's role as a mother and as a keeper of family memories. In this way, I call attention to Mary's often invisible labors. I then draw connections between Mary, the narrators in Irena Klepfisz's essay and poem, and myself, a woman without children. I call attention to the various labors each of us performs in order to suggest other ways of keeping account of the past in an ever-shifting present. Although motherhood may still be the most obvious way of performing these labors, it need not be the only way. I use other texts and other stories, including the tale of my own mother as a teacher and mentor, in order to show that these legacies can be transmitted in other ways, especially by those of us who are women without children.

Conclusion: Other Ghosts, Other Encounters, Other Communities

In the conclusion, I return to the Tower of Faces to reconsider the allure of other people's family pictures. This time I return with my grandmothers and invite readers to bring their ghosts with them as well. I ask what it means to publicly share family stories, stories of intimate loss, and to see them alongside other people's stories, including the trauma of the Holocaust. To illustrate what this might look like, I turn to some of those with whom I have shared my stories in the process of writing this book to offer a glimpse of the kinds of stories this writing has engendered with the hope that readers will bring their own stories and pictures into these discussions.

I argue that by all of us bringing our own losses to bear on what we witness in spaces like the Tower of Faces, or even in reading a book like my own, we just might be able to forge more meaningful relationships with others, even with those whose families and communal stories are radically different from our own. In so doing, we can begin to unravel the very substance of what constitutes family, community, and identity and, in the process, find more creative ways of engaging with one another in the future.

1

Looking Out from under a Long Shadow

Like these, my despised ancestors
I have become a keeper of accounts.

I do not shun this legacy. I claim it as mine whenever I see the
photographs of nameless people. Standing staring off the edge of
the picture. People dressed in coats lined with fur. Or ragged at
elbows and collar. Hats cocked on one side glancing anxiously
towards the lens. A peasant cap centered and ordinary. Hair styled
in the latest fashion. Or standing ashamed a coarse wig awk-
wardly fitted. The shabby clothes. Buttons missing. The elegant
stance. Diamond rings. Gold teeth. The hair being shaved. The
face of humiliation. The hand holding the child's hand. A tree. A
track. A vague building in a photograph. A facility. And then the
fields of hair endless fields of hair the earth growing fertile
with their bodies with their souls.

—Irena Klepfisz, *Bashert*

What does it mean to be a "keeper of accounts" after the
Holocaust? How do we preserve memory? Which memories get to be
remembered? And which memories are worth preserving? These are
some of the questions posed by poet Irena Klepfisz in this, the last prose
section of her poem *Bashert*. After the Shoah, how is it possible to imagine remembering anything but this overpowering legacy of loss, "the
fields of hair the endless fields of hair"? And yet, Klepfisz's narrator
does not limit the accounts she keeps only to the legacy of the Holocaust. For her, Jewish memory is replete with images and stereotypes of
Jews extending backward and forward in time. She invokes a full range
of Jewish figures, wealthy and poor, fashionable and shabby, arrogant
and humiliated, and sometimes just plain ordinary. By addressing these

diverse images of Jews, especially in photographs, the narrator insists on the act of remembering. She insists on "keeping account" of all of her ancestors. Like this narrator, many of us struggle to keep account and remember our Jewish pasts in the aftermath of the Holocaust, questioning what can be remembered, what should be remembered, and what has been remembered. Lest we forget everything but the Holocaust, I want to insist on seeing the ordinary, the arrogant, the despised, the beloved, as well as "the endless fields of hair." And this means taking seriously the everyday losses that mark the lives of ordinary American Jews.[1] I look to family photographs like those of my grandparents to address these more quotidian losses, stories of loss that have all too often been overshadowed by the devastating destruction of European Jewish life that is the Shoah.

In what follows, I will turn to a very specific set of experiences where I found myself both wishing and not wishing that the Holocaust were my own. One of these experiences was my first visit to the United States Holocaust Memorial Museum in Washington, D.C., in particular, Yaffa Eliach's stunning memorial made up entirely of prewar family photographs from a single eastern European town destroyed by the Nazis, the Tower of Faces. It was in the Tower that I felt caught, tangled up in my contradictory desires. As I will explain, it was the familiar family images in the Tower that brought these different legacies together. It was here that I found myself thinking about my own family photographs, images of family members who have directly affected my life but are known to me only through faded black and white photographs. And I realized that those memories also drew me to the European Jews pictured in the Tower.

For American Jews like me who were born well after the war, Jews with no familial ties to the Holocaust, these contradictory desires and experiences are common. Making the Holocaust our own is dangerous, as is looking elsewhere to other more familiar Jewish legacies in order to identify ourselves as Jews. Even the thought that there might be other Jewish stories worth telling remains taboo.[2] It remains somehow shameful and selfish to either take on the Holocaust as if it were our own or to turn to more ordinary stories and images of Jewish life. The former is an act of appropriation, the latter a betrayal of the Holocaust and those who died. All of this is especially troubling for me, an academic engaged in contemporary Jewish studies. After all, how can I possibly want to use my time and energy to address common stories after the

Holocaust? Why don't I put my energy into studying the Holocaust, the most urgent of Jewish legacies? How can anything else measure up to this central task? And how can I ask you to follow me into a seemingly less urgent domain? And yet, my experience in the Tower shows me that these different legacies can and often do touch. And in so doing, these different stories need not efface one another. By reconsidering what identifications are made possible when ordinary images and stories are shared outside of the intimacy of the family, as in the Tower of Faces, I want to show how these different images brush up against one another —how they connect and how they differ. In other words, part of what makes the photographs in the Tower so compelling is that they are traces of what were once precious ordinary lives. Remembering the ordinariness of these lives helps us to not allow the horrible deaths of the people in these photographs to efface what these images once meant to those who took them and to those who first held them. We can then begin to imagine how these more intimate legacies might be shared. In this way we begin to keep account of the lives of these people, not just their deaths.

Those of us with no direct family ties to the Holocaust and no children of our own live with an additional tension. To whom do we pass on these various legacies? Given that not having children has itself been cast as an affront to the legacy of the Holocaust, how might we let go of the biology of inheritance and imagine other forms of community that might keep all of these legacies alive? How do we pass on not only the memory of the Holocaust, but also all of the more intimate legacies of loss that mark our American Jewish lives, and how do we see all of these memories as a part of a larger communal story? When we bring these, our own stories, with us into places like the Tower of Faces, I believe that we cast new shadows on the Holocaust that enable us to see other things. In other words, by taking seriously the various other legacies of 20th-century Jewish life and loss that overlap with the larger narrative of the Holocaust, we see all of these stories and images differently and begin to appreciate how all of these legacies might be shared.

Tangled Up in History: Taboos, Images, and Imagination

To write about ordinary Jews and their grief in the shadow of the Holocaust feels strange. To insist that the lives of ordinary American Jews deserve to be addressed in their own right feels presumptuous.[3] But I know that I have to keep these things, the Holocaust and ordinary American Jewish lives, together. It is not possible to address one legacy without invoking the other, but doing so feels fraught. I know that I don't want to be caught taking away from the centrality of the Holocaust and its imprint on contemporary Jewish life even in America.[4] Many of us are afraid of being judged, of not having permission, of trespassing and getting caught. We are afraid of getting entangled in tales we could never have been a part of.[5] And we worry about feeling obligated to pass on these legacies.

Getting caught up in Holocaust memory is tied to the contradiction at the heart of what it means to identify with other Jews. Through identification we make a connection to all Jews, but we also acknowledge the differences that separate those of us whose families were not affected by the Shoah from those of us whose families were profoundly altered by it.

In *Caught by History*, cultural critic Ernst van Alphen turns to contemporary art, literature, and theory to address some of the taboos that surround Holocaust commemoration.[6] Van Alphen struggles to keep the legacy of the Holocaust alive in the present and worries about the distancing effect of much historical writing and even of museum exhibitions. Like me, he is caught in a dilemma, how to make the Holocaust come alive for new generations. And also, like me, he finds contemporary art and literature a way of challenging the distancing effects of those other genres. He uses the notion of being caught as a way into his argument and as a way of positioning himself. But here our dilemmas differ. He is caught in the shameful position of not being able to identify with Holocaust victims and of being bored by the sanctioned stories he was taught. For him, the challenge is to figure out how he might identify not only with the victims but also with the perpetrators. In his explicitly personal introduction, van Alphen confesses to a terrible boredom with the legacy of the Holocaust going back to his postwar non-Jewish childhood in the Netherlands. He writes about his frustration with the heroic narratives his culture gave him and explains that he could never reconcile the coherence of victory with the horrors of the Holocaust. There was no room in these sanctioned tellings for any critical engagement. As a child, he felt unable to explore the complicated moral questions raised by the war, including what it might have meant to identify, even fleetingly, with the perpetrators. Without this, he argues, he was never able to enter into the more complicated moral terrain of what it might have been like to have lived through the German occupation of his country and to have experienced the deportation of Jews, both neighbors and strangers alike.

Rejecting another set of official narratives, in this case the sanctioned Dutch narratives of the war and the Holocaust, van Alphen is caught in a morally awkward position. He argues that art and literature—not history, the authorized genre of Holocaust studies—has offered him a way out of this dilemma. Art and literature seize his imagination. As he explains, "Whereas the education I received failed to make the Holocaust a meaningful event for me, Holocaust art and literature finally succeeded in calling my attention to this apocalyptic moment in human history" (3). He goes on to say that his book is an exploration of why and how "this capture by art and literature" happened; he uses his personal engagement with particular artists and their works to "get to the bottom of the matter" (3).

I initially turned to van Alphen because of the title of his book, *Caught by History.* I was looking for something close to what I had been struggling with in terms of my own engagement with the Holocaust. I wanted to consider the various ramifications of my sense of being "caught" in this history. Yet, now, as I reread van Alphen, I feel torn. Although he and I are contemporaries,[7] his analysis cannot begin to capture what it meant for me to grow up under the shadow of the Holocaust as a Jewish girl in postwar America. What van Alphen and I share is ambivalence, but the tensions and contradictions are different. He is caught by his terrible boredom and is later freed from it by contemporary art and literature. My ambivalence is of a different order.

For me, being caught up in this history is first and foremost a matter of fear, the fear of being captured, overtaken, or seized as a Jew. The Holocaust made clear to me that, as a Jew, I must be prepared for such a possibility, even in America. I needed to have hiding places, escape routes, a place to go just in case.[8] I worried about being caught off guard. I hardly remember a time when I did not have these fears. At the same time, I have also felt confident as an American. As such, unlike van Alphen, I did find some comfort in the heroic narratives of my country's fight against Hitler. It is only more recently that I have begun to question some of these cultural frameworks, both Jewish and American, that have shaped my understanding of the Holocaust.[9]

Although there is much that I find unsatisfying in van Alphen's book, especially in his broader conclusions,[10] I admire the risks he takes in revealing his abiding disinterest and annoyance with a variety of truisms in Holocaust studies, and I follow him away from positivist history and into the terrain of imagination. By owning my own taboo emotions as van Alphen does, I, too, want to invite new generations of children and adults, with their own perhaps less than acceptable reactions to this past, into a more meaningful engagement with the Holocaust. In so doing, I also want to show how this past touches and can open up an engagement with more ordinary tales of Jewish loss.[11] And so I turn to art and literature as well as to family photographs in order to explore a different kind of taboo—the taboo against making connections between ordinary and extraordinary loss.

In contrast to van Alphen, I insist on doing this in the first person, not only in my introduction but throughout this book, in order to show how these enactments work in both intimate and quite public ways. Because art, literature, and memorials like the Tower of Faces are performative, as van Alphen has powerfully demonstrated, they make it possible for us to experience aspects of the Holocaust and these other more ordinary losses together in the present. This immediacy makes all of these tales compelling and dangerous. The challenge for future generations with no direct access to the Holocaust is how to build on these often emotional reactions without losing a sense of the differences between us and them, then and now, and here and there.

In order to demonstrate how these dynamics work, I turn to an account of two connected moments in my own life, one at the Holocaust Memorial Museum in Washington, D.C., and the other at a lecture given at Haverford College in 1996. I come back to these recollections in the present to illustrate some of the contradictions and tensions that continue to make it difficult for so many contemporary American Jews to value the other often all too ordinary legacies of 20th-century American Jewish life and loss. Through my account of these narrative moments, I will show not only how memory works, but also how particular memories, in their messy and contradictory articulations, help make the urgency of telling some of these other tales of loss in relation to the Holocaust more apparent. More specifically, I hope to make visible the broader, still inchoate desires of ordinary American Jews to have our own more intimate tales of loss not only seen and acknowledged, but also considered a part of 20th-century Jewish history.

The Holocaust Memorial Museum, Washington, D.C., 1994: The Tower of Faces

One of the most powerful aspects of my first visit to the Holocaust Memorial Museum in Washington, D.C., was the time I spent lingering in Yaffa Eliach's photographic memorial, the Tower of Faces. It was entering and then returning to these seemingly ordinary images of Jewish life, the visual archive of a single eastern European town, that captured my imagination. These photographs fascinated me. I fell in love with their familiarity. I had to keep reminding myself of their poignancy, the fact that virtually all of the people whose lives are depicted in these photographs were killed in the Holocaust. There was something about seeing familiar Jewish faces, postures, and poses in this public space in the capital of the United States that moved me. I wanted to imagine these people as my own. I wanted these photographs to be those of my own family's albums. But in the midst of this fantasy, I caught myself. I remembered where I was and what had happened to these people. I realized that I was not at the Smithsonian or some other national museum, but at the Holocaust museum. In this place, these seemingly ordinary images could not be so familiar. These photographs, unlike my family's, were the traces of a community of families, specific lives brutally destroyed by the Nazis. They offered tantalizingly familiar visions of European Jewish life before the Nazis. Yet the lives of the people depicted in these photographs were marked in a way that made them unfamiliar. Their homes, their communal, social, and cultural organizations and institutions, their everyday lives in this specific place were irreparably damaged. For the few who survived, there was nowhere to return, no physical place, no social embrace.

Compared to virtually all of the other images in the museum, I experienced these photographs as a relief. The architecture and design of the permanent exhibition seems to recognize this dimension of the Tower by allowing visitors to return to this display again and again. Visitors enter and reenter the Tower at two different levels, from two different vantage points, and although the photographs continue up beyond our field of clear vision, we are allowed to see what is visible from more than one perspective. From each perspective, we encounter families, friends, and lovers—a whole world of intimacies populated by many different faces. In the museum, we are invited to take another look. And

The Tower of Faces. Yaffa Eliach Collection, courtesy of the United States
Holocaust Memorial Museum.

yet, even as we are able to get ever closer to more and more of these
photographs, we are reminded of our distance from them. We look up
and see all of those we will never encounter, images upon images illustrating the extent to which the totality of the losses of even this one

town remain out of reach, outside of our comprehension. These are the impressions I have carried with me. They are my memories.[12]

It is difficult for me to write about this visit and these lasting impressions. I wrote these words a number of years after my first visit to the museum. Part of what interests me is that these are the impressions that have lingered. They are what have stayed with me and animated my initial response to the Tower of Faces. In other words, I am interested in what these impressions say about the attraction of this display for other American Jews like me who are not the children of survivors and who have no known relatives who died in or survived the Holocaust.[13]

In part, I feel as if I am saying something obvious. And yet, I want to resist this kind of thinking. I want to resist the presumption that there is a normal or natural response to this place or this display because I am increasingly convinced that the imposition of such norms defeats the purpose of these exhibits. By owning these memories, I want to begin to challenge the assertion of norms of appropriate reception of Holocaust materials. In other words, by valuing some of the more complicated aspects of my own viewing practice, I hope to learn more about what viewers like me bring to such places. Why do we linger each time we enter the Tower wishing that these were our family's photographs on the walls? Why do so many of us wish that the Holocaust were our story, knowing full well how horrible this story is?

American Jews and the Desire to Be Included in Jewish History

For many American Jews, the desire to be included in the narrative of the Holocaust is expressed literally in efforts to seek out a connection.[14] American Jews who do genealogical research hoping to find European relatives who died in or survived the Holocaust do so in order to feel like they and their families' histories matter. Many of them are desperate to see themselves as a part of an acknowledged history. They do this despite the emotional costs of such revelations.[15] For me, this is only part of the story. It is not so much that I want to place myself in this specific, already formed, and authorized narrative; rather, it is that I want a place for my own stories of loss. In many ways, this book is a wager that I am not alone in this uncomfortable, unspoken desire. Building on this desire as I experienced it in the Tower of Faces, I want to show how these other tales are both related to and distinct from the

Holocaust and how they, too, are a part of 20th-century Jewish history. By resisting the notion that, compared to the Holocaust, ordinary stories of American Jewish loss like my own do not measure up, I am looking at another dimension of what happens at Holocaust memorials and museums. In this way, I challenge the notion that these other stories of loss are somehow unworthy, not important enough to merit either my own attention or a broader and more public appraisal. To this end, I want to let myself stay with what I have come to recognize as my own desire for my family photographs to be seen on display and my longing for my family and its grief to be acknowledged. By staying with these contradictory desires, I want to appreciate what is lost when the Holocaust overshadows other Jewish legacies. Again, I need to stress that these are not desires that one is supposed to have. They do not conform to the set framework or cultural expectations that have come to shape how American Jews are supposed to approach the Holocaust. Those acceptable engagements do not include these longings. At this historical moment, these other desires are not normative. But I want directly to challenge these assumptions and argue that these heretofore inexpressible and unacceptable desires are in fact at the heart of American Jews' engagements with the Holocaust. When we address the other more ordinary legacies of loss that have shaped American Jewish life, we demonstrate how this interplay works. We can then begin to work through our shame in order to confront more fully what is so haunting about all those intimate images on the walls of the Tower.

Before moving on to this other way of engaging the past, I want to return to the Tower of Faces to show how these normative practices work. In the case of the Tower, viewers are supposed to identify with those depicted in these photographs.[16] We are supposed to make some connections between them and ourselves, our families and their families, our communities and theirs. But we are not supposed to linger on this connection. Instead, we are supposed to see this portion of our engagement as but one move in a linear progression. Identification is merely the first step toward a teleological end. Ultimately, the exhibit is supposed to encourage us to build on this heightened sense of identification in order to begin to recognize the devastation of the Holocaust. In other words, we are supposed to experience the horror more personally through our familiarity with family photographs, but our individual encounters are ultimately supposed to be dwarfed by the grander vision of devastation and loss that is the Holocaust. Even the loss in just this one small eastern European town is exponentially beyond anything most of us could ever begin to imagine.

In many ways, my own reaction conformed to this agenda, but again, I am most interested in those aspects of my engagement that resisted this memorial rhetoric. What haunts me still is not so much this sanctioned narration, but rather something more excessive in my desire to connect to those faces. It also seems to me that this excess resonates deeply with the logic of the permanent exhibit as a whole, pointing to another way of understanding our relationship to this past. Visitors to the museum are encouraged to go back to this site as a part of their journey through the museum. Even as we linger in other places, we are never far from the Tower. Through cutouts and bridges, we keep finding ourselves near but unable ever to touch these faces. We catch glimpses of them even when we are not in the actual Tower. In other words, not only do we literally travel through the Tower more than once, but the Tower also seeps through the rest of the permanent exhibit. At various points along the way, newly revealed faces, which only become visible at these distinct locations, confront us.

Our return to the photographs again and again in terms of the actual architectural space of the museum enacts not so much the authorized narrative of the display but the kinds of longings I have described. In a real sense, as I experienced it, it was as if the architect and designers understood that we would not be able to get enough of these images. And, as I have explained, even though I did not physically return to the museum for many years, it is my longing for these images that has returned to me again and again in recollection. And it is the persistence of this longing that draws my attention now. I want to know what it meant that I did not find myself in this strangely definitive Jewish family photo album and what it might mean to challenge this understanding of 20th-century Jewish history that places the Holocaust at its center.

Seeing the Connections, Knowing the Differences

And so, I return to where I began. I am left with my desire to see my ordinary Jewish family on display in Washington, D.C., my longing to have these uncanny European Jews somehow be my own. On the one hand, the desire I am addressing is very much about placing myself in this very specific historical narrative, the catastrophic central narrative of 20th-century Jewish history, the Holocaust,[17] but it is also about imagining something else entirely. It is about recognizing and legitimating the more ordinary tales of eastern European Jews who had already established themselves in America during this same historical moment.[18] What might happen if we were to imagine that these other narratives and images are worthy of public recognition? What might it mean to own the fact that these Jews also long to be seen? And ironically, why is it that, even to broach the topic of these other images, I find myself having to begin in the Holocaust museum?

In order to address these other more intimate legacies, American Jews need to engage the Holocaust because it provides, at least at the present moment, one of the only legitimate, morally permissible routes to these other legacies of loss. At least from this starting place, we may begin to recast our understanding of 20th-century Jewish history as a series of interrelated legacies. Exhibits like the Tower of Faces may enable us to confront the Holocaust in such a way that we can also allow ourselves to engage these other legacies of loss and disappointment.

I left the museum troubled by my own conflicting desires. All that I had seen in the rest of the permanent exhibition horrified me. I understood the terror of the Tower, a chimney of lives literally gone up in smoke. This Tower cast its own shadow over the entire exhibition and over me. It also cast a shadow over my own more ordinary desires.

Haverford College, Spring 1996: Making Public Identifications

In the spring of 1996, I went to Haverford College to hear literary critic Marianne Hirsch give a talk about family pictures and Holocaust memory. The talk was culled from her engagement with these issues in what would become her book *Family Frames*.[19] At the time, I was completing my first book, for which I had begun to think critically about using family photographs in my work.[20] I was also working closely with a few graduate students on Holocaust-related dissertations. It was with two of these students that I went to the talk.[21] I was greatly impressed by Hirsch's presentation and excited about her larger project.[22] More than this, I was taken by her account of her visits to the Tower of Faces. This was the first time I had heard a scholarly appraisal of this exhibit.[23] Hirsch's words struck a chord, and I was grateful. I was fascinated and relieved to hear Hirsch's description of the exhibit and her critical appraisal of how it functions in the broader museum. I also wanted more, and judging by the discussion following the talk, others also wanted to say more about the Tower of Faces.

The account Hirsch offered at Haverford is echoed in the final chapter of *Family Frames*. I now turn to her text as a way of capturing the texture of her presentation. When Hirsch visited the U.S. Holocaust Memorial Museum, she thought a great deal about the role of photographs in preserving and transmitting Holocaust memory, asking, "Do pictures provide the second- and third-generation questioner with a more concrete, a better access to the abandoned parental world than stories can? Or, as indexical traces, do they perhaps provide too direct and material a connection to the past" (248)? Hirsch then connects these practices to her notion of "postmemory."

According to Hirsch, postmemory is tied to the particular cultural, historical, and intellectual context of the second half of the twentieth century. As she explains, "I believe that this moment has given rise to new aesthetic questions and perhaps to new aesthetic forms. . . . Art Spiegelman's *Maus* functions as a paradigmatic and generative text . . . allowing me to mark out the parameters raised within my particular reading of postmodernity" (12). In *Family Frames* Hirsch goes on to explain that Art Spiegelman's delayed, indirect, secondary memory captures best what she means by postmemory.

> *Maus* is a familial story, collaboratively constructed by father and son. The Spiegelman/Zylberberg families have lived through the massive devastation of the Holocaust, and thus the details of family interaction are inflected by a history that refuses to remain in the background or outside the text. Their story is told, drawn, by the son, who was born after the war but whose life was decisively determined by this familial and cultural memory. (12–13)

For Hirsch, postmemory works as an ambivalent practice that captures both Spiegelman's "passionate interest and desire" in terms of his parents' history and his "inevitable distance and lack of understanding" of this same legacy (13). According to Hirsch, it is this deferred, mediated, secondary memory that has cast its shadow over contemporary life and helps explain the power of family photographs in the museum in Washington, D.C. As she explains, these photographs help bring whole new generations of viewers into the realm of postmemory. At their best they allow viewers with little connection to the Holocaust, both Jewish and non-Jewish visitors alike, to imaginatively identify with the generation of postmemory, the memory of survivor children (249).

After explaining the various and varied uses of photographs throughout the museum, Hirsch focuses her attention on the importance of family photographs and how they work in this context.

> The conventionality of the family photo provides a space of identification for any viewer participating in the conventions of familial representation; thus the photos can bridge the gap between viewers who are personally connected to the event and those who are not. They can expand the postmemorial circle. Photographs of the world lost to genocide and to exile can contain, perhaps more obviously than the names and narrative fragments handed down . . . the particular mixture of mourning and re-creation that characterize the work of postmemory. (251)

Hirsch asserts that given this, it is not surprising that the Tower of Faces is situated "at the very center of the museum" (251).

Although the museum's permanent exhibit is chronological, beginning on the fourth floor with the rise of Nazism, leading into the prewar "terror in Poland" and the Nazi euthanasia program, the Tower interrupts this linear narrative. As Hirsch narrates it, this break is crucial. After describing these exhibits, she continues:

> Next we pass over a glass bridge whose walls are inscribed with hundreds of names, each representing a town or a community destroyed in the genocide. In a radical break in chronology, we then enter a room shaped like a tower and constructed entirely of sepia-toned photographic images that hover all around us. An introductory panel explains that what we are seeing are several hundred photographs of the Lithuanian shtetl of Ejszyzski collected by a child survivor of the town, Yaffa Eliach, the granddaughter of the town's Jewish photographers, Yitzak Uri Katz and Alte Katz. (251–252)

Hirsch then takes us into the space of the Tower from this vantage point describing it in detail. "Some of the photos are eye level, others are out of reach, hard to see. We are separated from them by the bridge on which we are standing, which keeps us in the middle of the room, removed from direct contact with the images" (252). What we see from

The Tower of Faces. Yaffa Eliach Collection, courtesy of the United States Holocaust Memorial Museum.

this precarious vantage point are ordinary family pictures, the familiar poses and intimacies of our own family albums. Hirsch is also captivated by this familiarity, as are those around her. " 'Look, look, look,' I hear people saying all around me, 'we have a picture just like this one in our album.' Or 'Look, that looks just like Grandma!' Interestingly, in the minutes I spend in the room, I find that this identification easily transcends ethnic identity and family history" (252). It is here that I find Hirsch capturing my own excitement in recognizing these seemingly familiar faces. For Hirsch, the key to this process is the conventional nature of family photographs. She goes on to link these engagements in the Tower with the more common experience of looking through family albums stressing the contrast between the Tower and the rest of the permanent exhibition. "When we enter the Tower of Faces, we leave the historical account of the museum and enter a domestic space of a family album that shapes a different form of looking and knowing, a different style of recognition" (254). For Hirsch, this kind of looking transcends differences. For her, such "affiliative familial looking" enables viewers to become a part of a collective memory that may not be their own. They can "adopt" this stance in the space of the Tower.

Hirsch's narrative continues with a description of how visitors return to the Tower as they descend through the museum. As she explains, visitors reenter the Tower on the third floor, which is dedicated to the culmination of the Final Solution.[24] As Hirsch describes it:

> After walking through a railroad car used in the Polish deportations, seeing a model of the gas chambers and crematoria in Auschwitz, walking by a pile of shoes brought from Auschwitz and seeing an actual oven from Mauthausen, we cross another glass bridge, right below the one that listed all the names of lost communities. This bridge is covered with hundreds of first names—I find mine, my mother's and father's, that of each of my grandparents, those of my sons. After a few other memorial exhibits this bridge leads to the Tower of Faces on a level below the bridge on which we initially stood. (255)

Entering this portion of the Tower, Hirsch makes clear that the message is different, signaled by the words that are now on the wall describing the Tower. Here we learn that a mobile killing unit destroyed the town of Eishyshok (Ejszyski) in September of 1941 and that there were virtually no survivors. As Hirsch insists,

> This is a radically different encounter with the images. The lower room is much darker since the light comes from a distant skylight obscured by the opaque glass bridge on which other visitors are standing on the floor above. The room is square, and we can go right up to the images —we are no longer separated from them. We see the faces more closely; we look into the eyes of people who were alive. . . . The images are at once more accessible, because we are closer to them, and less so because there is so little light. (256)

Not only the black borders of the photographs but the full weight of the Tower as a funerary pyre come to remind Hirsch of all that has been lost. As she explains, "This album is also a tomb, . . . commemoration is also mourning" (256). Like the chimneys of the crematoriums in the death camps, here, too, life is seemingly reduced to smoke. It is during this second encounter with the Tower that Hirsch experiences its larger meaning. This time around she is no longer able to identify with the images on the walls. She becomes angry. She is in disbelief. She comes to see the devastation and brutal destruction wrought by the Holocaust. Although she ends her account by drawing attention to the layering of memory over time and space, the thrust of her account is with this, the cumulative effect of these two encounters with the Tower. Here its dark and devastating resonances get the final word. Although we identify with these images, ultimately, Hirsch argues, we are left with a clear sense that they can never be our own.

I have re-presented large portions of Hirsch's account not only because she offers a more fully developed description of how the Tower functions in contrast to my own more impressionistic account, but also because I wanted to show the points of overlap between our descriptions. When I first heard Hirsch offer this account I was struck by her notion of identification and its implications. I no longer remember if I was the first one to raise questions about the Tower in the question and answer period following her talk, but I do remember that there was a lot of discussion. During this prolonged exchange, I spoke about my desire to see these people as somehow a part of my own family. There was a great deal of discussion back and forth. Although I no longer remember the particulars of the discussion, what stands out for me is how the conversation ended. Lori Lefkovitz, a Jewish feminist literary scholar, spoke as the child of survivors. For Lori, as opposed to the rest of us it seemed,[25] there was no pleasure in identifying with these images. These people could have been her relatives. Like her extended family, virtually all of these people had died in the Holocaust. For Lori, this recognition was unbearable. There was no joy in this recognition. The Tower was not a place of affiliative longing. Instead, it was a creepy and disturbing place, made only more so by the expressions of cheerful desire, the familial longings of so many visitors like me who could not stop ourselves from making connections to our own more or less intact family albums.

This was my worst fear come to light. I had been caught red-handed in a terrible act. I had expressed a comfort and pleasure in identifying with European Jews who had been murdered in the Holocaust. I had said this in public. There was no turning back. Lori's comments confirmed my shame. They reminded me of the obscenity of my desires. Chastened, I was reminded that I would always be an outsider to this history. Even as an American Jew, I would never know what it felt like to have lost family in the Holocaust. And I would never have a right to make these kinds of connections. To be fair, this was not Lori's intention. She never told others what to say or feel. She simply spoke from her own experience in the Tower, and that was enough for me to draw these elaborate conclusions. Lori's comments simply confirmed lessons I had already internalized.[26]

"Past Lives" Revisited, 2003

As I worked with Marianne Hirsch's text to reconstruct her account of the Tower of Faces, I found myself caught between wanting to remember the talk she had given at Haverford and wanting to reconsider the larger argument of her book. In the final chapter of *Family Frames*, her account of the Tower exemplifies the aesthetics of postmemory, highlighting the powerful role of family photography in this aesthetic. Hirsch uses an image by artist Lorie Novak to frame the chapter, as she explains:

> I choose as my chapter title and emblem "Past Lives," a 1987 photograph by the Jewish American artist Lorie Novak. "Past Lives" is a photograph of a composite projection onto an interior wall. Novak populates this domestic space with a picture of the Jewish children hidden in Izieu and eventually deported by Klaus Barbie, superimposed on a picture of Ethel Rosenberg's face, superimposed on a childhood image, from the 1950's, of Novak herself held by her mother. (246)

For Hirsch, this layered photographic work clearly enacts the aesthetics of postmemory. It brings together "many ghosts," connecting public and private memories as well as different temporal moments and geographic places. Here Holocaust memory and American memories are intermingled in the intimacy of the all too familiar trope of mother and child. [27] For Hirsch, this work "begins to define the aesthetic strategies of mourning and reconstruction of her [Novak's] generation of postmemory" (246). Like the various works Hirsch discusses throughout her book and especially in this chapter, this work is haunting. Here, "space and time are conflated to reveal memory's material presence" (246). This is how, according to Hirsch, art and memorial works can enact postmemory. And yet, I am struck by this notion of Novak's "own generation."

Like Hirsch, I was also taken by Novak's image, not so much for how it formally engaged the issues of postmemory, but rather for how it helped me begin to clarify the various positions that Hirsch attempts to bring together in her notion of postmemory. Unlike Hirsch, I do not see these positions merging in an attempt to replicate the experience of a single generation, the generation of children of survivors and children of exiled European Jews.[28] I am much more intrigued by the idea of multiple generations and how American Jews born after the war, including me and my contemporaries Lorie Novak and Shimon Attie (another American Jewish artist whose work Hirsch discusses), bring aspects of our own non-Holocaust-related pasts into these encounters with the Holocaust in the present.

I am interested in how these engagements distinguish us from Hirsch or Lefkovitz and others of that initial generation of postmemory like Spiegelman. Rather than hoping to replicate or adopt the position of that single generation, a generation that is itself plural and contradictory, I want to acknowledge more fully the growing contradictions and distances that continue to distinguish ongoing generations from one another and from that literal generation of children of survivors. Although, as Hirsch rightfully argues, this generation of children were the first to exemplify the experience of exile or diasporic memory, they do not share a single stance with each other, much less with other generations who follow them.[29] By making these distinctions, I want to take seriously the very American and indeed explicitly postwar resonances of the images of Ethel Rosenberg and Lorie Novak and her mother in "Past Lives" as they interact with the legacy of the Holocaust and how they shaped my first reading of the Tower.

In many ways, my reading of Hirsch builds on the tension she sets up between identification and difference, the way photographs both enable and disable our ever knowing the pasts they depict. Like Hirsch I want to emphasize what can never be known, but I also want to be clear about what distinguishes different viewers from one another even in the act of identification. As I see it, what happens as viewers encounter the intimate images in the Tower of Faces is not homogeneous. Although Hirsch emphasizes, through her repeated use of the phrase "at its best," that the Tower and the Museum in Washington, D.C., "elicit in its visitors an imaginary identification—the desire to know and to feel, the curiosity and passion that shape the postmemory of survivor children," or that, "*At its best* [my emphasis], it would include all of its visitors in the generation of postmemory" (249), I disagree with this assessment.

As I see it, for those of us with no direct ties to survivors, such inclusion is not possible. Instead, within the Tower, our own ghosts confront us.[30] For us, the challenge is to distinguish between the various layers of desire that both separate and connect us to these faces. In part, this means seeing more clearly what separates me from Lorie Novak and each of us from both Marianne Hirsch and Lori Lefkovitz. It also means seeing the distance between Hirsch and Lefkovitz on the question of postmemory.[31] Here, even at its best, the generation of children of survivors does not share a single position, especially in relation to the Tower of Faces. Although Hirsch encourages all visitors to enter the circle of postmemory, Lefkovitz insists that this invitation is fraught. There is no single authorized stance for all to appropriate even in the generation of postmemory. Instead, the Tower lends itself to a broad range of responses. In other words, in the Tower, the gaps among those with personal connections to the Holocaust and the gaps between them and those of us without these ties, are *never* bridged (251).

If anything, at their best, these gaps are made wider, creating spaces where images and memories of other times, other places, and other losses can all come together. It is in these gaping spaces that images like those offered in Lorie Novak's "Past Lives" find their place. It is here that postwar and even prewar memories become visible. Although they are often shaded by the legacy of the Holocaust, as in Novak's work, they are not effaced. They seep through. If we don't turn away and instead look more closely, we can see the faces of Ethel Rosenberg and Lorie Novak and her mother as they fade in and out of the faces of the deported children.

By acknowledging this layering as ongoing, I question Hirsch's claim that the Tower can bring those of us without personal connections to the Shoah into the generation of postmemory, into the generation of children of survivors. As I see it, Hirsch's insistence on a single stance takes away from the power of her mediated vision and instead reinforces the dominant American Jewish legacy of privileging the Holocaust to the exclusion of other memories. It is this desire that I want to challenge. By rigidly safeguarding against the Holocaust's displacement by any other legacies, a justifiable fear becomes all-consuming as it keeps us from seeing other losses, those other pasts that we necessarily bring to our engagement with the Holocaust. Ironically, I believe that by not acknowledging these other memories, we are kept from more fully appreciating all that the Holocaust means for us in the present. If we allow the interplay of connections and differences between ordinary and extraordinary losses, we can more fully come to understand how all of these losses are a part of our everyday lives.

Although the circle of those who remember may expand, this opening up is not about allowing more people to participate vicariously in any single experience of children of survivors and the children of exiled Jews as Hirsch's notion of postmemory suggests. Instead, this is an expansive process. Here remembering the Holocaust is about owning our own memories of loss and letting them help us more fully appreciate what the Holocaust denied to so many others. In other words, we reanimate the pictures in the Tower with "our own knowledge of daily life" (256). In order to do this, we need to be open to all of the other losses that we necessarily bring to the Tower, including those right in front of us in this place. Only by recognizing *all* of these layered memories can we begin to make distinctions between what is and what is not our own. As I see it, we are obliged *not* to try to lose ourselves in other people's pasts, to become a part of a single generation of postmemory as Hirsch suggests, but instead we are obligated to take more seriously the stuff of our own more intimate memories of loss so that we can begin to see the boundaries that distinguish us from others. In this way, we can avoid the kinds of vicarious appropriations of other peoples' experiences that often mar even well-meaning engagements with those who suffer. What I want is for visitors to be able to acknowledge the desires and experiences we bring with us as we enter the Tower. I don't want to forget these other losses. Rather, by more fully bringing these often more intimate legacies of loss together with the photographs on display in the Tower of Faces, we can begin to touch, in Hirsch's words, "the death that took those lives so violently" (256). It is the interplay between these disparate memories that animates the Holocaust for us in the present.[32]

What distinguished my position from Hirsch's is that I resist the desire for an ideal position, a single all-inclusive authorized stance in relation to Holocaust memory. I suggest that it is only possible for us to see ourselves in relation to the Holocaust through the shadows and layers of the various memories, both public and private, that we bring to places like the Tower. We cannot assume the position of a generation, the generation of children of survivors who themselves do not share a single stance. I see these efforts to remember and commemorate the Holocaust as ongoing. In this way our engagements with the ghosts who haunt our individual imaginations continue to shape how we engage with the Holocaust and touch that past. This happens in much the same way that Lorie Novak's installation works. By including postwar and American Jewish legacies as the templates that make visible and tangible this more distant legacy of loss, Novak's work illustrates how these different legacies of loss touch and illuminate each other.

This more mediated, shaded, and shadowed engagement with Holocaust images preserves the tensions between connection and differences at the heart of photography's allusive and elusive presence. Without a single ideal stance, distinctions are maintained. We can be more honest about the lack of fit between ourselves and others, our memories and theirs. By not striving to find consensus, we lessen the chance of misappropriation. Given this, although the generation of children of survivors has clearly helped shape and define our understanding of the displaced memories of all of us who come after, this generation's process has not produced a single stance. Instead, the process of identification as I understand it offers an ever-expanding range of positions.[33] I want to respect these distinctions, the distinctions between Lorie Novak and Marianne Hirsch, and between each of them and me. Given this, a gap opens in the Tower and all of these differences are present. The point is not to overcome this multiplicity, but to appreciate the interplay among and between these various and distinct legacies of loss.

It was dwelling on these questions that prompted me to begin writing about the story of my father and his two mothers in the shadow of the Holocaust. Since my first visit to the museum in 1994, I have thought about the implications of these kinds of interactions, the ways that different losses brush up against one another. For me, what is crucial is that in those moments when they touch, they illuminate each other. One loss is not replaced or effaced by the other; they coexist, somehow clarified in that touching. My initial visit to the Tower of Faces was my entry into these relationships. It drew me to my own family photographs, the very photographs that I had wanted to see next to the ones in the Tower, the pictures of my paternal grandmothers.

When I left Haverford with Tania Oldenhage and Michelle Friedman, who were then still my graduate students working on Holocaust-related dissertations, we were intrigued and troubled by Hirsch's notion of "postmemory." Like van Alphen, we were all born well after the war, but we each have very different relationships to this past. Tania was born in Germany and she is not Jewish. Michelle and I are both American Jews, but unlike me, Michelle is the child of a child survivor. These differences among and between us have always been important to our engagement with each other's work on the Holocaust.[34] And, yet Hirsch's framework did not quite capture what it was like for us to work together. We never assumed common ground. This is the piece of Hirsch's account of "postmemory" that did not resonate with our experience, even then.

Over the years it has been an abiding insistence on recognizing and honoring our quite different positions that has allowed each of us to more honestly and critically confront the legacy of the Holocaust. And, in this respect, Tania's position is most telling because it is most removed. She enters this space the child of Germans who lived through the war. Like Hirsch's postmemory which ideally enables all visitors to enter vicariously into the generation of the children of Jewish survivors, the gaping space I describe is also inclusive but in a different way. It is open to American Jews, Germans, and Americans of various backgrounds as well as to survivors and their children and grandchildren. I believe that there is room in the Tower of Faces, as Hirsch suggests, for Tania's ghosts and for my own, for van Alphen's Dutch ancestors and for Michelle's Hungarian grandmother. The point is that our experiences cannot ever be the same or in any simple way shared. Given this, what happens in the Tower is a gap that is open to these differences. The point is not to overcome this multiplicity but to appreciate the interplay among and between these various distinct legacies of loss.

In this sense, what happens in the Tower is clearly not simply a Jewish enactment. Although I focus on my American Jewish experience, a relatively privileged position in the prevailing cultural narrative of Holocaust commemoration, by challenging even my own trepidation in claiming this space I am suggesting a broader opening. As I see it, this public site already invites a broad and diverse range of visitors into an engagement with their own ghosts. I want to offer permission to all who visit this site to see these other legacies, especially those seemingly lesser legacies of loss. This would also include those legacies that are at odds with the very narrative of the victims of the Nazis, the memories of the next generation of Germans, Poles, and Austrians, to name but a few. Although I am especially concerned about the taboos in my own community about recognizing more ordinary America Jewish ghosts as they appear in this space, my wager is that we are not alone in this prohibition. By letting go of these restrictions, we can begin to see that the Tower is filled with all kinds of ghosts fading in and out of the consciousness of individual visitors to the museum.

In the conversation that Tania, Michelle, and I had in the car on the way home from Hirsch's lecture, we tried to imagine using "postmemory" in our work. We initially found the term alluring, a big broad term that might enable us to stand together, but it was difficult to deploy. As soon as one of us tried to use it, we were confronted with the differences that distinguish each of our positions from the other's. Revisiting Hirsch's text all these years later, I see that the problem was not in the interplay she so beautifully describes, but rather it was that after seeing the various overlapping images, we were unwilling ultimately to contain our hauntings within a singular stance, the position of the second generation. What I propose, instead, allows us to engage with van Alphen and Hirsch as well as with Michelle and Tania, respecting the fact that we are all haunted by quite different ghosts even as we confront the legacy of the Holocaust. The goal of a critical engagement with the Holocaust does not require us to relinquish those legacies, but it does require us to acknowledge them and, in so doing, to appreciate what makes them distinct. Knowing these differences, we are able to share our various haunting stories with one another.

Returning to the Tower of Faces with Michelle and Tania

By telling less extraordinary narratives outside of the bounds of our families or even the Jewish community, we might begin to forge other kinds of communities and connections. In other words, by opening up the space of Holocaust museums and memorials like the Tower of Faces to these other tales of loss, those embedded in our own memories, we begin to recognize how commemoration always involves an interplay between various pasts and an ever-changing present. None of us enters these spaces without memories of our own. By acknowledging these other ghosts and indeed embracing them, we begin to change our expectations about what it means to commemorate the Holocaust. In this way the Holocaust is no longer something totally outside our comprehension. By allowing ourselves to bring our own losses with us into spaces like the Tower of Faces, we come to appreciate anew the human dimension of this catastrophe.

It is not possible to banish these other ghosts from places like the Holocaust Memorial Museum in Washington, D.C., nor does their presence in Holocaust studies need be denied or shunned. Instead, if we look at these elusive ordinary figures more closely, we can see how they animate our engagement with the legacy of the Holocaust and how the Holocaust animates our engagement with them. Instead of denying or trying to get rid of these ghosts, I want to respect what they have to tell us about the labor of remembrance.[35]

I want to invite not only my own ghosts to linger but also those of others. Instead of trying to remake our ghosts into versions of the same, a kind of postmemory, I return to the Tower with Tania Oldenhage and Michelle Friedman. This time, I imagine us there together telling stories, our own and those of others—German stories, Hungarian Jewish stories, and American Jewish stories from both before and after the war—with no compulsion to find common ground. Instead, we tell these different and even contradictory tales of loss. The catastrophic and the ordinary are all there, but, this time, there is no shame.

2

Postmarked Pictures

Ordinary Legacies

As we have already seen, for many American Jews, the allure of the Tower of Faces is a sense of connection and familiarity. It is as if these people whose pictures are on display in the Tower are our own. Through these deeply intimate connections, viewers also come to appreciate how intimacy can usher us into larger and more public narratives. We want to claim these images and stories, not only because we long for connection and for larger notions of family and community, but also because we want to have a sense that we, too, are a part of Jewish history. And yet, many of us whose families were fortunate enough to have left eastern Europe well before the war feel that we cannot lay claim to this most important of Jewish stories because we are not directly linked to that dramatic history. In other words, because our relatives were here and we escaped that fate, we are not a part of the communal narrative that is the Holocaust.

In this all-too-common telling, the Holocaust is at the center of 20th-century Jewish history. Given this, many American Jews struggle to figure out how to see ourselves as really Jewish. Many of us proclaim our connections to other Jews and to an intimate God to address this lack. Some of us attempt to reform ourselves into more authentic Jews by embracing an ancient tradition, and still others have turned to Jewish nationalism, to the State of Israel, to compensate and counteract the otherwise dominant narrative of the Holocaust. We use these other versions of Jewish identification as a way of seeing ourselves as a part of the Jewish people, a community increasingly linked, not so much by a shared space or place in the world, but by a shared past.[1] We want to believe that we are connected to other Jews through time, that we have a common history with ancient roots.[2]

The problem is that, for many of us, making these connections across time is not so easy. Our own families' histories do not go back that far. For American Jews like me who are a part of the vast majority of eastern European Jews whose ancestors came to this country from 1880 to 1924, there is little that links us to that first generation who came to the United States or to those they left behind. Most of us have few, if any, connections to the faces on the walls of the Tower in Washington, D.C., much less to any of the specific eastern European locations identified throughout the museum. We know little about where our families came from. If we are lucky, there may be a few strands of an incomplete narrative, a place name, a family name, but little else. And because most of us come from the ranks of the poor and uneducated, we also have few material possessions that have been passed on to us from that past to bear witness to these historical connections. There are no books, no ritual objects. Again, if we are lucky, we may have a few scattered photographs. These are our only connections to a larger historical narrative. And yet, this more immediate history is the piece of the story that many of us rarely engage. The loss and disconnection that mark this inheritance is too great. Although we long for these connections, finding them in their specificity is often impossible. It is something we have hardly begun to grieve. The fact is that we know little about our closest ancestors, and this makes the effort to learn more daunting. Confronting the loss of our families' stories is painful.[3] And, even if we try, we are not sure that these incomplete narratives will ever really matter.

This, too, is part of what attracts us to the Tower of Faces. The photographs we have, the ones that are often the oldest and most precious in our own families, images we know so little about, date to around the same era as those on the walls of the Tower. The Tower seems to tell us that perhaps our photographs are also important; they may tell us something about a larger Jewish past. But if we do not simply place our pictures on these walls and somehow make them one and the same, what do the images in the Tower offer those of us with other family photographs that we need to engage?

When we look at the photographs in the Tower, we find traces of at least a time, if not a place, that is vaguely familiar. We see a resemblance that is comforting. Like the pictures in the Tower, our family photographs also date from the turn of the last century, the few decades before and after, but unlike our own pictures, the family photographs in the Tower are labeled and publicly validated.[4] They are clearly important. Not only do they offer us a sense of our links to a time before we, our parents, and if we are lucky, our grandparents were born, but they also validate those earlier moments in ways that we cannot yet do with our own images. Again, they show us that those legacies mattered. They also suggest, albeit in a different way, that our images might also carry larger meanings.

Unlike my partner, whose father's family can trace its roots back to the time of the American Revolution, most American Jews of eastern European descent do not have these kinds of family histories. We cannot trace our families back much beyond the mid-19th century. And yet we do not talk much about this void. Instead, more often than not, Jewish figures in public and private life, the famous and the infamous, attempt to erase this gap by making links to an earlier, more mythic era in European Jewish life.[5] They claim to be the descendants of the famous, the learned of another era entirely, or as I did, they attempt to reclaim a seemingly timeless ancient form of Judaism in the present as their own. These efforts are all symptomatic of the kind of disconnect I am talking about. Because most of us are heirs to some of the least educated and the poorest of what was once the culture of the Pale, those who fled to the United States at the beginning of the 20th century, we are uncomfortable with our actual pasts. Few of us are the heirs to great rabbinic dynasties despite our efforts to lay claim to these histories, and at the end of the 20th century and the beginning of the 21st, it seems that, increasingly, this need to be a part of an important Jewish past is being manifested in our desire to lay claim to the Holocaust. In other words, this desire for a more authentic and important Jewish identity may also drive many of us to claim those faces in the Tower as our own, to insist on our connection to the Holocaust, and to blur the distinctions between our families and theirs. In all of these ways, we long to place ourselves within an authorized Jewish narrative. We find ourselves leaving our Jewish homes in order to re-create ourselves as more authentic Jews.

In part, I believe that these efforts are linked to a more basic desire to fix our identities, to plant ourselves on some firmer ground than what we actually have. And yet, I want to argue that to really do this successfully, we need to take more seriously the intimate legacies closest to home, our own family histories. By claiming this site of intimacy as the site of identity formation and identification, we might begin to appreciate how even the most ordinary emotional connections and relationships across time and space can actually help us feel more at home in the world, even if only for a time.[6]

For American Jews, the desire to forge connections with other Jews is linked to notions of endogamy, to seeing Jewishness in familial terms, and yet ironically, those notions of the Jewish people as family often replace the more intimate and messy legacies of our own more immediate family relations. To more fully embrace intimacy as a building block to a notion of the sacred that makes our relationship to God itself a form of intimacy, we need to look more closely at the broken and partial stories of our own actual ancestors. As we get closer to home, this includes an appreciation for what intimacy can never do. We need to remember that we can never fully know even those we love the most. Our connections are ultimately always partial and incomplete. It is these qualities of intimacy that make these relationships so compelling, drawing us in again and again.[7]

This is part of what my first book, *Jews and Feminism: The Ambivalent Search for Home,* was about. It is also connected to my efforts to become a more authentic Jew in Israel in 1982. In my book, I wrote about trying to find a home in the textual legacies of my various peoples, especially those most formal and official legacies—the rabbis, liberalism, and liberal Judaism. And even there I think I was looking for a foundation, a solid platform upon which to stake out my own claims to a Jewish identity in the present. I wanted to add weight and authority to those desires. I was not quite comfortable embracing the ordinary legacy of my own family. And again, I do not think I am alone in these struggles. These very desires for solidity and clarity are, I suspect, disproportionately related to how little those of us who want them the most actually have at our disposal. In other words, for those who can trace their families' histories back in time and space, the need to claim this kind of history is less urgent than it is for those of us who cannot. We want what we do not have, and because we do not have these things, we want them all the more. This is the dilemma as I have experienced it time and time again. But instead of becoming more observant, creating mythic stories, or appropriating the tragedy of the Holocaust as my own, I am looking more closely at what many of us do have, the traces of those ancestors closest to us in time and space, the bits and pieces of the ordinary lives they left behind both here and in Europe and the few physical objects, especially the photographs, that link us to them.

What happens if we look closely at these ordinary and mundane traces of our own families' pasts? What do these common objects tell us about who we are? What do they tell us about the contours of our family's specific immigrant legacies and how they continue to shape our lives? What are the kinds of Jewish lives our grandparents left behind in Europe? What kinds of lives did they create in the United States? How are these stories of promise, loss, disappointment, and desire a part of Jewish history? How might we begin to include these tales in what constitutes Jewish history?

Doing this work brings together collective and individual narratives. It enables us to link our memories to historical narratives, those stories that have, until now, mattered most in the broader context of Jewish imaginings. And yet, to move from memory to history, from family to people, requires that we forge these intimate links, that we take more seriously our ordinary tales, however small and inconsequential we might believe them to be, and make them matter. I believe that without these common recollections, we lose a sense of the familiar, even in the most grand, the most traumatic, and the most dramatic historical narratives. We forget the simple fact that human beings lived all of these stories.

For me, Abraham Ravett's short nonnarrative film *Half-Sister* was a way into these tangled questions. This film about Ravett's belated reckoning with his family's immediate past, its Holocaust past, helped me appreciate the need to look more closely at ordinary stories, those legacies of loss closest to my own home. For Ravett, although the Holocaust looms large, casting a shadow over his family story, it is the family story that he struggles with. In *Half-Sister* Abraham Ravett attempts to figure out his place in his immediate family, a family created after the war. Ravett's parents had each been married to other people and each had children before the Holocaust. He articulates how his belated learning about the existence of his half-siblings (his mother's one daughter and his father's two children) changed his self-understanding.[8] The film is about how Ravett had to unlearn his place as an only child in his own family after discovering that each of his parents had other children, other families, before the war. Here the small and the grand come together. Ravett had to come to see himself anew. As an adult he learned that he was and was not an only child. He had long-dead half-siblings. Abraham Ravett's own sense of self changes as he begins, belatedly, to see himself in relation to these half-siblings, siblings whom he could never have known and whose very deaths were, in part, the foundations of his own existence. His parents would never have met and married if they had not had to start their lives all over again in the aftermath of the Shoah.

This knowledge leaves Ravett both more and less alone than before. His place in his family and in the world is altered most profoundly by these impossible relations, the devastation and loss that happened before he was born. In this case, the extraordinary story of the Holocaust is made small. Its effects, in their specificity, come to shape how Abraham Ravett understands himself and his place in his own family as a child born to survivors after the war. In *Half-Sister*, Ravett reenacts his process of discovery, the belatedness of his overt knowledge, and his ongoing struggle with his multiple and contradictory desires to come to know just one of these siblings, his mother's daughter. And all that Ravett has of his half-sister is a single image. The film is very much a meditation on this single photograph as a way into this complicated terrain. I will return to this film shortly. For now, I simply want to signal this initial connection.

In what follows I want to offer an enactment of my own. I want to demonstrate how I came to reassess the loss of my father's mother, Lena Levitt, in relation to Ravett's film. The formal connection between Ravett's meditation on a photograph returned to him (or to his family) belatedly and the belated return of the portrait of my father's parents drew me to this film. In order to show what this connection has opened up for me, I will move back to a retelling of my family story and my various engagements with Ravett's film. In this way, I want to enact the interplay I experienced between these very different legacies of loss. And I suspect that these moves will be familiar to many of my readers. What I am illustrating is the often less than conscious ways that our memories are triggered in our everyday lives. I offer an especially detailed account of Ravett's film because in addition to the formal connections between the tragic story of Ravett's half-sister and my family story, his film enacts visually the way this kind of memory works. In its enigmatic movements across time and space, its odd juxtapositions and connections, Ravett brings the viewer into the haptic,[9] tactile landscape of living memory. He explores visually how the past remains a part of our everyday lives in the ways our imaginations and desires continually shape and reshape our engagements in the world.

My Family Story in Pieces

It has taken me a great deal of effort to begin to find my grandmother. I have had to dig through layers and layers of family lore, of secrets and silences, only to find that there is hardly anything left to hold onto in the place where my grandmother once lived. My labors have echoed those of Walter Benjamin. As Shelley Hornstein explains, for Benjamin to

> approach . . . [one's] . . . buried past [one] must conduct . . . [one-self] . . . like a man digging. . . . [One] must not be afraid to return again and again to the same matter; to scatter it as one scatters earth, to turn it over as one turns over soil. For the matter itself is only a deposit, a stratum, which yields only to the most meticulous examination what constitutes the real treasure hidden with the earth: the images, severed from all earlier associations, that stand—like a precious fragment or torso in a collector's gallery—in the prosaic rooms of our later under-standing.[10]

For me, mining the site where my grandmother once was has meant digging through my father's buried past. I have had to make my way through the various layers of sediment that separate him from me, and that separate him from his mother. This has been an ongoing labor, and the work has been slow. It is now over twenty years since I first began these efforts. I have had to return again and again to try to find other angles, other ways in, and it often feels like I have to begin all over again as if from scratch. My shorn nails are dirty, and my hands are aching from the effort. And, even still, there is so little I really know. What I have found over these many years is like that which Benjamin writes about. The fragments I have found are already so out of context that I can hardly decipher their meaning. By the time I get to them they have already become something else, both precious and incomplete.

Part of this process has pushed me to forge relationships of my own with relatives I hardly knew. I have sought out distant cousins to help me see what I have not otherwise been able to see. And I am especially grateful to two of these cousins who once stood on the periphery of my father's family: Frances Levitt, a daughter of one of my grandfather's brothers, and Philip Pearl, the son of one of Lena's brothers.[11] These cousins, both oddly outsiders to my father's various families,[12] are the ones who have most illuminated this past for me. Through the stories they have been able to tell me, stories about what they remember of my grandmother, I have been able to piece together something less ephemeral and more concrete.

What they have offered are sideward glances, their passing visions of her life.[13] For Frances and for Phil, Lena Levitt was not at the heart of their memories but instead a presence within their own differently focused family stories. She only became central in the context of my questions and our belated conversations. By asking them about her, I produced this effect. What Frances and Phil offered me were the memories of children looking on from a distance. And in both instances, these memories were combined with the adult stories they heard about these other relatives from their parents over the course of their own complicated lifetimes.

From Frances, I learned of the ambivalent feelings of a more self-consciously Americanized cousin who carried her own legacy of traumatic loss. Frances is my father's first cousin on his father's side. She is the daughter of his father's brother Louis Levitt, the older brother who took my grandfather in and offered him a job as an assistant in his prospering tailor shop. My grandfather and his young wife, Lena, settled in Schenectady, New York, because this brother had forged the way. My grandparents were each originally from Europe and had apparently met in New York City where they first lived after arriving in this country. When Louis offered my grandfather a job, they moved to Schenectady. Unfortunately, not long after they arrived, the entire family was in a terrible car accident. In the car were my grandparents, my grandfather's mother, and Louis and his young pregnant wife, Bessie Levitt, and their two young daughters. Frances was one of the little girls in the car. She was there when her father died. He was the only one who died. The accident led to a permanent rift in the family and many open wounds that never healed. Part of the reason for this rift was that after Louis's death, Frances's mother lost the family's business to my grandfather. Bessie Levitt was left alone to fend for herself and her children when, sadly, she was perhaps the relative most capable of maintaining the tailor shop. Bessie eventually opened a hat shop and was able to support her family on her own.

The accident happened in 1925, just a year before my father, his parents' oldest child, was born. In my efforts to rediscover Lena's grave with my father and his sister, we also found the graves of Louis Levitt,

and his wife Bessie Levitt, Frances's parents. We also found the grave of
Rose Levitt, the matriarch of my grandfather's family, the grandmother
who lived with my father's family.[14]

In describing this household, the home of her paternal grandmother,
Frances remembers herself looking on with both disgust and longing. As
a child, Frances saw this home from a distance. To her, it was an exotic
household comprised of her foreign-speaking relatives—the home of
her grandmother, her uncle, his wife Lena, and their children: my father
and his siblings. It was also the home of the uncle who took over her father's business after his tragic death and ultimately destroyed it. By the
time Lena died, Frances and her family were already estranged from my
father's family as they each, in their own way, grieved the loss of her father, the man who had linked them to one another. From her perspective, I came to see my father and his siblings as the children of immigrants. I had not fully appreciated the foreignness of this household, an
eastern European, Yiddish-speaking home in the midst of a middle-class
section of Schenectady. This was a place with few immigrant Jewish
families. Listening to Frances, I began to consider my father's childhood
and his mother as foreign and exotic. From her, I learned about uncomfortable neighbors who were troubled by this smelly foreign household
and would call Frances's more Americanized mother, asking her to tell
these relatives to take better care of their children. I heard about the
shame of difference and both the attraction and repulsion Frances experienced in relation to these old-world relatives, including Lena, her dark
and mysterious aunt.

Mostly from Frances, I learned things about my father's childhood. I
came to realize more fully that my father grew up outside of the norms
of American middle-class culture. Through the pretenses of my cousin
and her mother—who, despite their own struggles, had learned to conform—I began to understand some of the shame that came with having
been a part of my father's family when it was intact. And even after
learning all of these things, my grandmother keeps slipping out of my
reach.[15]

Nevertheless, Frances also confirmed other things, things I had and
had not already known. She reminded me of my grandfather's limitations, his incompetence in business. Although her account was more urgent, it confirmed something I already knew. It is true that my grandfather was responsible for the demise of what had been his brother's
once thriving tailoring business. Although the Depression made all small

businesses precarious, my grandfather had never been equipped to run his brother's tailor shop. And yet he inherited this business, which might have been better served by his now dead brother's wife, Frances's mother, a woman with many more skills than my grandfather. This was something I had not known.

In addition to these things, Frances has been the only person in my extended family to offer me a glimpse of my grandmother's presence, her taste, and her style. On the one hand, Frances has reiterated the fact that she saw my grandmother as a dark beauty. This is something she claims to see in me and likes to remind me of. On the other hand, she told me about her own forbidden peek into her aunt and uncle's bedroom. Here she spoke about how beautiful she found the deep green satin bedspread set in that room. As she described it to me, it was the be all and end all of glamour to the little girl who discovered it by sneaking into this private space. She still remembers it vividly.

From Phil Pearl I gleaned other things. I was able to get a glimpse of the relationship between my grandmother and grandfather and what went on in the private space of their bedroom. Phil told me about my grandfather's sexual appetite. He told me about the role these more carnal desires played in his married life and, perhaps, in the death of his young wife. According to Phil, his father, Lena's brother Harry Pearl, believed that my grandfather was to blame for Lena's death. According to him, it was the insatiability of my grandfather's sexual appetite that compromised Lena's health and ultimately her life. According to Phil, this, along with my grandfather's incompetence in business and the family's precarious financial status, made all of this all the more dangerous.

It seems that the family could not afford to have more children. And it was my grandmother's responsibility to make sure that this did not happen. According to Phil, this is ultimately why she died at thirty-six. As Phil explained it to me, illegal abortions were a common practice among immigrant Jews in the Albany area in the 1930s. People knew where to go to obtain such services. Lena had used these services, perhaps even more than once. And according to her brother, her death was the result of a botched abortion. In her attempts to end an unwanted pregnancy, she lost her life. By the time she went into the hospital, it was too late.

According to her death certificate, Lena Levitt died of septicemia. This may very well have been the result of an ill-fated abortion. Septicemia was often the cause of death in such cases, especially in the 1930s before there was penicillin. Although the evidence of this or any other abortion does not exist where Lena is concerned, this account echoes many accounts of such procedures—not only anecdotal evidence from memoirs about this period but also more formal accounts of what abortion looked like then and how such deaths were accounted for before abortion was legal.[16]

Phil Pearl told me this story in the late 1990s after I urged him to tell me what he knew. By that time, I had already requested and received a copy of Lena's death certificate. Earlier hospital records had long since been lost in a fire, so I could not learn anything else about her past medical history. My initial attempts to obtain these records had been precipitated by a series of rumors about Lena's death that circulated around the time of my grandfather's death in 1988. Some said it was a "toxic pregnancy," while my father insisted that she had died of blood poisoning from a rusty nail. There was some consensus that she had died of blood poisoning, but there was a lack of clarity about what had made her ill in the first place. There was also consensus on the fact that, had there been penicillin, she might never have died. When I wrote for a copy of Lena's death certificate, I hoped to find out whether or not she was pregnant at the time of her death. Of course the certificate said nothing about such matters. Again, it only echoed the all-too-common cause of death in such cases, septicemia.

What I gleaned from my cousin Phil and his recollections was some greater clarity.[17] This was confirmed by another story Phil told me about a discussion he had had with my grandfather about sex. This was a conversation between a grown man and a still very young boy. Phil was a few years younger than my father. Apparently, my grandfather initiated this conversation with Phil around the time of Lena's death. He asked Phil if he knew about sex and then proceeded to tell him how much he liked it.[18]

My discussions with Phil and with Frances over the last number of years have been some of the most fruitful of my efforts to learn more about Lena Levitt, her life, and her death. They have offered shape and texture to my otherwise utterly vague sense of what this woman, who was my grandmother, might have been like. These accounts have helped me imagine her in more animated ways. I have been able to put them together with the more impressionistic things I have learned about her from my father and his silence. But all of this has come to me very late.

Haptic Viewing

> Haptic visuality implies a fundamental mourning of the absent object or
> the absent body, where optical visuality attempts to resuscitate it and
> make it whole. At the same time that it acknowledges that it cannot
> know the other, haptic visuality attempts to bring it close, in a look that
> is so intensely involved with the presence of the other that it cannot
> take the step back to discern difference, say, to distinguish figure from
> ground.
>
> —Laura Marks, *The Skin of Film*, 191

Cinema scholar Laura Marks insists that film can touch us. It can even
leave its mark on our senses, perhaps especially as it attempts to caress
an absence. Using what she calls "haptic visuality," Marks argues that
many intercultural film and video makers bring viewers into the intimacy of loss. Instead of replacing or pretending to revive what has been
lost, they allow us to come in closer, to sense the presence of another to
whom we no longer have any physical access. Although Marks' study of
intercultural cinema does not address the work of Abraham Ravett, it
might have.

Many of Ravett's works, especially those films about his Holocaust
survivor parents, engage in precisely the kinds of mourning Marks sees
expressed in haptic visuality. Like the intercultural artists Marks writes
about, Ravett also struggles with how to forge a relationship with a
past he can never know, his parents' pasts and the intimate relationships
that had structured their lives before the war, their other families. As I
have already indicated, he does this most specifically in his 1985 experimental[19] film, *Half-Sister*, which is about his belated conscious engagement with the memory of his mother's first child, his half sister, who
was murdered by the Nazis. In this film, Ravett insists that although he
cannot know his half sister, he can use film to bring himself closer to her
absence. In this twenty-two-minute film, he offers "a look that is so in-
tensely involved with the presence of [this] other," all the while knowing that he can never resuscitate her or make her whole. He can only
hover around the places she might have, but could never have, been in
his life.

Like my family story, at the heart of Ravett's film is a single photograph. This is a studio portrait of a woman and child: the child is his
half-sister, the woman is an aunt or cousin.[20] The photograph was taken

before the war. It was returned to Ravett more than forty years after his half sister's death. It is this double move, the death as well as the intimacy conveyed by the returned photograph, that continues to draw me to Ravett's film. Although he insists on the impossibility of his desire to know his half sister, he nevertheless reproduces the immediacy and intimacy of this familiar desire. In this way, Ravett's film offers viewers access to a mournful intimacy that I believe, in its specificity, enables other viewers to reexperience with him not only his loss, but also intimate losses of our own.

As I have already suggested, *Half-Sister* has offered me a way into the tangled questions at the heart of this book. And as I now hope to show, my own ongoing engagement with this film demonstrates how ordinary Jewish losses are often already intertwined with the legacy of the Holocaust and its representations. In this case, *Half-Sister* triggered memories of my lost grandmother as early as 1994 when I saw the film for the first time. It was while watching this film that I remembered learning about this family trauma. More specifically, the film helped me appreciate how coming to know about the death of my father's mother, the fact that my father had had another mother whom I had never met, the woman I am named after, has haunted my own imagination in vivid although not always articulate ways. When I watched Ravett's film for the first time, I was struck by both the formal similarities between our stories as well as the differences. Although, like Ravett, I too came to experience the loss of a distant relative through the belated receipt of a long-lost family photograph sent to my father in the mail, the differences between our experiences have often stopped me in my tracks. Even so, my ongoing engagement with Ravett's film has allowed me to touch my own story of loss.[21]

The film's ability to tap into the vivid, silent gestural realm of my grandmother's absent presence in my own life has drawn me in. It has allowed me to experience viscerally the process of trying to make a connection to a grandmother I never knew. The film makes vivid an otherwise inarticulate legacy of loss. It allows viewers to touch with our eyes that which is otherwise completely removed from our experience, the object at the heart of these losses. These impossible, visceral desires to touch that center has moved me to return to this otherwise enigmatic film again and again.

In saying these things I already feel a discomfort. I know that I am not supposed to make analogies[22] and, at the same time, I find myself working against an urgency that has yet to be named. As I have already argued, I know that it is critical to make these connections between different Jewish losses. This is not only because the future telling of Holocaust history will increasingly depend on those of us with few, if any, direct memories of the Holocaust, but because there are also these other legacies of Jewish loss that need to be reckoned with. These other losses need to be engaged now before American Jews like my father, who lived through the first portion of the 20th century in this country, are no longer alive to tell their stories. Paying attention to these stories makes it possible to see them more fully. This includes seeing how they have been transformed and distorted by the shadow of the Holocaust.[23] In other words, we are able to more fully appreciate how the Holocaust's looming presence has already begun to transform these other narratives of the Jewish past when we acknowledge the interactions between different losses. I believe that it is precisely these interactions that continue to shape the lives of those of us who were born after the Shoah.

Half-Sister: *Circling*

I find it difficult to write about Ravett's film, not only because I have so much emotionally invested in it already, but also because it is difficult to watch. I have lived with this film for a long time. I have watched it over and over again in different venues, trying to learn from other people with whom I share it and from the repeated act of viewing the film itself what it is that draws me to this film, what it does and what it means. I brought *Half-Sister* to the Association for Jewish Studies (AJS)[24] with some of Ravett's other films about his parents, and I showed it on its own at the American Academy of Religion (AAR).[25] Each time, I

Image from *Half-Sister,* the photograph.

tried to see what I could glean from others, hoping, perhaps fantasizing, that if only the right people watched it, they would be able to reveal its secret meaning to me—as if there were one neat, convincing, and authoritative interpretation. I know that that fantasy was about not trusting myself; it was about my sense of my own unworthiness as a reader/viewer of film and as a reader of the Holocaust. For years, these fantasies kept me from writing more than conference proposals and drafts of readings.

I was stopped in my tracks when I began writing about Ravett's film. Initially, these fantasies of knowledge kept the film at bay, giving me excuses to publicly engage with it without actually having to pin down what it was that has haunted me about the film from the very beginning, from the very first time I watched it in a darkened screening room in Temple's film school during the spring of 1994. As I returned to my own words, I found myself rewriting and trying to explain that I have let go of my quest to find a definitive reading, and I have also learned how to appreciate this very process of thwarted engagement as itself an important part of my story and of the film's meaning. Moreover, my engagement with *Half-Sister* and its impossibility has become enmeshed with my efforts to unravel the story of my grandmother, itself a tale of thwarted desires. In both instances, I came to appreciate that there are no definitive answers, only repeated engagements, repetitions, and reiterations with slight variations and nuances distinguishing one from another. Iteration is how that which is strange becomes familiar, normal, or natural. It is through repetition, the ritual of reiteration, that we internalize new knowledge, new ways of seeing and being in the world, including the fact that all we might have are these very iterations.

When I would bring Ravett with me to these various events to talk about his films, he was often elusive. He never told audiences what he was trying to do. He spoke of his privilege as an independent filmmaker. He explained that he had the ability to make intimate films, films that were ultimately for himself. He did not have to worry about his films' commercial viability.[26]

In his various experimental films about his parents, which include *Everything Is for You,* 1989 (58 min.), and *The March,* 1999 (25 min.), Ravett offers an uncompromised engagement with the slippery experience of memory, loss, and desire. In all of these films, and particularly in *Half-Sister,* he describes his own efforts to remember—not just getting some past thing back, but a process in the present that is ever shifting—

as a kind of circling. For Ravett, this circling is visceral. He uses this term to characterize his process of moving in slowly toward his half sister in the film. He gets closer and closer but is never able to touch her, the sister who is the object of his desire. Instead, he brings the viewer with him, as we visually get closer to what visual traces he has of his half sister.[27] We see the picture, more specifically the image of the little girl's face, over and over again. He moves this picture in as close as it can get to the camera and then pulls it away. We see it close up, we see it at medium range, and we see it far away. He shows us the letter that accompanied the portrait as well as the envelope addressed to him, and then we see the envelope with the face peering through again and again and yet again, multiple versions of the very same image covering the surface of the envelope so that it is virtually all we can see.

What Ravett offers viewers is a visual enactment of the often internal and intimate process whereby we come to take in new knowledge. Here memory and desire, longing and loss are experienced together. They are a part of our everyday lives. The repetition of this process, the desire to keep finding different or other ways to touch that which is lost, animates this film. In other words, Ravett uses film to animate his desire to know his half sister. He re-creates these desires mimetically.[28] This is how he attempts to make his parents' past and his half sister come alive in the present. In so doing, he also makes clear how these desires are always distorted and thwarted in the process of engaging with them. He demonstrates how what is remembered is always made different in the act of remembering. In his efforts to remember his half sister, other things come to take her place. She not only recedes, but other people, objects, experiences replace her, obscuring his and our access to her memory.[29] Nevertheless, in this film, he keeps trying to conjure her up again and again. In part, I am drawn to this elusive and frustrating experience in and of itself. But there is also more to my desire for clarity and my resistance to writing more fully about this film.

The fear of letting go, of telling or knowing the meaning of this film, is that such knowledge might destroy not only Abraham Ravett's efforts to give life to his half sister, but also my own desire to give life to my dead grandmother. Pinning down these efforts and wrapping them up in a nice neat package seems to end the possibilities opened up by an ongoing engagement with these lost relatives. The illusion of animation ends. By deferring answers, we keep open the hope of ultimately finding an answer, and more importantly, the process of hoping itself, which is a form of magical life giving in the present. In part, I feared coming to a conclusion because there is a delight in the experience of repeated engagement, in this case, in my repeated viewings of Ravett's film. Although I thought that the pleasure I experienced was in the promise that maybe this time I would finally discover the definitive reading of the film, I now suspect that I knew all along that there was no such thing. That was only a cover story. By keeping Ravett's film in motion, showing and reshowing it without actually writing about it, I had been able to participate in the illusion of life giving, the very illusion of moving images that is film. In this way I experienced not only Ravett's memories and desires to revive his half sister, but also my own desires to believe that all my dead could also be revived. In other words, in the process of watching this film, my memories and desires also felt alive and filled with potential. The potential is not teleological, as if we will come up with an answer or some kind of resolution. No, the point is that in watching the film through its twenty-two-minute duration, I could believe that my dead could be revived. Ravett allows us to touch these intimate desires as we watch his film.

Here I am reminded of Resnais' *Hiroshima Mon Amour*. Just as Resnais attempts to make a film about Hiroshima that is not a documentary, Ravett also refuses such simple conventions. In order to get closer to the traumas that are the subject matter of both of these films, each filmmaker takes an indirect approach. Each film insists on a more roundabout method. In using these methods, albeit in different ways, they are each able to reproduce some of the otherwise less than tangible sensations that make up these experiences of loss. "Circling," as Ravett describes it, is both a strategy for getting closer to an elusive legacy of loss and a way of reproducing the effect of that distance or loss. This is the way we experience these memories. This is what both Ravett's film and *Hiroshima Mon Amour* enact. Both demonstrate how the haunting presence of loss is experienced as a part of daily life. So although Ravett's film does not allow narration to conquer forgetting as in Resnais' film, it does get at the process that cultural critic Michael Roth describes, the way certain traumatic memories often linger in inarticulate ways in our everyday lives. Moreover, as Ravett demonstrates, this haunting continues even after the trauma becomes known.

For Ravett this means that the sister he never knew he had, the sister whose presence reemerges through the receipt of this letter and photograph, helps bring to light some of the feelings that were already present in his life. The film enacts the elusive presence of this absence. It shows how knowing and not knowing continue to shape a particular traumatic loss as Ravett comes to understand his own abiding preoccupations with women and children anew. In the film, he looks again and again at his ongoing relationships with women and girls. The discovery of his lost sister continues to affect Ravett's relationship with his mother and with other women in his life, his wife and daughter, as well as other women and girls who remind him of who his sister might have been and never was able to become. In the film he shows us how these preoccupations become conscious as well as how knowing deepens all of these already present preoccupations. The film also makes more acute the limitations of these elusive connections. He is ever aware of the fact that this is the only way his sister lives.

In Ravett's film this elusive presence and the absence of a coherent narrative persist even as he learns more about his sister's life and death. Ravett offers the viewer a way into what this experience feels like, the interplay between intimacy and distance. He does this formally in the way he structures the film. Just as we think we know what the film is about, we are confronted with a flood of disparate images we cannot understand or neatly assimilate. Although we share something of the headiness of recognition, making certain connections between the disparate pieces of the film and the figure of Ravett's half sister, we are also plunged back time and time again into the dreamy landscape of loss in all of its idiosyncratic specificity. And we cannot assimilate this. We cannot fully understand or even take in Ravett's vision. There are always pieces that do not fit, images and gestures that leave him and us unsure. In all of these ways, this film reminds us of how difficult it is to communicate loss in all of its specificity. And because the film is about the experience of a belated loss, it also shows us the distortions of time. Ravett uses this temporal distance to make more vivid how the process of remembering is only partial. There is so much forgetting, and the very acts meant to help us remember can add to our forgetting. They can end up taking the place of the things we hoped to remember.

Ravett's film offers a kind of recognition but no resolution. By identifying with at least a few strands of the film—a photograph returned, an imagined sibling we never knew—we enter into the terrain of memory and forgetting. We come to reexperience the all-too-common experience of loss, the desires and the frustrations, the inaccessibility as well as the ways we, too, are able to touch that to which we have no other access in our daily lives. Ravett demonstrates this through his use of transitional objects: clothing that resembles the outfits his aunt and his half sister wore when the portrait was taken, women's and little girls' shoes, hats, and coats. He also shows this in terms of how he uses dolls, little girls and their dolls, mothers and daughters. All of these objects trigger memory.[30]

On another level, the silence of this film, its literal lack of words and sound for the vast duration of the film, is itself significant. It literalizes a kind of inarticulateness that is also a part of loss. But, in this case, silence is not only about absence, it is also about potential. Like the French woman's silence in *Hiroshima Mon Amour*, *Half-Sister's* lack of voice holds out the promise of reanimation. At least for me, there is an illusion of hope, a deferred hope. And yet here again, if this loss is articulated it might disappear, and those who have died might really be gone. This is the magical logic triggered by the film, and it is also, in many ways, a desire the film has helped me to begin to let go of. Parts of Ravett's film make visible these elusive desires as they flow in and out of our consciousness. In this respect, the specificity of Ravett's film and the desires it enacts make room for viewers to take hold of those pieces that speak to them. Because we cannot master the entire film or understand all of it, we have permission to grab hold of these moments in the film that speak to us. This also speaks to how we grasp the Holocaust more generally. Let me offer an example.

At one viewing of the film, a friend called attention to a dreamy sequence of underwater shots, a sequence that when repeated shows a group of dolphins swimming together in a confined space. He wanted to know more about these images and asked Ravett to explain it to us. Although the filmmaker did not directly respond, I found myself haunted by the question and its specific resonances for my friend. What I knew was that this particular viewer brought to this film his own experience of loss, and although his experience was never articulated, I began to make connections. My friend had inhabited the same womb as a sibling who had died before he was born. What resonated for me was precisely this intimate connection, the fact that dolphins are marine mammals whose name comes from "delphus," the Greek word for womb. Part of what interests me about all of this is the way the film evoked these perhaps less than conscious connections.[31] Of course, in this case, the connections are all my own. What we bring to the film from our own experience helps illuminate it for us even as the film helps us better understand our own, often less-than-conscious memories.

Given this, *Half-Sister* is not so much a film about loss as it is a reenactment of it, a remembering of a past that was never fully experienced by the one who remembers. In this sense, it shows what this process looks like or, better still, what it feels like. It demonstrates what happens when a loss that was heretofore unknown becomes known in a distant present. It is about how these resonances and traces can become more tangible and visible even as they can never become fully known. It is about a kind of partial reckoning that also acknowledges how such memories are already a part of us, even before they are made conscious.

Through this particular film, Abraham Ravett shows what it has meant for him to learn about the existence and brutal death of his half sister in the Holocaust. As an adult, almost fifty years after her death, he uses film to show what it has meant for him to become conscious of the ways he had always known about this loss. He demonstrates this through his attention to his own relationship with his mother and his fantasies about mothers and daughters, how little girls come to learn about becoming mothers through playing with dolls. This helps explain, at least for me, why there are so many images of little girls and dolls running through this film. The enactment of this preoccupation does a number of things. Not only does it figure this displaced knowledge, but it also represents mother and child,[32] the distance between animate and inanimate objects and desires, and the peculiar lifelessness of the photo. Here the stand-in quality of the dolls offers a kind of playacting, a way of showing what cannot be experienced in the flesh. Moreover, Ravett shows this happening always from the perspective of the child, the one who came after. In these ways, the film shows how Ravett lives with the knowledge of this loss in an ongoing present. It shows how he imagines his lost sibling, a child who was brutally killed over fifty years before, a child who would have been, could have been, his older sister, a sister who might have grown up but never did.

He also gets at his sister's haunting presence by showing her appearing and disappearing over and over again, more or less directly, in his own life where she is remembered as a woman, a child, a girl, and an adult. He offers only a brief overt account[33] of her tragic death but uses various shots of fires, smoke, and long shadows to signify her terrible end as he re-members it in the present. These frightening shots of fire juxtaposed with the images of girls, dolls, women, children, and aging women together, offer a certain fleeting coherence to the film.

Pieces of the Past

This is my narration, how I remember the film and not its actual sequence. I want to highlight this precisely because, as I will show, the film actually begins quite differently from the way I remember it and the way I discuss it in what follows. I come back to the film looking at the way it is ordered in a later section of this reading.

For Ravett, this critical engagement (or reckoning) is triggered by a photograph, a sepia-colored portrait of a woman and child, his half sister and a relative, taken in the 1930s. The photograph was mailed to Ravett by a distant relative. The sequence of images that remains most vivid for me in the film is the camera's slow and loving embrace of this missive in all its parts—the envelope, the letter, and the photograph, slowly, lovingly.[34] (I had mistakenly remembered this sequence as the beginning of the film.) Coming in closer and closer, pulsing, the camera seems to make these inanimate objects come alive by noting each individual frame of film that makes up the whole as moving image. Here each frame is redeployed in an attempt to give life to that which is lifeless. In this way, Ravett uses film against itself, reconstructing the film as a series of individual shots, one frame after another pulsating into the appearance of life. He literalizes the process of animation. The moving pictures that are the stuff of film are literally re-membered.

The film is soundless except for the rhythm of the projector's own breath for virtually the entire film, and something was lost for me when it was rendered silent on video. Having watched it and rewatched it both ways, I note the loss of the projector's voice and wonder if it could be added to the video, although the actual labor that the sound enacts would be lost in such a translation. As I viewed the film both ways (hearing the sound of the projector and not hearing it), I told myself that it was this, the importance of the projector's voice, that explained Ravett's insistence that his work be experienced as film; he wants his film projected on a screen and not flattened out and silenced on video. I thought he wanted us to hear the sound of the projector, the pulsing beat, the breath of light as it projects each image onto the screen of a darkened room. As I experienced it, the projector offered a kind of mechanical animation or approximation of life through the physical experience of projection. The virtual lack of dialogue in the film is one kind of silence that is distinct from a lack of all sound. And so, despite the lack of a narration, hearing the projector during Ravett's film did feel like hearing a kind of voice. Its breathy rhythm approximated the cadence of Ravett's various cuts and edits. Let me explain this point a bit further, when screened in a small venue where the projector's sound is not filtered out, the film breathes. The sound of the projector follows the rhythm of the film's play of images during the long duration of the film without any voice.[35] At least this is how I experience it.

As the camera moves in closer and closer to the surface of the paper and the cardboard surface of the formal photographic portrait of woman and child, Ravett uses the camera to attempt to touch the skin of the photograph, no longer paper but rather the external texture of something we long to render alive. As these intimate close-ups continue to offer only something approximating skin, Ravett shows us more directly what he really desires. Briefly we are offered a close-up image of a hand, the texture and color of his skin. As Marks suggests, this is a kind of haptic enactment where the film mimetically re-creates for us the feel, the texture of both skin and paper. It uses vision to imitate touch.

The portrait Ravett presents offers the trace of another era, another time, when such photographs were commonly taken in studios to mark special occasions. Despite the formality of the image, its familiar troping, as Roland Barthes reminds us, the effect of a photograph, even a portrait, "is not to restore what has been abolished (by time and by distance) but to attest that what I see has indeed existed."[36] In this case the photograph offers evidence that a child once existed, that Abraham Ravett's mother did have a daughter. Part of what is so painful about this particular image is that it appears to be the only image that still exists of this lost child. And here, unlike the moment of her death, she is not alone, completely separated from her family. In the photograph it appears as if mother and daughter are in fact together. And in this wishful reading, the woman in the picture is her mother. We see woman and child standing together in a studio portrait formally dressed in winter coats and hats; the little girl stands carefully posed on a chair that allows her face to come up to almost the height of the woman's face. Here, I wanted to believe that she was forever figured with her mother, that it is their shared mother who links Abraham and his half sister, the two unlikely siblings, forever, but my wish is an illusion since the woman in the photograph is not their mother. And yet, this desire is easily assumed by viewers who are never told explicitly who the figures are in this photograph. We are never told that the woman is not the little girl's mother. This was something I only learned much later from the filmmaker.[37]

Again I recall the envelope, the letter, and the portrait. The camera focuses on the outermost layer of this correspondence, the envelope with Ravett's address. Looking at this postmarked paper, we begin to see the face of the little girl from the photograph slowly peeking/bleeding through the envelope, not once, but again and again. By the end of this sequence, almost four different faces are taking over the space of Ravett's name and address, blotting them out.[38] In this case, the multiple images of the child's face and the sameness of these images remind us of the impossibility of using film to reproduce her. She cannot be animated. All we have is evidence of the existence of the single photograph again and again, nothing more. There are no other images to attest to her existence. In watching this process of reproduction, we end up noting more keenly the distance between these siblings. The filmproducing brother cannot, himself, attest to his sister's existence solely through the evidential qualities of film. He must use film to offer other ways of making her legacy known to himself.[39]

These attempts at animation deserve further discussion.[40] The term "animation" aptly captures the desire at the heart of these efforts and Ravett's specific use of film to enact this desire. To animate is to give life to, to enliven, to fill with spirit, resolution, or courage. It also inspires action or the effort to impart motion or activity. In these ways the meanings of this term link up to a more imaginative process, the work of animation, as in the making of a design or image as in a cartoon where there is an illusion of motion. As a noun, animation has become synonymous with the art or process of preparing an animated cartoon.[41]

These definitions are reminiscent of the decks of cards that children used to use to both learn how animation works and to enact the process. The deck offered a series of simple images that were actually slight variations on a single image. When viewed quickly in order, the deck appeared to show the image in motion. The trick was to view the cards fast enough to capture the appearance of motion. In some ways, this is precisely what Ravett does as he makes the face of his sister slowly appear to bleed through the envelope again and again. The difference is that in this case, the repeated image of the face of this lost child appears and reappears with no variation, one next to another, and it is slow rather than fast. These images could not have the same effect as the cards precisely because there is no variation, and without variation, animation, the illusion of life, is impossible.

All of these possibilities of lifegiving are raised in this film. In his repeated images of the child's face and in all of his efforts to revive his sister throughout the film, Ravett, as he continually reminds us, shows us the impossibility of these efforts. There is no magic that can bring his sister back to life, but the desire remains. Even the illusion of projection cannot animate this image. And yet, the effort to enact these desires makes them visible.

Returning to the Beginning

I always think of this film opening with the receipt of the letter, with the letter triggering the images that follow. Given this, I was startled while watching the film again, after an extended period of not watching it, to realize that I had remembered it incorrectly. Rewatching the film on video, in silence, alongside my mother, I uncomfortably noticed this discrepancy in my own memory. In part, my discomfort was exacerbated by my desire to help my mother understand the film. I was especially invested in the letter and portrait as a way for my mother to share my particular reading of the film with me. I wanted her to make the specific connections I had made with our own family story—our receipt of a long-lost photographic portrait—the connection I had made as I initially watched this film. Anxiously, I sat with my mother staring at these enigmatic images waiting for the part I remembered and so wanted to share with her. I wanted to just get there already, which helps explain why in my memory the crucial scenes for me came first, the image of the photograph and letter.

Instead of seeing this image, I watched again the various segments of the film that unfold before we get to see the letter. We watched the opening footage, the target image of the film's beginning, descending numbers—8, 7, 6, 5, 4, 3, 2—cut to strands of white leader film with flashes of bold yellow and reds, and then the beginning of an image. Slowly the camera pans what appears to be an old black and white photograph of a group of little girls, each of them holding on to a doll.

Based on the clothing of the little girls, their cropped haircuts, and the quality of their dolls, the photograph appears to be from the 1930s. The photograph may be European, but that is less clear.

The camera slowly scans the photograph. The slow scan is confusing; it almost makes it seem like we are watching an old film. After the scan, the camera pulls back to show us the photograph, still and lifeless. Instead of zooming in to explore the texture of this image, its skin, Ravett moves slowly enough to make it seem as if the image itself is moving. Here the objects of the camera's gaze are both once living children and their inanimate dolls. But the juxtaposition of these little girls and their dolls also comes to echo the portrait of woman and child that follows. Here the little girls seem to be playing out the roles of mother and child. The dolls allow them to imagine and pretend what it might be like to be a mother, or in the case of ever more sophisticated dolls, what it might be like to be an adult woman. These playful desires echo a certain fascination that Ravett continues to have with mothers and children, little girls and grown-up women. In this way, the dolls act as transitional objects.[42] They come to stand in for the real thing, for mothers and daughters who are otherwise inaccessible. They allow for a kind of imaginative engagement with these inchoate desires. Like the film, they demonstrate Ravett's attempts to play at being a mother or a brother, without really being able to actually be one. I see these things more clearly than my mother did, although I have watched this film many times and she saw it only once.

There are various other images of dolls throughout the film, a recurring rag doll worn and clearly played with, perhaps a precious toy from the filmmaker's daughter's own doll collection. Even the images of little girls have something of a substitute and doll-like quality. Not only are there lots of archival shots of little girls, ghetto footage of girls carrying chairs on their heads, but there is also more contemporary color footage of innocent little Catholic girls all lined up in white, little veils on their heads, about to take their first communion, as well as individual little girls in the present depicted at play or just looking into the camera.

The little Catholic girls taking their first communion also remind us of other kinds of communion—the acts or instances of sharing thoughts and feelings like the intimacy between siblings, a form of intimacy that remains impossible for Ravett and his sister. But there is more. These shots are also eerie. This familiar contemporary color procession becomes an alien and mysterious religious ritual complete with frightening authority figures draped in long dark robes, especially as Ravett reverses this film showing a negative version of what appears to be this footage. But it also seems to include the inversion of some older footage of cassocked figures as well.[43]

For Ravett, there are no rites of passage to be shared with his sister. There are no wedding dresses, no marriages, and no children that they can celebrate together. There is also, oddly, no aging. There are two other clearly visible family photographs, both studio portraits, included in the second half of the film, but the identity of those depicted in these photographs is never made clear. The first of these is a wedding portrait that may or may not be of Ravett's parents. The other image is a family group portrait, a seemingly older photograph of ancestors, an image from the turn of the century; but again, we never learn anything specific about those depicted in these family pictures.

To account for all that Ravett can never know about his half sister and what might have been, he must again improvise. He can only offer "what if" scenarios, progressive images of girls and women, all of whom remind him of who his sister might have become. The girls and dolls scattered throughout the film are both substitutes and reminders of the impossibility of actually touching his lost half sister. But they are also, in essence, the tangible traces of what he does have, stand-ins that are a part of his life and his imagination.

A Closer Look: For the Intrepid Reader

The early sequences of archival images make explicit the specific historical context of the loss Ravett presents. And it is for this reason that he embeds the two moments in the film where there is actual conversation into the first portion of the film. Together these sections set up the mostly more contemporary footage that follows. With this agenda in mind, we return to the beginning of the film.

After the slow pan of the photograph of the little girls holding their dolls, Ravett moves to another image, a more ominous piece of old film footage he reshoots and shows in negative.[44] There is something eerie about this inversion; the figures we have just seen in this format appear ghostly. The images are strangely familiar; they are part of a now common repertoire of Holocaust images, the rounding up of Jewish women and children forced onto the back of a truck. It is only after this sequence of images that we finally come to the letter and portrait that I had imagined coming first. This belated entry of the returned photograph is less dramatic than I remembered, and only in retrospect do the connections I am drawing between Ravett's half sister and these other images make sense.

These Holocaust connections are reinforced when, not long after the letter and portrait sequence, Ravett uses a piece of vintage footage from a ghetto.[45] Here he uses specific footage to express his desire to revive his sister from another angle. The footage he refilms is itself made up of a few different short reels spliced together. The first depicts a group of children carrying chairs out of a building; this is followed by other ghetto shots, poor and starving people in a doorway—men, women, and children. These are ominous depictions, a transport. The film is dark and full of shadows. Moreover, the footage is cut off; it is incomplete. We never know what became of these people, where they were going and what happened to them.

Like the photograph of the woman and child, this footage is old and partial. The copied and reproduced footage is repeated and also turned inside out, shot and reshot as a negative. In each instance, the image remains in motion even as those depicted go nowhere, repeating again and again the same series of motions. What links the portrait and the vintage archival footage are the little girls. The girls in each look alike. We wonder if they might be the same person. Although in both instances, and not unlike what Ravett did with the opening image of the photograph of the little girls holding dolls, Ravett films and refilms older images, images from approximately the same time and place as the portrait of his half sister. There are also other connections. Not only do both sequences depict children, presumably eastern European Jewish children, but there is also something else. Within the first portion of this ghetto footage, standing alongside the children carrying the chairs is another child, a little girl, who, like us the viewers, watches this procession. She, too, is a passive observer. But there is more. Not only are we encouraged to identify with this little girl, but we are also made to believe that she is also familiar. Based on her clothing, her haircut, and her approximate age, we begin to realize that she could be the same little girl we first saw in the portrait. Here Ravett plays with resemblance as it, too, triggers desire and memory. We watch the little girl as she looks on, hoping for other signs of connection, but as in the earlier sequences, our desires are never fulfilled. The footage cannot be stopped. The little girl never moves. We are not allowed to make a definitive identification or connection. Even as Ravett shows us the negative that produced this positive image, we are unable to identify Ravett's lost sister in this context. Instead, we have only the trace of a resemblance and a kind of proximity. In this case the images are already multiplied. This is film footage and not a single photograph, but even still, the desire to capture the lost child, to find her again, to see her in motion cannot be met. What we have is another little girl who stands aside and watches motionless, even in the context of a series of moving images. Here again, we are confronted with a little girl like Ravett's sister who lived during that time in that place, but in this case we do not know what became of her. Although we know her situation was already grave at the point when this footage was originally made, we do not know her name or her fate.

In this portion of the film, which consists of footage that is repeated later in the film, Ravett asks us to imagine that the little girl in the photograph has reappeared. He shows us how it might be possible to imagine such a reappearance. He asks us to believe that there is other visible evidence of her existence. Is this other little girl the same little girl we saw in the portrait? We want her to be, but again, all of this labor, this longing, and these desires are never made explicit. There is no narrative voice in Ravett's film to tell us what to see and what to feel at any of these moments. That is left open. Only the pulsing beat of the projector and Ravett's editing link the disparate images and their many versions.

In the midst of all of these ungrounded feelings, the film offers a few words, a verbal account of the loss of this beloved child. In two instances, the pulsing rhythm of the film is interrupted by words. In these two instances, Abraham Ravett's mother speaks. In the first of these, we return to an image from early in the film. Here an older woman sits on a milk carton outside. It seems to be autumn; she is wearing a raincoat and appears to be talking, although the first time we see her in this shot there is no sound. We only watch as her lips move.[46] When the film returns to this scene, the sound is turned on, and we hear an account of the struggle of mother and child to survive. We learn about a carriage, echoes of child's play, girls and dolls, young mothers and their children out for a stroll. In this case the carriage is filled with bread, offering a lifeline. We are able to begin to link some of the disparate pieces, the ghetto scenes, the woman and child, the old woman, and perhaps the woman in the portrait.

Between this sound segment and the one that follows is our first glimpse of the ghetto footage I have already discussed. Here it is shown and reshown in its entirety.

When the second sound sequence begins, the shot is more intimate. The same older woman, the mother, is seen again, but this time seemingly safely indoors. She sits on a couch with a young man, her grown son, the man in control of the moving camera. He asks her questions about her first child, his half sister. We learn her name, Katchia.[47] Despite the familiarity and seeming safety of this domestic interior setting, the story that the mother tells is horrifying. She describes the last day of her daughter's life, the camp, the hunger, the fear, and the children's barracks that is emptied as the loudspeakers announce that the children are going to heaven. Her voice breaks, she has not seen her child, she is desperate, but there is no way to interrupt this process.[48] It is May 1944. She carries a carrot, something, anything to show her child that she loves her, but there is no access, she never sees her again.

This scene is followed by the blurry yellow streaks of film leader that slowly lead into footage from another time and place. This footage is less professional, perhaps footage taken by an amateur on vacation. In retrospect, piecing together the various images—a podium, a series of aging adults in bright colored clothing—I suspect that this is home-movie footage taken at a gathering of survivors in Jerusalem. During most of this sequence there are no familiar faces; it is only toward the end of the reel that we see a younger version of the filmmaker's mother, the woman whose voice we have just heard. This footage gives way to an X-ray image, again a still image that the camera seems to make come alive through its own movement and the pulsating rhythm of the film. This is then followed by a series of contemporary outdoor shots. The camera slowly pans a rural vista; there is a barn, there are trees, a field, and smoke, and eventually, we see flames in the distance. Of course there is more to the film, the interplay of shadow and light, variously aging women, mothers and daughters, and ultimately, from my perspective, an image of Ravett's mother with his daughter, a loving caress, the aging grandmother holding the young girl who is her granddaughter, a girl about the same age her own daughter was when she died. The caress is palpable, the touch that was not possible in the narrative she told of the last day of her daughter's life. And of course there is no closure. This is not the final scene of the film. The haunting continues.

Returning to My Ghosts

My father's family and his past were always a mystery to me. They were territories he was unable to share in any direct way with even those of us who love him most—my mother, my brother, and me. This "not knowing" has always been a source of puzzlement and discomfort for each of us, especially for me and for my mother. Although my father has in various ways encouraged us to get closer to him, he has not quite been able to guide us in these endeavors, and, on top of that, he has also never admitted to his desires for our help in finding ways of articulating these things. I now want to try to retell the story of my efforts to piece together the jagged-edged shards of a long-since broken narrative without reopening the still fragile old wounds that have marked my father's life. This has been an ongoing process that has profoundly shaped my relationship with my father and his family. In these efforts, I feel most profoundly connected to Abraham Ravett and his film *Half-Sister*. Again it is hard to begin, and yet I feel I must begin all over again, precisely because the stories I have to tell both are and are not my own; they are family stories mediated by a generation.

Unlike Ravett's stories, my stories are about my father and his past and not my mother's. It is the story of my father's mother's death, a story whose absence, perhaps more than its actual contours, has shaped me as my father's daughter. The urgency of my tale is, of course, less overt, more submerged, less obvious than Ravett's. And yet, the complicated interplay between past and present as depicted in his film resonates with my efforts. While the Holocaust is at the center of Ravett's story, it is not a part of my own.

Mine is a tale of ordinary loss. It is a story about relationships and events that set the course of my father's life, the loss of his mother, a loss that eventually led to the entry of Mary Levitt, the woman I knew as my grandmother, into my father's family. This time the story is about confusion. It is about my inability to understand how all of these members of my extended family were related to me and to one another. To offer just a single example of this confusion, I return to Mary Levitt, the woman I knew as my paternal grandmother.

For me, this woman's place in the family was itself mysterious. It was never fully explained because, for much of my life, the initial loss that initiated her entry into the family could not be articulated. What this produced for me was a vague notion of who was family. I had all of these relatives who were more or less related to each other on my father's side of my family, but I never knew how they came together. There were strong unspoken taboos about asking questions about any of these things. Questions about relationships within the family were never voiced. These prohibitions were unspoken but very much in place. No one dared ask how he or she was related or not related to anyone else or even how other relatives were or were not related to one another. The question of what made anyone kin in this part of my family was fraught.[49] And for me, this was exacerbated by the fact that these people all seemed to live together. I was confused by their close proximity to one another. They all lived in and around Albany, New York, and my family did not. This meant that I came to these questions and these people from a faraway place, but this distance was also temporal. The crucial events that created this confusion happened well before I was born. And all of these paternal relatives lived hundreds of miles away from my family and me. At first we lived on Long Island and later in Dover, Delaware.

Because we were the out-of-town relatives, everyone in Albany seemed to come together whenever we visited. It never occurred to me that this was done for our benefit, and that this was not how they regularly interacted. I only figured this out much later. I felt so outside of this web of family relations, that for a long time I just assumed that the distances and disconnections were mine alone.

I come to the story of my two paternal grandmothers through my father. This is how our tales are bound together. He is my link to all of these other people to whom I am related. And so, what I have come to experience in relation to this inheritance is itself ambivalent, a combination of often contradictory things. Most acutely this has included feelings of shame and discomfort. I cannot differentiate between the legacy of my grandmother Lena's death and the life she once lived. For me, these things are conflated and fraught. And I cannot talk about Lena without also acknowledging Mary, my beloved grandmother. And yet as I try to broach Lena, what I know best in my body are childhood fears associated with a mother's sudden disappearance and death, poverty, and the loss of a home. These are the most overt portions of my father's early life that live on in me. They are the most powerful pieces of the legacy of his first mother that he, her first child, has given to me. These are things I carry as his first child.

What's in a Name? An Interlude

I was named Laura, an American English name beginning with the letter "L." Each of my father's siblings' first children were also given "L" names. His sister's daughter was named Linda, and his brother's oldest daughter was named Layne. We are all named after our grandmother Lena Levitt.[50] This was not something that was articulated as each new child was born. None of us was told that we shared a name, much less that we carried the name of the mother whom our parents had lost when they were children. This was something we each only learned much later, but the clue was there. It was in our names. We share the initial, even though none of us has ever really learned what our grandmother's Yiddish/Hebrew name was, what she was officially called, or how she was identified, named by those who loved her.

According to eastern European Jewish practice, one honors a dead relative by passing on her or his name. And it is only in recent times that the name has become an initial, not the actual Yiddish or Hebrew name, but an American name that sounds similar to the original, an equivalent beginning with the same letter as the original.

Although I can finally transcribe the name from our grandmother's gravestone, I am not so sure that even the name inscribed there is the name that she went by. And really, such a renaming comes too late for me and for my cousins. I was given a Hebrew name as a child. That is the name that has identified me in Jewish liturgical contexts since. Sadly, that name is clearly not my grandmother's name. Although I did know that my Jewish name was Yiddish, the rabbi who first taught me Hebrew in the 1960s insisted that we all have Hebrew and not Yiddish names. I no longer remember if I even ventured to articulate a Yiddish name, was it "Leba" or "Lena"? What would I have said? What I do remember is that my friend Brenda offered her Yiddish name to the rabbi only to be told that "Brina" was not an acceptable Jewish name. I think I took my cue from his response to her. In 1967, she had to have a Hebrew name, and so did I. I no longer remember what Hebrew name the rabbi gave to Brenda, but like Brenda, I too was renamed. My Jewish name became "Leah." I do not know if my cousins were ever given Hebrew names or if this has ever mattered to them. Neither of my cousins had a bat mitzvah. And I do not know what they have done on those occasions where they have found themselves in need of such a name. What I do know is that even this effort to remember and honor our grandmother was not fulfilled. The name got lost in too many translations.[51]

The Story, Continued

In terms of what I remember, instead of mourning my father's mother, a woman we did not know had ever existed, we the children of the next generation simply loved the woman we always knew as our grandmother, Mary Levitt, our grandfather's second wife. All of us were very attached to Mary. For my father she was just "Ma." For me she was "Grandma." Mary mothered so many people that it is hard to remember that she did not give birth to any children; instead, she mothered as sister, as daughter, as wife, stepmother, aunt, and grandmother. Mary mothered many of her own younger siblings upon her mother's death, after the birth of her youngest sibling, her sister Paula. Mary then became mother to my father, aunt, and uncle after marrying my grandfather, and much later, she helped raise my first cousins as well as some of her many nieces and nephews who also lived in Albany. At least that is how I imagined it, especially when it came to her relationship with her other grandchildren. From far away, I envied my cousins their closeness to Mary. It seemed to me that she was a regular part of their lives in a way that I had never known any grandparent to be.

And yet, even from afar, she was the grandparent who insisted on spending time with my brother and me. She went to great lengths to visit us on a regular basis, arranging elaborate bus trips to Delaware. These trips were especially complicated because she never had a driver's license.

Along with my first cousins, my family celebrated Mary's extended family, the siblings she was closest to, their children, and grandchildren. We attended their bar and bat mitzvahs and many of their weddings. They were family. Those related to Lena were family, but in a more secondary sense. We were not as actively engaged with them. These connections were nebulous. This, too, was part of the ambivalence I experienced in relation to Lena.

As I have come to understand this, my father and his siblings didn't want to have to tell their children about losing their mother; they didn't want to pass on that bitter knowledge. But, despite their best intentions, we got the message anyway. Like Ravett, there are things that all of us know without ever being told.

We knew something was amiss but could not put our fingers on it. What we garnered was something less overt and perhaps more ominous. And we knew better than to ask. What we got instead were glimpses of loss. At least this is what I imagine my cousins also received from their parents. It remains difficult for any of us to discuss any of these matters even now. There is a distance between us. At least my brother and I have never been very close to any of them.

For me, this sense of loss has included a haunting sense of fear, a lack of trust perhaps. As I reflect back, I see this legacy as a kind of emptiness that includes a vague fantasy of a beautiful mythic female past, the loss of an object of many desires, the desires of children for their mother, and the desire of a man for his wife—a man who, in retrospect at least, had once married for love and lust. And even if this man, my grandfather, had married again, even in part for love, the initial loss had made that first love all the more bittersweet. At least it has appeared that way in the imaginations of his son, my father, and me, his grandchild. Or is this my mother's interpretation? Is it one of her frustrated analyses of the Levitts and their peculiar distances?

My mother struggled to understand my father and his estranged family, but did so with her own ghosts. Her family used distance as a form of retribution. Given this, for many years my mother was hurt by the estrangement she experienced in my father's family. These feelings tapped into her very real fears of distance, a discomfort she learned well in her own extended family. She had no way of understanding this other family's distance even as she experienced it personally. For her, it made most sense to imagine that it must have been something she did to keep them away, that it was her fault. The problem was that this explanation was also frustrating. She never could figure out what it was she had done to deserve this treatment.[52] So sometimes she lashed out, exasperated by their inscrutability—my father's inscrutability and his family's. She made up stories, more coherent narratives, out of the bits and pieces she had. Some of them were disturbing. They reflected both her pain as well as some truths about my father and his family. My mother needed control and narratives that made sense of this silence. I am very much her daughter. I, too, have been enamored by the promise of narrative. I worry that I want relief, and that to get relief I will just accept any plausible tale. And so, when it comes to stories about my grandfather and his wives, I cannot distinguish between my mother's stories and explanations and my own. Given this, I know my telling echoes some of these frustrations, hers and my own.

Nevertheless, even if the romantic story of my grandmother Lena was not really the case, and the whole of Lena Levitt's life with her family was in fact fraught, this is not how my family, and it seems my father, has decided to remember it. Nor is it how his siblings seemed to have remembered her. At least this is my impression, for when they did eventually speak of her and this lost past, the visceral contours of her actual lived experience were not there. I do not know what she smelled like, the texture of her skin, or the sound of her voice. Neither my father nor his sister has much to tell me about these tangible traces. As I understand it now, the tensions among and between the mythic, soothing narratives, perhaps not even formulated into words, that these children told themselves and each other and the more terrible memories of yelling and screaming in another language, the foreignness of their mother's tongue, and the horror they experienced in response to her sudden disappearance and death can still hardly be articulated. What I eventually heard from my father was something less real. I got some carefully crafted tales of a boy who had lost his mother at age ten and whose memories had been both guarded and reconfigured in his imagination.[53]

These soothing stories, as I now refer to them, had grown up and been nurtured within the architecture of my father's boyish heart.[54] For over fifty years they were hardly ever articulated or shared with others. In all of that time, they were barely ever put into words. Within his imagination, as I now want to imagine it, my father's mother became someone he needed her to be for himself, someone whom, for most of her existence, he could not share with others except, perhaps, his brother and sister, but even this I do not really know.

In this way my grandmother, Lena Levitt, was born anew after her death within my father's imagination. And, by the time he was able to tell me about her, all he had was this mythical person, already a figment of imagined memories and no longer a living person. These mythic internal tales were about all he could eventually remember. What has been hardest for me to do is to try to get my father to re-member the once living person who was his mother. In many ways, I have been no more successful than my mother has been in trying to make this happen. So instead, what I carry in my heart is this vision of my father's imaginings and the traces I can put together from the evidence that has come to light so belatedly after her death.

Those who knew Lena Levitt, especially those closest to her, those whose lives depended upon her—her children—can no longer speak of her physical presence, at least not directly. By the time she emerged from their hidden imaginings, she was already transformed into something else. These efforts came too late. When she did emerge from these shadows, she was no longer familiar even to her own children. Her presence had long since receded; she was well out of even their reach. They had buried her and, along with her, most of their own concrete feelings and memories, the stuff of their everyday lives together with her as her children. By the time I was to see images from that time, it had already become "once upon a time." It remains hard for my father to turn back. The layers of all the many years and all his many efforts for so long in order not to have to feel and remember these things make it impossible for him to do so now.

For all of these reasons, it is no longer possible for any of us to remember Lena, to come up with a semblance of her presence in the world. Her touch, the cadence of her voice, the names she used to address her children, are all long gone. My father and I suspect that his siblings could hardly remember her body in any overt way because they were so young when she died.[55] And, along with this, and perhaps as tellingly, for a very long time they did not even know where she was buried. That, too, was lost to them. Phil Pearl's father, one of Lena's brothers, the uncle who had regularly taken them to visit her grave, died in the early 1950s. After that they stopped visiting her grave. No one had a car to take them. Only in the past few years at my own urging have my father and his sister rediscovered her grave.

Ravett: Another Take

I strongly identify with Ravett's position in his film *Half-Sister,* his distant and distorted loss, his difficulty in grasping a past that has already shaped who he is in the world even without his conscious knowledge of having ever had a sister, much less the specific events surrounding her death. I cannot help but think of Lena, the grandmother I never knew I had, the woman I am named after, whose life and early death I also only learned about belatedly more than forty years after she died.

Moreover, I cannot help but identify with the desire to animate that portrait, the photograph that appeared belatedly but nevertheless seems to both make present and re-present this lost relative even as it makes clearer the distance between us and her, between then and now. Although we can never know those who died before we were born, something also happens when someone is forgotten. The portrait—and I, too, had, for a very long time, only a formal portrait of my grandparents—is not alive. Even if a photograph could capture the past, it is hard to look to a formal image to find some semblance of life. Here the staging, the structure of the portrait itself, is a hindrance. Precisely in its ability to successfully take on the form of the portrait, this image only comes to resemble all too many other photographs just like it, pictures of other people done by the same or another photographer during this same historical period. In *Half-Sister,* women's clothing, costumes, and dress-up are all a part of how the film attempts to conjure up the resonances of the portrait and create, notice, and use transitional objects to approximate the mother and daughter who cannot be touched otherwise. Here the dolls are crucial. They are dressed up, and attention is given to every detail, including their shoes. It becomes a generic portrait. Again we experience a shared sense of loss.

Of course there are differences, indeed dramatic differences, between the story of my grandmother's death in America and Ravett's half sister's murder at the hands of the Nazis. My grandmother lived to become an adult. She came to America and married. She had children. She also died, before the war, in 1936, perhaps before Ravett's sister was even born. Yet like Ravett's mother, my grandmother came from eastern Europe where Yiddish was her first language. Like my grandfather, Ravett's mother also spoke broken Yiddish-inflected English. And, although I never heard my grandmother's voice and by the time I met my grandfather he had already spent another forty-plus years in this country speaking English, I recognize a connection between Ravett's mother's voice and my grandparents' voices. Even as I have come to find a few people who actually remember my grandmother, who heard her voice, I only know that she spoke English with an accent. I know that she spoke virtually no English when she was at home where she continued to speak Yiddish. This astonishes me as I think of my father as a boy growing up in a home, where English was a second language, not the language of his parents' everyday life. In this house, English was a foreign language. The hope of becoming a real American was imagined as something distant. It was to be achieved in a language very different from my father's mother tongue. And having accomplished this extraordinary goal, my father cannot speak his mother tongue. He can barely understand it. Thus, despite this early upbringing, he now has only a limited understanding of Yiddish. He cannot speak it himself.

We now return to *Half-Sister* within the larger context of Ravett's other films. We do this to see how this film connects not only to some of the other films he has made about his parents (and to see, more immediately, how, in part, his engagement with this film lead to *Toncia*, a film solely devoted to his mother's telling him about his half sister's death), but also to see how it connects to his seemingly completely different film, *Jack Haber*, a film pieced together from found footage purchased in an antique shop in Brooklyn. *Jack Haber* is a film about a stranger and what might be gleaned about an ordinary life from the traces of film he left behind. I want to connect these two films, and Ravett's other works about his parents, to my own struggles around what stories I need to tell. I am interested in how our intimate connections to the not-so-distant past lend urgency to these efforts. I am also struck by the differences between Ravett's films about his parents and this other film.

And yet, the more we struggle with trying to make distinctions between these films the more we see how much these distinctions are not really that important. Instead, what is striking is a different kind of connection and movement between these disparate tales. In many ways, we all find it difficult to just stay with our own stories of loss. We need to get away, we long to go elsewhere, but even in these ventures away, we find ourselves circling in on precisely the portions of our tales that we find most difficult to confront. We move outward to get closer in. And so, as I tried to figure out these connections, a friend suggested that I listen to an episode of the radio program *This American Life*, "The House at Loon Lake."[56] The show is about a young boy's lingering fascination with an abandoned house he first comes across as an eleven-year-old on vacation in New Hampshire. The house is crumbling but its contents are all there, as if, all of a sudden, the family had to run out, leaving everything as it had been. Food is still on the table. Personal items are all still there over fifty years later. Why did they leave? What happened to this family? These are all open questions that capture the young boy's imagination. He feels compelled to learn more, and slowly, over time, he brings his mother into this mystery. She, too, comes to explore the house. She helps him try to put the pieces together, directing the boy to the town's cemetery to see what it might tell them about what happened to those who once lived in this house. As the narrative continues, we slowly come to learn more about the family who once lived there and what happened to the house.

As I listened to the show, alone in my office and not yet adept at adjusting the sound system on my computer, I was startled by the voice of the boy's mother and the things she had to say about her own family. She had an accent, a European accent that was familiar to me from years of work on Holocaust narratives. As she slowly talks about her own fascination with the house, she reveals that for her, there is a more personal connection at stake. She knows what it means to have to abandon one's home. As she explains, her family had to leave their home in Czechoslovakia to escape the invasion of the Nazis. Her family had to leave virtually everything they owned behind as they fled for their lives, never to return. In part, the boy's mother speaks of her own deep longing. She hopes that perhaps someone, even an eleven-year-old boy, a stranger, might have found her family's home and wanted to know their story. She wishes that someone might have paid attention to the stories that her family's home and their things might have told. As she explains, "things" speak. They long for someone to hear their stories. And, although this was not exactly what my friend had in mind when she first led me to this program,[57] it was more than I could have imagined finding.

The radio narrative led me back to Ravett's film *Jack Haber*. Not only did Ravett "hear" or "see" what Haber's film had to say, but his engagement with this footage, his attempts to learn more about this stranger, also helped him engage, perhaps more indirectly, with the limitations and possibilities of learning more about his own family's past. Here the urgency to be known, to leave a trace, was something Ravett picked up on in the film footage he found. This also echoed other less overt traces closer to home that still needed to be heard, seen, and engaged. I do not have a neat way of conveying this indirect process, but my sense is that we are drawn to stuff whose tales cry out to us because they touch cords in our own lives. As we begin our engagements with this stuff, we must face our own legacies, which are often less than conscious. In the radio story, the little boy is drawn to an abandoned house and in the process connects to his mother and a more intimate tale of family loss, another abandoned house. The Holocaust tale is revealed in the process of engaging with a more ordinary American story of loss. The movement goes both ways, back and forth. In the end, the boy is also able to give the things he has salvaged from that abandoned house back to someone in that family who wanted them, someone who longed to understand her own family legacy. My efforts are a part of this process. As I will explain in the next chapter, my father also had things, hidden things, whose stories longed to be told, and in his case too, there was a stranger who happened upon these things and, like Ravett, did research to learn more about their stories. This stranger ultimately returned my father's things to my family. And like the now grown boy in the radio story, this stranger, through the fruits of his own labor, offered data about my family's past to my father and me. This data included various names and dates, and the places my relatives lived in and around Albany.

Whose Story?

In part, *Half-Sister* was and continues to be my way in. Again and again I am reminded that the story I am telling is my own. As much as I understand the story as a family story, as something I share with my father, my cousins, and my aunt, the truth is that the urgency around the particular tale I tell is always my own. It is not shared. Although what I have to say touches other members of my extended family, I am not capable of telling what this story means to anyone else, including my father.

What I have to tell is my version of my father's story—as mediated and distorted as it has become in getting to me. What is mine is this now very different tale, a narrative that has shaped my life in ways that are different from the ways my father's story has shaped his own life. In part, this telling may be connected to my cousins and even to my father and my aunt,[58] but it is ultimately my take on the story of my grandmother. It is the telling that I need to articulate now. And despite the fact that I have known this in some way or another for a very long time, I am startled again and again as I am reminded of this simple truth. Although our family stories are intertwined, they are never the same. The angles are always different, and that means that what gets noticed, what

Laura Levitt at Lena Levitt grave. From the Levitt family collection.

stands out, what is highlighted or important can and does shift from one person's perspective to another's, even as we share the contours of what is presumably the same story.

As I reread what I have written, I am struck by how much I still want to be able to find the definitive story of my father's mother, Lena Levitt, and in this way lay claim to a tale that is not just mine. I somehow feel obliged to do this and then to share the story with my cousins as if we really were much closer than we actually are. Is this the continuation of my father's role as crafter of the childhood pact, a pact between siblings not to mention their dead mother once their father remarried? As the oldest child, my father, I suspect, felt responsible for his siblings and for making sure they could all survive in this new household with a new mother. As I write these words, I am struck by how this makes some sense of my own position in this ongoing legacy.

Although I am not the oldest grandchild, I am the first child of the oldest of Lena's children, and in that respect, my father has passed this sense of responsibility on to me, his oldest child. I feel responsible to my cousins as the one who must make some sense of this legacy. But even with this obligation in place, what I have to offer is not something whole. It is just my own story, my own sifting through the various pieces I have collected. Here I am thinking about not only Benjamin's notion of the labor of digging up and sifting through one's buried past,[59] but also Mary Gordon's tales of what it is like to try to put together the story of her long-dead father's life.[60] Gordon's *Shadow Man* is a daughter's struggle to let go of the mythic father she had created as a little girl, a father figure who enabled her to become the writer she now is, and to come to terms with who her father was in his actual life. The book is an account of Gordon's search for her elusive father. She traces his published writings and official records, and she tries to meet with those still alive who once knew her father, including members of his family she had never known. In her final narrative in the section "Telling Stories to My Father," which includes a series of parables each entitled "This Is What It Is Like," a woman receives packages all her life "from the estate of your father" and finally decides it is time to go through these packages and figure out what it is that has been bequeathed to her. She rents a space and starts unpacking. She hopes that by sorting through these boxes she will finally understand her father. But after unpacking everything, she realizes that she cannot put all of these things together. "When she tries to put things together to create a shape, nothing holds." And so, "She gives up the idea of a coherent shape" (201). Instead she is left with an array of disparate things, shards and pieces that must be "constantly accessible, constantly interchangeable, constantly ready to be in different relations to one another" (201). She leaves the following things on a bench in plain sight:

> A broken spring from the inside of a silver watch
> the marble finger of a god
> a skull with missing teeth
> a pot with a hole in the bottom, unable to be mended
> a luminous, rough-textured cup that cuts the lip and there-
>   fore can only be looked at, not drunk from
> a gourd that rattles in a playful way
> a blue-gray feather, motheaten to a tender shade
> a porcelain child's valentine, chipped
> a pistol misfired
> a devotional weapon whose use cannot be ascertained
> fragments of messages: "If only once more I could see your
>   face." "Among the dead there are so many thousands
>   of the beautiful." (201–2)

I feel like I am the member of my family (however true this may or may not be, it is how it feels to me) who has been sent all of the packages, and I am the one who has collected them and now feels obliged to sort through them and finally report back on my findings to my father, to my family, and to you, my readers. The time has come, and, like Gordon, all I have are pieces, idiosyncratic pieces that do not all add up to the woman who was my grandmother. Instead, it is as if I have put together a film filled with blank segments. There is no continuous narrative. Even as I splice the pieces together over and over again searching for a narrative thread, there is none. And so I find comfort in *Half-Sister*. It feels familiar and honest even though I cannot truly say that I understand it. Like Gordon's narrative, it is incomplete, discontinuous, a set of glimpses at something, someone, who can never be made whole despite our very best efforts.[61] And despite my knowing this, I notice how my desire to smooth over this simple truth slips into my thoughts and my writing again and again. I want to be able to tell the story as if it is a whole tale complete with a narrative arch, but there is no such thing. I have only pieces culled over many, many years of digging and searching. I need to write it down as it is and acknowledge that this is how it must be. And perhaps like the end of Adrienne Rich's poem "Transcendental Etude," I, too, can remind myself that as I work with all of these things that are in my lap I need not make them into something brilliant or eternal. I can just have them as they are.

> Such a composition has nothing to do with eternity,
> the striving for greatness, brilliance—
> only with the musing of a mind
> one with her body, experienced fingers quietly pushing
> dark again bright, silk again roughness,
> pulling the tenets of a life together
> with no mere will to mastery,
> only care for the many-lived, unending
> forms in which she finds herself. (77)

Like Rich's narrator, I can outline the shape of the loss of this woman I did not know and whose absence has reverberated over time, over generations. I can talk about what it has felt like to try to approach her legacy through the gauze of my father's not telling, his buried feelings, and those moments when he has ventured to show me something of that precious past, snapshots taken out from years of hiding, a lost portrait come to light, the finding of a grave on my insistence, and the return to the home his family once shared, again at my request.

Maybe I am obsessed. I wonder why I care so much, why I feel so strongly about this past, about remembering. I know that there are those who are often designated to be in such positions in families and other intimate groups and that this has been my role, but I still find it startling to realize that this is not just the way people are, that this is just that, a role, one of many possible ways of being in the world. As I write these words, I am reminded of the ways I learned this craft. Early on, I was just a mimic. I learned my mother's stories since she was the one who told actual tales. I memorized her stories and assumed that they were true. It took me a very long time to figure out that these were just, in fact, my mother's stories, my mother's take on her family and their past, and, occasionally, my mother's take on my father's family and their lack of stories. In the void that was my father's family story, at least in my immediate family, my mother tried to fill in, to make some sense of what was not articulated. In part, this entire project follows my mother's lead. It is less neat and less frustrated. And I hope it is also less angry. I do not blame my mother for her anger. I appreciate her frustration. My mother had a hard time tolerating silence, the lack of narrative. For her, silence had to have a reason. This was her only way of explaining the gaps, and it made sense given the volatility of her own family of origin and their silences.

Despite my following her lead, I was never quite satisfied with my mother's tellings of my father's family stories. The narratives did not fit. They felt wrong. They did not make sense given my own experience of this part of my family. I loved these relatives. Actually, I adored them. And the narratives my mother came up with just didn't feel quite right to me, although I still think there are glimpses of deeper truths in my mother's stories. I hear her struggling with these issues in the car on the way home from yet another family trip to Albany. It is the mid-1970s. She is groping yet again with her own discomforts, her feelings about not quite belonging to this family. She thinks that their distance from her is a response to something she has done to them. She wants to know why they don't like her. Or, do they like her? What did she do or not do? What did my father do or not do to distance them? But these are not the right questions. I knew this even then, but I also wanted to know more. I wanted to understand, but there was always something about this family that resisted being known. This is also something I knew more intimately in relation to my father. It is part of how he still relates to the world and also, in part, how he has always related to me. Few people even now really know him. Even we, his family, do not know so many of his secrets. We cannot see the dark recesses of his heart.[62] But I must return to that car trip.

I was a teenager and it was only then that I first learned that the woman I knew as my grandmother was not my biological grandmother, that my father had had another mother. I learned this truth in that car driving home from a family trip to Albany. It was in my mother's frustration that she let slip this long-held family secret. And so I am in a sense, yet again, indebted to my mother for finally saying this out loud, for telling me this truth even in this way.

It was not long after this incident that my mother, my brother, and I dramatically locked my father in the house with us on a Saturday night in order to get him to tell us about his childhood. My mother's revelation made clear how little we actually knew about my father's childhood. Although I suspect that my father loved the attention, the process of getting him to talk was awful. It was like pulling teeth. My mother was so frustrated; she groped, often forcefully, to get him to talk, to feel, to say something real. Even then I appreciated the urgency of her efforts, but I also felt the disconnection between what she was doing and what she was hoping for, her intentions and her actions. You could not force such things out of my father. They had to come on their own, slowly, in dribs and drabs. It would never happen in an evening or even in a few days. It would take time, a lifetime, to discover some of these things. There was no drama then, and even now there is still no catharsis. That was what my mother, the English teacher, hoped for, but really it was just not going to happen. Like Ravett's film, my father would remain inscrutable. And although I too had wished for a catharsis, I am learning to appreciate what comes when we let go of those desires. Although it all would have been so much easier, and it would have made a much better story, the truths of my father's life are just more textured, less straightforward. Like *Half-Sister*, my father's life is messy and halted. It does not flow. Even when I work to carefully craft the various pieces together, there is no crescendo. It just isn't dramatic. And even though I have known this for a very long time, the desire for such a story still creeps into my text as I try to put down in words the truths I have learned.

Postmarked Pictures: A Postscript

Dear Reader,

This postscript is my belated engagement with the title of this large chapter, "Postmarked Pictures." I have purposely delayed this discussion as a way of enacting the lateness that marks all of my engagements in this project. I have done this to make clear that these kinds of engagements always come, in some sense, too late. And yet, despite this, I hope to suggest that in the end, for Ravett, for me, and, I suspect, for many of us, the presence of loss, of specific losses, however inarticulate, have always been a presence in our lives, even before we receive word of their particulars. We are often haunted. Our knowledge of the past remains sketchy, the traces retrieved—in Ravett's case and my own, a letter and a long-lost image—allow us to touch what were hitherto completely inaccessible stories. In these cases, the haunting has been transformed— we know who and what we might be grieving. Ravett powerfully enacts this haunting presence in *Half-Sister*. In a somewhat different way, with the help of Ravett's film, I have attempted to animate the image of my grandmother, to begin to imagine who she was, who she might have been, and how her death and the shame and secrecy surrounding her death shaped both me and my family. In this sense, like Benjamin's digger, I have taken an image "severed from all earlier associations" and placed it within my own "prosaic room of later understanding."[63]

And now the image I send out to you has been marked by my efforts to turn it over again and again, to look at it from a range of other angles. It has my fingerprints all over it. What I offer you is an image profoundly marked by my own ongoing engagement with it. Dear reader, what you now have before you is an image covered with the traces of my desire to know, to understand, to make known, and to mourn this woman who was my grandmother. I have not placed her away in a gallery out of reach, but rather, like Ravett, I have tried to make her come alive and, in so doing, to touch her. I have also asked you to touch her as well, to circle in closer with me. I imagine that in the process, perhaps you, too, have left your own fingerprints on this text and her image as well, placing her in conversation with those who haunt your own imagination.

And so I find myself returning to the title of this chapter, "Postmarked Pictures." For me the "Post" is after, later in time, but it is also about something that circulates, as in the mail. It is something sent from one place to another, a package addressed to someone from someone else. It is about an exchange and a sharing. It is a form of connection, the passing on of property or information from one person to another purposefully. But, going back to the belatedness of this "post," for me the return is late, perhaps too late. That which has been returned has become something else. And yet, it has been returned. In this case, the portrait of my grandparents belongs to those of us who now have access to it. In other words, it remains mine, but is now in some sense also yours. Taking possession of this image as presented here comes with the weightiness of those still inaccessible earlier associations and with traces of all that has transpired since. In this sense, the image of my grandparents or Ravett's half sister, although now clearly signifying loss, once meant something very different that also cannot be forgotten. Despite their mundane, scripted familiarity, for Ravett and for me the generic poses of a certain era of studio portraiture hold out the promise that, at least at the moment these pictures were taken, those depicted were, in fact, still living their ordinary lives, lives still filled with the promise of a yet unknown future. It is the loss of that unknown future and its promises that we mourn. The receipt of these visions of a past we did not know allows us to bring to light that which was once hidden. Moreover, the return of these lost studio portraits—at least one portrait—with both a familiar and a previously unknown family member helps us draw the connections, to see ourselves in relation to these other people. The woman I thought was Ravett's mother and my grandfather offer us a way in. And although the salience of these images is with the heretofore unknown figure in the picture, it is this imagined intimate relation that allows us to make these connections across time.

I think that these shared relationships also help us realize that there must have been other clues to this person and to this unknown past that were already present in our lives and we had not fully recognized until now. These include certain fascinations, silences, and preoccupations. For Ravett, some of these are his attention to little girls and to dolls. In my father's family, there has been a fascination with certain resemblances among and between my aunt, my first cousins, and me. This recognition is part of the gift of the return. It constitutes the context of a more metaphorical package. It also helps explain why we are so drawn to these pictures. They make visible that which was hidden, although always already present. As these legacies begin to unravel, other once hidden aspects of these pasts also come to light.

3

Secret Stashes

At times I feel crazy, thinking about my daily obsessive, joyful, sorrowful digging. I feel slightly mad.
> —Jane Lazarre, *Wet Earth and Dreams: A Narrative of*
> *Grief and Recovery,* 107

Writing about grief and recovery and the imbrications of different losses in her own life, the writer Jane Lazarre describes her ongoing efforts to deal with the loss of her mother when she was seven. In her book *Wet Earth and Dreams: A Narrative of Grief and Recovery,* Lazarre explores this legacy in lucid and powerful ways.[1] For her, as it is with me, the effort is a kind of digging into the past, over and over again, in ways not different from those Walter Benjamin suggests. Unlike my father, Lazarre does this work in words and not in pictures. By contrast, Lazarre's efforts are narrative and as such closer to my own. But for me this effort is more mediated. I am a full generation removed from the loss of the mother in my father's precious picture. She is not someone I could ever have known. And here I find myself closer to Lazarre's son, whose experience of his mother's grief is also indirect. Writing about her son and his relation to her mother, a grandmother he never knew and whose existence she did not talk about with him, Lazarre narrates:

One night he calls me after seeing an old movie about a mother who is banished from her daughter's life. He describes the plot, the mother poor and unloved, watches her daughter's marriage into a wealthy family through the crack in the doorway in a church. . . . He is crying as he tells me the story, and I keep asking, but why are you crying so much? "I don't know," he repeats. Then finally, "I just know I have always been haunted by your mother." (112–113)

The first time I read this passage I understood. I, too, have been haunted by a banished grandmother whose existence was a mystery. Like Lazarre and her son, many of us are engaged in a process of reckoning with ghosts. And as we dig deeper in search of these ghosts, other things come to light; other secrets, and other stories emerge. Sometimes buried objects also reemerge—old photographs, books, films—that complicate what we thought we already knew. In my case, although I had understood that there were no pictures of my grandmother, Lena Levitt, until the portrait came back to my father in the early 1980s, it turns out that there were other pictures. This chapter is about a stash of those other pictures and some of the dangers of these discoveries. I locate my father's predilection for hiding things and their belated reemergence in a broader cultural desire that is especially powerful in the realm of Holocaust memory. In this case, I bring together my father's secret stash and the 2,400 family photographs found at Auschwitz-Birkenau, the remnants of one of the last transports of Polish Jews to the camp. I look closely at Ann Weiss's *The Last Album: Eyes from the Ashes of Auschwitz-Birkenau,* the text that introduced me to this story and these images, and I then turn to *Before They Perished . . . Photographs Found in Auschwitz,* the two-volume compendium of these images and evidence about where they came from compiled and published by the Polish State Museum at Auschwitz-Birkenau.[2] By looking at these texts next to each other and in relation to my father's story, I raise questions about any heroic telling of the recovery of once lost images. I offer a cautionary note about redemptive readings of the discovery of what was lost and now is found, and those who find, revive, and publicize them.

My Father Hides Things

My father hides things. This is part of how he has dealt with the losses that have marked his childhood. Not only did my father hide a stash of family snapshots, the stash at the heart of this chapter, but he hid other things as well.[3] To hide is to conceal. It is to keep something out of sight, or secret. It can be a way to seek refuge, as well as a way of dealing with shame or grief, as in averting one's gaze. It can also be a way of protecting oneself, as in hiding from a pursuer. These are all aspects of my father's efforts to conceal and protect parts of his childhood however conscious he might have been about these various efforts. But I am not sure what he had eventually hoped to do with the things he hid, or who he hoped might find them. I suspect that these efforts to store away some of his precious possessions did allow him to grieve some of what he had lost after his mother's death and what he lost shortly afterwards when his family lost their home in Schenectady, New York, as the Depression deepened.

Even now, my father has few words to explain these efforts. He just did them. He cannot explain. Even when I sit beside him looking at the remnants, the few things that have been recovered, he cannot tell me why he hid them. He cannot say what they mean to him now or what they once meant. These are not questions my father can answer. He cannot in any direct way give voice to these remnants. Rather, like the boy in the radio drama "The House at Loon Lake" who went in search of the stories of the abandoned house he found, I have been the one who has had the need to attempt to give some name, some voice, to these no longer lost objects and the tales they might tell. Like the young boy's mother in the Loon Lake story, I too believe that these objects have stories to tell and that it is those of us who find them, those of us in the present who feel something compelling about these things, who are ultimately responsible for attempting to articulate these stories, however partial our knowledge of them might be or however dangerous their exposure might be.

Let me begin with one of these other stories of hiding from my father's childhood—not the stash of photographs that will be my main focus here, but another cache of things my father hid. I want to use this other tale to shed light on some of the problem of finding a voice, of giving meaning to these acts of hiding for the little boy who was my father, for my aging father, and for me, his adult daughter, who comes to these efforts so late in the story. As I hope to make clear, this first story is linked to the story of the snapshots my father hid. It has helped me to flesh out the meanings my father has associated with the gesture of hiding since his childhood. And by placing these stories alongside another more charged tale about discovery, the story of the 2,400 family photographs found at Auschwitz-Birkenau, I want to make clear some of the limitations and possibilities opened up by these kinds of discoveries in the present.

As I tried to begin telling this story, I went back to my old files, no longer sure when or where my father had hidden a box of his things when he was a child, a cache that was found over forty years after he hid it in the floorboards of his family's home. At first, I remembered this as an earlier gesture. I thought that he had hidden these things when his family was living in Schenectady. But it turned out that it was later, and I was confused about which of the many homes of my father's family in Albany might have housed this secret. I had to call my father and ask. Although this seemed like a simple act—pick up the phone and ask the question—it was more fraught. Increasingly, I felt uncomfortable asking my father to remember these things because I already knew how little he can recall. But I just wanted to find out in which house he had hidden the box. So I called. And then I got going; I couldn't help but try again to ask the more difficult questions: Why did you hide it? When did you hide it? Did anyone else know about this? These are the questions that now pain me. I so want him to finally come clean and tell me the truth, but in this case, the truth is just not so simple. Neither the little boy nor the grown man has answers to these questions. He just did it. What he remembers is that it was around 1937, a year after his mother's death, but perhaps it could have happened before? It had to be before 1940 because that was the year the family moved to Albany— but these are questions about the photographs and not the box.

He knows where he put the box. As he explained it to me, the second floor of the house was not complete; there was an unfinished space, and it was here that he moved a floorboard and placed his box of possessions. He also recalls the content of the box—some drawings, cartoons of various characters he had made up, a Hebrew school report card from the Nott Terrace Synagogue—the Orthodox synagogue where he attended Hebrew school, the place where he was made to say Kaddish for his mother, and eventually, the place where he had his bar mitzvah. There was also a blue and white *Tzeddakah* box.[4] This was something my father suspected might now be valuable. It was the one thing that the man who owned the house and found these things decided to keep. I don't really object to this, and neither did my father. After all, this man had gone to great lengths to find out all about my father and his family, and his efforts have been a great gift to me and my extended family. Most of what I know about where my father's family lived and about what the public record has to say about when they arrived in this country and what they did for a living are the fruits of this man's labor. Giving him the *Tzeddakah* box was the least we could do to thank him for his efforts. I wish I still had his letter. I only remember bits and pieces of his narrative. What I have are photocopies of a few handwritten pages of information he recorded from the census records and other official sources.

While on the phone with my father as I was writing in the spring of 2005, I also asked when this man first contacted him since I could no longer remember. My father guessed around 1980, and this seems to make sense based on what the man had written about ownership of the house. The last people listed lived there from 1949 until 1982, and these were my grandparents. From this information, I infer that the man who found my father's things was the next owner. That means that he would have had to have contacted my father around 1982 or sometime not long after that. As I recall, he had not being living in the house for very long when he found these things.

What I know is that this story has come back to my family and to my father from a stranger. The man and his family had decided to do some renovations, and in the process, they discovered my father's treasures under some old floorboards on the second floor. Like the little boy in the radio story "The House at Loon Lake," this man was moved by what he found and felt compelled to learn more about the boy who had hidden these things. He wanted to return these items, and he set about doing research on the house and its various inhabitants. And when he came upon the boy's family, he learned more about them as well. Eventually he tracked down the boy's now living relatives, those still in Albany, who led him finally to the man who had once been that little boy, my father.

This stranger did research for us that no one in the family had ever done, giving us a map to our past, to public records about our own history. He also got my family talking about their past. It was almost as if the fact that a stranger could find this story so interesting meant that it really was worth exploring for ourselves. His discoveries also gave us tangible things through which we could trace our past. And for me, the fact that this man had found something my father had hidden, a box of my father's secret things, confirmed what I had guessed. My father hides things. My father had always, it seems, hidden things. This discovery was the evidence that gave me proof of this and helped me begin to see much more clearly how important hiding has been to my father. And now we could talk about it at least a bit more openly.

This story about my father's hidden box is a lot like both the *Jack Haber* film and the "The House at Loon Lake" story. Here again inarticulate things, traces of a life once lived, longed to be heard. And in each instance, a stranger is able not only to return the property to its rightful owner and/or his heirs, but also to tell some of those stories. In this case my father's inarticulate childhood yearnings, the desires that led him to hide these precious things, came to light, and a stranger was able to figure out at least part of the story. The stories, of course, are incomplete, but in all of them, strangers—Abraham Ravett in the case of *Jack Haber*, the little boy in the Loon Lake story, and the man who found my father's hidden treasures—reveal objects and expose their longing.

My father, secretive, shy, and even quiet, has a very different public persona. He is passionate about his opinions and makes them public every chance he gets. For many years he had a regular newspaper column, and even now he writes opinion pieces and draws political cartoons for his local papers. In addition to this, he is an artist, and as such, he has produced thousands of images, paintings, and drawings of men, all of whom resemble himself.[5] This seems to suggest a very public person, a man comfortable in revealing himself, in being open and known. But this is not the case. What he does not say or draw or write is as voluminous as what he does.

Part of what I want to suggest here is that the excess expressed in these various modes of self-display very much hides the shy person who is my father. And in this sense, the silent witness of his paintings and drawings is most revealing. These images offer access to this other more intimate part of my father. Here alongside the actual physical objects that my father has hidden, they allow me to touch the less articulate but still visible traces of this other part of him. These objects and images offer access to what has remained unsaid, what he still cannot say more directly. This is the inchoate legacy expressed in the things my father has hidden and in the less overt impressions, feelings, and moods evoked by his drawings and paintings. But, as I will show, just having these once hidden objects come to light, both is and is not revealing. The secret may be out in the open, but that does not mean that it is readily decipherable. Both his painted portraits and his formerly hidden treasures remain difficult to explain. But I want to understand, to makes sense of my father's gestures and how they have shaped my story. And

Images from the Irving Levitt collection. Courtesy of the artist.

as the stakes become higher, the trauma deeper, it is difficult for me not to be swept away by my desires for a kind of revelation. And as we will see, in the case of Holocaust-era family photographs, the desire to clarify meaning can be overpowering.

In terms of the Holocaust there is all too often a redemptive fantasy at work. If only we can find traces of this lost past and bring them to light, we will not only discover some new, secret knowledge about this past, but in so doing, we can also help resolve the trauma. Although I appreciate this desire and struggle with it in my own efforts to engage with my father's past, I want to resist this practice. It offers a much too easy resolution of precisely the ambiguities that continue to haunt all of these efforts to reckon with the past. Given this, I insist on valuing the partial, the incomplete character of all these efforts. Here I am reminded of a different visual clue from my father's past, a more familiar work that also does not speak directly, my father's 8mm silent film, *The Thud of His Defeat,* which he produced in the 1950s when he was in twenties.

The Thud of His Defeat

The Thud of His Defeat takes its title from the final line of a poem by Stephen Crane from his collection *War Is Kind.*[6] The poem reads as follows:

> "Have you ever made a just man?"
> "Oh, I have made three," answered God,
> "But two of them are dead
> And the third—
> Listen! Listen!
> And you will hear the thud of his defeat."[7]

This poem was first published as a part of Crane's second and last book of poems, a collection that seems to confirm his bleak vision of the world. In his introduction to *The Complete Poems of Stephen Crane,* Joseph Katz writes of Crane, "His is a vision of the world in which the gods have departed and man is left alone to fend for himself."[8] As I read it, Crane struggles not so much with "the gods," but with his Christian faith and the legacy of the cross. In part, it seems to me that he is taken by the notion of suffering and its centrality to Christianity. Life is filled with suffering and it does not always feel like it is justified. And yet, the idea of Jesus' suffering and death help Crane grapple with the pervasiveness of human suffering. The just are not singular but plural, indeed a trinity, and although all of them die, the three here suggests a kind of Christian hope against hope.[9] After the death of the second man at the moment when resurrection seems most unlikely, Crane leaves open the possibility of hope, yet he posits no guarantees. Even still there is this hope against hope in the figure of the just man. Given this, I am interested in what it means to be a "just man."

What makes a person "just"? What, more specifically, makes a "man" just?[10] "Just" as an adjective is generally meant to connote that someone is honorable and fair in his or her attitudes and actions. The just person conforms to notions of rightness either in terms of what is valid according to the law, what is suitable and proper, or what conforms to sound reason.[11] In this poem "just" is clearly what is in accord with God's will, God's judgment. God is both asked the question and given the final word. The just are virtually all gone from this earth, but still the question is asked. And the answer commands the questioner to listen hard, to pay close attention. The doubling of the word "Listen" is emphatic. God demands that this defeat be heard, but what is to come out of this listening, itself a biblically inflected command, remains unclear.[12] We know this is what God wants us to do, but not what we are to make of the sound of this final defeat.

In another way, the poem is an indictment. What is our role in the demise of these three just men? Is the human condition helpless? In this way, the God of this poem can be read as offering little comfort. This God offers no overt salvation. He is defeated or perhaps just defeating, taking the wind out of any hope for human justice in this world. This is all in keeping with the tone of the other poems in *War Is Kind* where justice is hard to find, especially in the guise of human men. There are few rewards in this life and much pain, irony, and death. Just men must die. Their fate is death, which implies that God is either cruel or uncaring, or that his message is much more complicated and contradictory, the message of the cross indeed.

But let's say we are to listen hard and heed God's command. What is it we must hear? Crane has God say "the thud of his defeat." A "thud" is a dull sound, the sound of "a heavy object striking a solid surface." It also refers to the blow or fall that causes such a sound.[13] The voice of

God urges his questioner to be attentive, and in so doing, he will hear the dull sound of the final just man's defeat. I wonder too about this notion of defeat. Defeat often means that someone else has won, that a victory has been decided and one side has clearly lost. But in this poem, the defeat of the just man is not dramatic. It requires a great deal of attention just to hear what confirmation we have about the outcome of this final battle. His defeat is signified by a thud. Is the dullness of this sound, its bland and uninspiring tone, a way of indicating that this loss, this failure, is itself just not that momentous? This, too, is a possibility.

Why was my father attracted to this poem? What made him choose these sparse few lines for the only narrative film he ever made? I will never fully know the answer to these questions, and yet . . . here again I find clues in the less overt messages of my father's choice. The connections he seemed to make to this poem link me to some of the hidden parts of himself and to the losses that continue to attract my attention.

The poem, for better or for worse, is something my father gave me. Although I did not remember its exact lines, I knew its basic structure. It is one of the only literary poems my father shared with my brother and me as we were growing up. We saw his film, and we were repeatedly told that it was named for this Stephen Crane poem. We even had a sense of how our father saw Crane in different lights and at different moments in his own life because he had also painted images of Crane more than once. He made a traditional portrait of the author as well as a more abstract rendition, and both of these paintings were framed and hung on the walls of the living room of the house we grew up in. The more abstract painting is still there. The other is with my brother. When the film was shown, often to my mother's high school students, part of the end-of-year ritual of their Great Books class, the students were also shown my father's portraits of Crane. The portraits and the students were a part of the ritual of these very literary screenings. I attended many of these events.

Oddly, in all that time, I don't think I ever really thought about the poem and its meaning or even what it specifically meant to my father. And although I knew that it resonated with a kind of suspicion, a fear and pessimism that my father has expressed to me in other ways, the message or content of the film were lost to me in these public screenings. But as I rewatch the film (now on video) as an adult far away from my parents and their home, I see other messages. In the silence of a small screening room in the library at Williams College, I hear a more intimate message from my father. I hear the voice of his fear, his distrust, now communicated visually. "Don't trust anyone. Don't lean on them. You never know when they might not be there." He would often communicate these things to me by telling me that "walls move." You can't trust that they will be there to lean on. This was a warning. Watch out, you never know when walls might move. Although he talked overtly about "walls," I thought that what he meant by this was that other people are not trustworthy. It was this message about caution and not trusting that I began to see expressed in my father's film. And yet, I also found this confusing. It contradicts some of the other lessons I have learned from my father, the more overt ones.

Despite these cautions, my father has always been a strong believer in human goodness, in our ability to make the world a better place. On the one hand, my father taught me that walls move and not to trust other people. But on the other hand, he both preached and practiced social justice. Now, as I viewed his film, I was beginning to see that my father has always kept these contradictory beliefs in tension. In his most overt and public statements, my father never expresses his more pessimistic vision. No, in public he is, as he always was, a true believer, especially in the promises of America and its democratic institutions. I internalized most readily the message my father gave me overtly, the message of hope. But I am slowly realizing that I also took from him this other, less positive vision. For a long time, I did not recognize this. It was only when I found myself profoundly at odds with this country's system of justice, the backbone of my father's faith in America and its democratic ideals, when as a victim of a violent crime in my late twenties this very system failed me personally,[14] that I railed against my father's optimism. I was angry with him and myself for believing in these promises. At that time I questioned his faith but did not remember the other lessons he had taught me. It is only now, many years later, that I am beginning to remember this other story. As I reconnect to the quieter lessons my father taught me, as I review his film among so many other things, I am seeing this other link between us.

What I am beginning to see is that the other side of my father's optimism was a more troubled tale, a vision of the profound injustice of this world. As I come back to Crane's poem now, I am able to see the connections between my own disillusioned vision of the world and what my father might have found compelling in Crane. As I began these musings I did not know that they would lead me to this place. I suspect that

I have resisted making these connections in the past, in part because I have not wanted to see myself sharing these more painful things with my father. And I suspect that when something terrible happened to me, he, too, tried to resist making these connections to me as well. Neither of us has been sure what the other could handle. And now I suspect we both were wrong.

There is something else that is strange for me in connecting to my father through Crane and it is the gendering of these poems. For me, Crane offers a powerfully masculine vision. It is a vision of pain and suffering in the guise of war, a war where women and children stay home and men, their men, fight for them on the front. And this is also true of my father's film. It, too, offers a vision of man's suffering, the suffering of men. These works are both by and about men, by and about what men do to other men, what men do to themselves, how men inhabit this world, and the stupid, mean, and cruel things they do to themselves and to others. For Crane, women are clearly idealized, and in that way they are unreal. And yet, I do feel implicated in both Crane's poem and my father's film. I, too, am not sure that the world is just, that men or women can be trusted. And perhaps, like Crane's narrator, as pessimistic as he is, I still feel compelled to turn to God for answers. Although we do not know if the man asking the question heeds God's call and "listens," we do know that God has responded. He has answered the man's question, and in the face of injustice, in the face of what appears to be utter defeat, he urges the man to listen. This feels compelling. Maybe I really am a theist after all. Is my father? In part, my father's film is his attempt to wrestle with this poem and its meaning, but, for me at least, the poem also offers a hope against hope. It is a partial, less heroic vision of faith, a response in the face of defeat.

I now turn to my father's visual narrative, an interpretation of the poem. Like Abraham Ravett's *Half-Sister,* my father's film *The Thud of His Defeat* communicates its message indirectly. In it my father reflects on his efforts to hide things, to store them away as hidden treasures, and he also questions what constitutes a treasure and whether there is anything redemptive to be found in any of these acts. Both literally and figuratively in his film, my father plays out these different scenarios. He offers a series of defeats, but in another way he also shows that one can do something else with these stories. By sharing them, he suggests that there may be more to these narratives than meets the eye.

My Father's Film

My father's film, *The Thud of His Defeat,* takes its title from the final line of Crane's poem. The film is only about twenty minutes long, about the same duration as *Half-Sister.* But it is not an experimental film; it is an amateur production in the best sense of that word, a labor of love done on 8mm black-and-white film stock.[15] It was a collaborative effort completed with the help of my uncle, Harold Wilson, my father's brother-in-law, his sister's husband. Harold was a builder with a knack for film and photography. He is the same man who would, in time, initiate my own entry into film and our family's home movies. Harold shot the footage for *The Thud of His Defeat* and helped my father edit it.

The film was conceived as a kind of parable, not unlike many of Crane's poems.[16] The film presents a stark tale about the relationship between two men, one black, and the other white. The landscape is urban. All scenes were shot in the city parks and city streets of Albany, New York.[17] The two men are presented as down and out. They are, in the terms of the time, bums.[18] It seems as if their racial difference hardly matters. And yet, I suspect that there is something about the hopelessness of the two characters in this film that is both black and white. Their lives are stark, their prospects few. Both are poor, and my father might have been trying to illustrate that among the poor, racial differences may be less of an issue. So although it strikes me as unusual in the 1950s that my father chose to hire an African American actor to play one of these roles,[19] it does make some sense within the logic of the film and my father's experience growing up poor in these same city streets of Albany. My father graduated in the 1940s from a high school that was "integrated," but here the term is really a misnomer.[20] My father attended Philip Schuyler High School, the public school on the wrong side of town. All of the students—black and white—were poor. He was one of the very few students to graduate with a college preparatory degree.[21] I suspect that this high school helps explain my father's ease in casting a black actor in his film.

What strikes me now, perhaps more than anything else, is that my father somehow got it into his head that he could make a movie, and that film was the way in which he wanted to engage with Crane's poem. Watching the film again carefully, alone, I am struck by how well done it is. Although there are some awkward edits and a less-than-compelling suicide scene, the film is gripping. Soundlessly it tells a story, a strong tale of decay and hopelessness. The opening sequence brings us into an urban wasteland. Eventually the two drifters will take their respective places in this desolate landscape. They will become points of despair within this larger vision. They will be depicted as bereft but in contrasting terms. And in all of these ways, the film, the two characters, and the urban setting offer an indictment of the presumed promises of postwar mid-twentieth-century American life. The dreams depicted in this film are nightmares. These are empty, unfulfilled lives lived in a place of little hope, Albany.

The silent film begins with a long pan. Slowly, a figure emerges. He stumbles into view, and as he gets closer we see that he is drunk, and then he moves out of view. At this point we see, amidst the rubble, a small hand-painted sign on which are the words of the final line of Crane's poem: "The Thud of His Defeat." I recognize the handwriting as my father's, but other than that there is no signature. There are no credits, just this one single sign, appearing briefly with no voice-over, no audio narration. I did not remember this sign, and perhaps this is not surprising given how brief this sequence is in the course of the film, but now I am struck by this trace of what I already know, that this is the title of the film. Someone finding this footage in a bin somewhere would have a clue to what my father was getting at even if he or she had nothing else. This is not unlike what Ravett found among Joseph Haber's film footage.

Over the course of the film, the two men depicted are restless. Each in his own way tries to fill himself up, distract himself, but with little relief. The first man—the black man—stumbles. He is drunk. We see a bottle in his back pocket that he frequently pulls out to soothe himself. He seems to have nothing else to do with his time. He wanders and he is lonely. He longs for human contact. He begins and ends the film in the park.[22] The second man—the white man—is gaunt and sallow faced. We see him leaving a rundown row house, a place with broken windows and ragged shutters on an equally shabby street. He is a creature of this place, a man of these streets. This is where he lives and where he will die. As he leaves the house, he carries with him a beat-up, misshapen old suitcase. Like the suitcase, the man also looks beaten down. This man calms himself with cigarettes. He lights up as he gets to the edge of the street. He sits down on the curb just outside the house and takes a few drags. During much of the film he is seen smoking as he wanders through the city.

This second man eventually makes his way into the park. This is where the two characters meet for the first time. As the second man sits down at the edge of the river, still very much an urban site with a railroad bridge just overhead, he tries to settle down. He pulls an apple out of his suitcase and tries to eat it. But after taking a single bite, he spits it out and throws the apple away. It is at this point that the other man comes into view. He seems excited by the prospect of engaging with another human being. But despite his best efforts, he cannot rouse interest in the other man. The black man cannot get this other man's attention. He tries all kinds of tactics but nothing works. He performs, he goads and cajoles, but his companion will not engage. He walks away irritated by the company. Despite this rejection, the first man pursues the second. He comes back again and again trying to make a connection.

Holding his suitcase close to his body, the second man keeps running away. We watch as the black man follows this sad fellow into the streets of the city and its changing neighborhoods. Here we notice distinctions of class and status, a majestic bank building, more refined parks, even a golf course. And in all of these settings, again and again, when the black man reaches out to the other man he is rebuffed. As these encounters multiply, the mood of the film becomes more tense. Increasingly, we realize how much the depressed man resents these encounters. We know the narrative is building. We know something is going to happen. Although there is an actual fight at one point, even this physical exchange offers no resolution. Instead, what does become more evident is that the white man is suicidal. He wants to kill himself and is looking for just the right place to do it. He crosses railroad tracks and busy streets as both the camera and the black man follow him. Finally, after all this wandering, he returns to the park. And here the first man surprises him one last time, but this time, when he gets no response, he grabs the suitcase and runs. It is as if he is taking the consolation prize. He wants a companion, but when he cannot get that, he decides to vent his frustration and take what he can. This is how I am reading the film although even my father's recent narration stresses that the black man always wanted the suitcase. Getting the suitcase is his motivation all along. I suspect that this version of the story might be how my father's script reads, but for me this is not how the visual narrative unfolds.[23]

In any event, the camera returns to the second man, now even more bereft than before. He no longer has the suitcase and the few worldly things he has packed within it. This is the final blow. He leaves the park and returns to the city streets. Here he finds an overpass, a viaduct where he will ultimately take his own life. We watch as he considers his options one last time.[24] He looks around, up and down and all around. And then we see him pick up his foot as if to go over the rail. Here the film itself is rough. The technique is awkward. There are a series of cuts with a few scenes shot from above, from the viaduct, and then an abrupt cut to a few scenes from below, a few views of the empty street below. The entire sequence ends with a shot of the man's body sprawled out in the street below.

The film then returns to the first man who has finally found a secluded place in the park, a spot under a tree where he can open the suitcase. Here again he is met with disappointment. After all of his efforts, whatever dreams or hopes he had of finding something of value, some comfort or pleasure or compensation in the contents of the suitcase, he finds no such thing. What he discovers instead are a few pieces of old clothing. There isn't even any loose change in the folds of these garments. The suitcase is worthless. There is no hidden treasure. All of its pockets and compartments are empty. The robbery has been meaningless. The film ends after the man has kicked the empty suitcase. He falls to the ground. He is on his back with his arms spread out facing the heavens. In a strange way, he almost looks like Jesus stretched out on the cross. This is a familiar and highly troped pose and may not be what my father intended, although it is a striking ending to a film based on Crane's clearly Christian poem.

Before I draw any conclusions, there is one more moment in the film that I want to comment on. In many ways, this is an embarrassing cliché, but it is something I want to call attention to, anyway. In the spirit of Alfred Hitchcock, my father, the director, makes a brief appearance in his film.[25] And, like Hitchcock, he shows up incognito. Unlike the two characters at the center of his film, my father is not depicted as a bum. He is a well-dressed man on the street in dark sunglasses. He is wearing a light-colored sports jacket. He is supposed to be cool; at least that is how I imagine my father thinking about his character. And yet this is not quite what we see. There is an excess to his character, visible on many levels. We see it in his posture. The man in the sports jacket and dark glasses is quite self-conscious. In his brief scene he is supposed to be just passing, a man about to cross the street when he encounters one of the two main characters. The meeting is seemingly by chance, no big deal. Nevertheless, what we see in the version of this scene captured on film is not that simple. For me, it is jarring. My father virtually trips off the curb. He is awkward, and this awkward movement makes us pause. We notice him in ways that we, perhaps, should not. His funny footwork tells us that this guy is less distant from the misbegotten characters in this film than we might have otherwise thought. He, too, is uncomfortable, out of place. His movement and his whole demeanor are awry. In some ways, it is a comical moment, a bit of levity for those who know that this is the filmmaker.[26]

I am both charmed and embarrassed by this moment. I do and do not want to see my father in this light. I am struck by how uncomfortable he is in his body. As I watch the film again, I realize that I had entirely forgotten about this scene, yet it comes back to me as I catch sight of my father on the screen. I remember my mother calling attention to this moment in the film each time we watched it while I was growing up. My mother's take on this scene is not quite the same as mine. She is charmed while I am uncomfortable. It is the performance of the filmmaker's signature that my mother wants us to see. She sees Hitchcock and is more than willing to smooth over the awkwardness. And perhaps Hitchcock is also awkward, but that is not something that my mother is concerned about. This is my issue. I am touched by my father's awkward appearance. His self-consciousness is intimately familiar. It is both painful and embarrassing. I recognize and identify with my father, whom I now see trying to take on the role of director. His now long-ago but forever fresh attempt to approximate this cultural ideal, an ideal taken from film and repeated in his own filmic production, is very familiar. What I see is both the longing and the inability to inhabit a cultural ideal.[27] This inability to approximate such a cultural ideal is something with which I struggle as well. Like my father, I too have tried to inhabit the space of all kinds of cultural ideals, American, Jewish, and feminine and later feminist, and I have not quite lived up to those standards. And I love this imperfect young man who cannot quite be Hitchcock but who made a movie. He has created a film just for himself, a film that is able to articulate his despair, his fears of defeat.

What I find so remarkable about this depiction is that the film has not shown me that life is hopeless, but rather that it is filled with possibilities. My father could make a movie; he could create something out of his own despair. Even in this place, he has been able to show me that we are oddly capable of sharing our fears with others. He connected to Crane in the desperate words of the poem, and through his film, my father has touched chords in me, my struggles with faith and hope in a terribly desperate world.

In my father's version of "the thud of his defeat," defeat is presented in the guise of two lost souls. These two just men may or may not be already dead; they may simply be waiting for the third just man to join them.[28] It may also be that my father is the third man. It may be that the film offers the final thud, the sound of the man landing on the street after his leap off the viaduct. Or it may be that the Christlike image of the black man is a sign that all that is left is the hope of a second coming. I do wonder if this last reading was the hope of the black actor who played this role and who, in the early 1950s, understood the meaning of the poem in ways my father might not have fully appreciated. I wonder if Crane's Christian theology combined with the actor's own real despair might have inspired this improvisational final moment.[29] And, even if this was the actor's idea, that still does not explain why my father chose to end the film this way. Might this adumbration of the poem's message be a part of what my father had always found alluring in Crane's poem, its mysterious Christian hope against hope? And, given this, it might also be possible to read the entire homage to Crane as symptomatic of my father's poor Jewish immigrant longings to simply be a part of the dominant culture, to belong and to share, in some way, in its faith?[30] Here we see the story of only two men. I wonder why he left out the third man. Is he part of the secret stash, the character hidden away but haunting the film? I do not know for sure what my father intended, but I do know that all of these interpretations are possible.

I feel compelled to say one last thing about the soundlessness of this film. Given the importance of the word "thud" to the title of the film, and given the final line of Crane's poem, I am struck that there is no actual thud in this film. Without a soundtrack, this film can never supply what the poem so insistently urges us to listen for—the "thud" of the just man's defeat. Even the one literal death depicted in the film, the action that should rightfully be accompanied by noise, passes in silence. I suspect that my father read Crane's poem as nonredemptive in this way, that for my father, there may have been no hope against hope, no relief. There is a Godot-like absurdity to it—we want the satisfaction of an ending, the landing, an auditory closure to all that anomie.[31] His two protagonists are defeated. And yet as I have already indicated, to me the film seems to offer itself as a gesture of hope. It does so at a different register, a place outside of the film's visual narrative but rather through its own impossible existence and endurance.

A Coda

What I remembered most vividly about this film before I watched it again as I began this project is that it is set in Albany circa 1952–1956. I remember recognizing this old and decrepit urban landscape. Part of what stands out for me over a lifetime of viewing this film is hearing about its Albany production. My father hired his brother-in-law to film and got two actors to play the roles of the two men. For weeks on end, my father and these men got up early and filmed in the streets and parks of downtown Albany. They did most of their filming in the neighborhood near the capitol. Most of these places no longer exist. And as I recently learned, this includes the viaduct, the place where the second man commits suicide. In a sense, all of these places, like the characters, have been defeated. And yet, I am tempted also to conclude that they have been rescued in the sense that they continue to live in the footage of this very film stock. What has been salvaged is one of the many decimated urban neighborhoods in Albany where my father and his extended family once lived. In this sense, this is also a lost Jewish geography, a quite unextraordinary place in this country where my Jewish family once lived and that now no longer exists.[32]

The neighborhood of my father's personal past, salvaged in this film, is now covered over by the high modern marble and concrete New York State capitol complex erected by Governor Nelson Rockefeller in the 1960s. In this sense, the film offers traces of a now literally buried terrain.[33] This is another secret, another inadvertent loss captured by this film. And as in the poem, this too is an ambivalent legacy. While a thud, even a silent one, is not redemptive—still I find hope in this bleak film. Maybe "hope" is too strong a word. I find solace in remembering, in drawing close to those hidden places and stories that have not disappeared entirely, have not entirely succumbed to urban blight, literal and figurative. The film allows me to draw near to my father and his interior life adumbrated in this silent black-and-white film.

Another Phone Conversation

While I was writing this, my father relayed the film's narrative to me over the phone. He retold the story. In this telling he focused on the suitcase, explaining how it is the motivation for the first man's pursuit of the second. He follows him because he wants the suitcase, only to discover that it holds nothing of value. I now remember that this is the way my father has always narrated the story; it is his interpretive hold. And this was part of why I thought about his film in the context of this discussion of secret stashes. But as I opened myself up to the film and to the poem, I did not find what I thought I would find. I did not find an empty suitcase. Instead, I found another secret stash, this time of implications, lessons embedded in both the film and the poem, which leave me more convinced that it is these subtle messages that are at the heart of what my father has always given me. These are the things I learn from his visual representations and from the various things that he has hidden and that he has eventually come to reveal to me in precious pieces.

Although my father's film seems to be an early effort to let go of his pain and his loss, to dramatically show the dangers involved in dreams of hidden treasures, it also performs a kind of promise, the promise of cultural production. The film enacts the ability of creative work to hold, to carry, and to deliver precious things to those who engage them. This cultural production is part of what brings my father and me together. It is some of what we share with each other. We are both producers of this kind of work, and we are readers and viewers of each other's creative constructions. I don't think that this was always so clear to either of us. It has taken a long time for me to appreciate this, in part because we do very different kinds of work.[34] My father has always considered himself a writer. He has always written, but for most of my life that has been more in the mode of his public persona as politician and advocate. His creative self, the artist and creative writer, has usually been hidden. Although for many years I thought that I would share that public life with my father, what I have come to discover is that the world we share most keenly is not that world at all. What we share is the creative, the often quiet and less than overt parts of ourselves. I think this is what my father realized as he read my first book. He recognized something in those pages that spoke to this part of himself. I suspect that there was some sense of recognition. Again it is not something we can talk about directly. But I am beginning to appreciate the ways he has acknowledged these connections in the past and continues to address them in the present.[35] And I am coming to accept these more intuitive perceptions as a different mode of communication and production.

A Revealing/A Revelation

I was in Dover, Delaware, visiting my parents during the winter of 1997–1998 to celebrate Hanukkah. This was not long after the publication of my first book. The book was very much in the air. Both of my parents had read the book, and each had been moved by the ways that I had written about them and the home I grew up in. My mother was especially touched by my account of the photograph of her mother, the image I used as the frontispiece for that book. She was able to talk about these things and did so.

So the story is that not long after my father read my book, he showed me these pictures; he went into his library, his storehouse, and came back with something to share. This is something that he does. He says, "I want to show you something" and goes into his stash of who knows what and comes back with something to capture our attention. This is something he has done all of my life. In the enactment he becomes the center of attention. All of us focus on what he has to show us. I think he likes this process. He is in control. It feels safe and contained. And when he did this with the snapshots, he was in charge. We had never seen these images, taken in the mid-1930s. After we looked at them and he explained some of them, he went off and put them away. What I can no longer remember is why we didn't insist on keeping them out, why we didn't immediately appreciate their significance, why we didn't ask questions. I wanted to. I don't want to inflate my role in this, but I think there is something about the unspoken pact between my father and me that became more overt with the publication of my book, *Jews and Feminism: The Ambivalent Search for Home*. It was as if after reading my book, my father just knew that I would know what to do with his secret photographs.

Once he put them back, these photographs remained away for another year or two. It was not until I asked him to show them to me, to us, again that we were able to appreciate them. This second time, my father had to remember which images I meant, which pictures I was asking to see. My mother also got into the act. She brought out some family photographs of her own, only to be told by me that these were not the ones I had in mind. After a few of these false starts, my father finally came up with the pictures I was looking for.[36] Of course, this also makes me think that there must be other things he still has hidden away. The only open secret is my father's illusive manuscript, the book that he cannot bear to reveal to anyone but promises to eventually share with my mother. In fact, I think he has shown her notes, some piece of it, but somehow that really hasn't lived up to the magic of his secret opus. This story, the story of my father's novel—is itself an abiding family myth. For as long as I can remember, I have known about my father's novel, his book, a text he has been working on forever and has hidden away somewhere. This was the one story about something hidden that has always been visible, a part of my family's story about itself. We understood that my father had a book he was writing hidden away somewhere in our house that he would eventually complete and not only show us but have it published. But it is now less clear to me that there is such a complete manuscript; it seems that this stash may exist very much in pieces.

In the case of the pictures, once I got him to show them to us again, it was as if we finally understood how important they were. I don't know why this wasn't clear the first time. I don't remember what I saw or did not see then. The second time, my mother took charge. They were the only pictures we have of all of the members of my father's family of origin together, my father with both of his parents and his siblings. It was only after my mother announced their importance that these pictures really came out of hiding. This time, my parents made copies of them. They also enlarged the one photograph with all of them together and sent out copies to all of my cousins and my father's sister. I got my own copies. My parents then framed the enlargement and put it on display with other family photographs, including the image of my father's parents that had been sent to him in the early 1980s. Each of these images has a special place, not only on the shelves in my parents' den, but also in our family's imagination. They are now crucial to our family narrative. For those who ask, my parents will now talk about my father's family and his long-lost mother.

Books and Libraries

In my father's world, books are sacred objects. Authors are to be worshiped, especially those who write literature. Novelists, poets, and playwrights are among those ensconced in his pantheon. For my father, literature was not simply a subject he studied formally, but a larger vocation. He haunted bookstores. In Albany he sat at the feet of a man named Lockrow who owned his favorite shop, Lockrow's Bookstore at 52½ Spring Street. More than any of my father's other fellow book lovers and collectors, Harman Lockrow was a mentor to him. He encouraged my father to collect books. My father began this collecting as a college student in the late 1940s. By now he has an impressive collection of first editions. Mr. Lockrow taught him a great deal about the publication history of many of the books he collected. This is still the basis for much of my father's knowledge about these things.

Because my father held writers in such high esteem and valued their published works, I think it was always a challenge for him to take his own writing seriously. When he met my mother he had published a few poems. She liked to think of him as a poet and a writer. This is a vision that still haunts our family. And because my parents have always been so invested in this vision, it has become almost mythic, making it that much more difficult for my father to scale the heights of those expectations. I suspect that this is also why he continues to hide his notes for that magnum opus he is supposed to be writing. I am not sure he can imagine writing anything that is not exceptional, that does not meet his own very high standards.

For as long as I can remember, my father has had "his boys." These "boys" are his favorite writers. They are the writers he worships and whose standards he can hardly fathom reaching. I could name names—mostly 19th- and 20th-century Americans—but I don't want to get lost in the reverie. Instead, I want simply to note their looming presence and the ways I see them both inspiring and hindering my father's sense of himself as a writer. My father longs to be a writer, but I would argue that his imagination has really always found its most powerful means of expression in visual form, mostly through literally thousands of drawings and paintings, and even in his single film. In these works I see my father as less self-conscious. I have often found it hard to read through all of the various writings he has shared with me that go back to the early 1950s. Although I greatly appreciate these texts and the fact that he wrote them, I do not find them as compelling as his images. They don't touch me in the ways that his artwork has always moved me. In his pictures and even his film, there is a sense that he is not trying so hard, that he just lets himself go. There is something freeing about his pictures that I do not sense in his writing. He is not judging himself against the legacy of his boys.

All of this is a bit awkward for me to write about. As I have suggested elsewhere, unlike my father and my brother, I am not an artist. I do not have those talents. But even as I write, I also need to say that I am not a writer in the ways that my father ever wanted to be a writer. I am neither a novelist nor a poet. Mine are the words of a scholar, albeit one who writes in the first person, a scholar who cares about writing and hopes to be able to communicate to a broader audience. In this way, I am grateful not ever to have to compete with my father's boys. And yet, there is something about my writing that speaks to my father's love of books, his sense of history. It was, after all, the publication of my book that led him to reveal these long-hidden family pictures. And here I do feel that my writing about him, about these hidden legacies, does make a kind of sense. It feels as if my father trusts me as a writer, that as someone who writes I will know what to do with these things. And, for me, the connection between us is a link between his artworks and my writing. For my father, books have been a perfect place to hide things. For me books are the perfect place to unveil things. For both of us books provide safety for what is precious.

By the early 1950s, my father had begun to amass his library. And thanks to his mother Mary Levitt, he could confidently amass these possessions knowing that she would take care of them. For many years when my father's life was still in transit, this library lived boxed up in his parents' home. In the early 1950s, he hid this particular stash of family pictures in the pages of Frank Norris's 1899 novel *Blix*. When I asked my father to explain this choice of texts, his answer was enigmatic. He said he thought it was a clever choice. The book was not valuable. It was not one of his prized first editions and therefore not where someone might expect to find something of value. This was an undated reprint of the first edition of the novel published by Grosset and Dunlap. Grosset and Dunlap appear to have bought the plates for the original edition and reprinted it under their own company name. Although my father owns first editions of many of Norris's works, he purposely chose this volume, a large square yellow book that would in no other ways call attention to itself.[37]

In terms of the content of the story of this book and its relationship to his decision to choose it as his hiding place, my father was very dismissive. He thought the book was dated and not of much interest to anyone at this point. What he did tell me was that *Blix* is a sentimental work. Looking again at the book, my father discovered a note in his own hand that said that he purchased the book during the summer of 1952, August 15 to be exact. He assumes that he must have put the pictures inside the book then and that they remained there until he showed them to us in the late 1990s.[38] This is about all my father has to say about why the pictures were in this book. Even as he told me this just a few years ago, I could still hear a certain glee in his voice, a satisfaction with his own cleverness. It felt childlike. I had the keen sense that even now, he takes pride in how well he hid these things.

Inside the Book

I am less sure than my father about the meaning of his choice of *Blix* as the place where he would hide these family pictures. My first cursory reading told me early on that there were some formal connections between the family described in the novel's opening pages and my father's family of origin. There are also major differences As if in some kind of funhouse mirror, in the novel we find a solidly upper-middle-class Episcopalian family of four, a widowed father and his three children. This family resides in a comfortable middle-class home complete with the requisite parlor described in vivid detail, including a view of the bay.[39] This family, even without a mother, is quite well taken care of. They have both a housekeeper and a cook to attend to their domestic needs. They are quite different from my father's poor Jewish family trying to hold on to their small home in Schenectady, New York, a house without a view. There are, of course, other differences. The novel is set at the end of the nineteenth century in San Francisco, while my father's family story is set during the Depression in the 1930s. Although there is a ten-year-old boy in the novel, he is the middle child and not the oldest, he is not the center of this story. This boy plays a minor role in relation to his older sister, and he has no brother to bond with. My father was ten when his mother died and he, too, lived with his father and two siblings, but the only help in his household once his mother died was his grandmother, an immigrant Yiddish-speaking Jewish woman who had little knowledge of how to best raise young children in America. There is little to connect these stories.

The thrust of Norris's novel has less to do with the family and its dynamics and more to do with the love story between Blix, the oldest daughter, and Travis, the man who falls in love with her and gives her this peculiar and endearing name.[40] As Norris scholars have noted, *Blix* is a highly autobiographical novel. It offers a lightly veiled fictional account of Norris's courtship with the woman he would eventually marry, Jeanette Black.[41] In the novel, the newspaperman and aspiring novelist and writer, Condy Rivers, plays the role of Frank Norris's alter ego. As many commentators have noted, this sweet and indeed sentimental story contrasts sharply with some of Norris's most famous works. Nevertheless, *Blix* offers rich insight into this important relationship and its powerful role in spurring Norris's career. Like Condy Rivers, Frank Norris had the support of a spunky young woman who believed in him. Her inspiration helped him take himself seriously as a writer. Eventually, as he writes more and more, Condy leaves his job as a reporter in San Francisco and eventually goes to New York to take a position at a major publishing house. This is not unlike Frank Norris's experience writing for the magazine, *The Wave*.

Perhaps there is something about this story and its happy ending that spoke to my father in 1952. Maybe he simply identified with this hopeful and talented writer who was destined to live a tragically short but highly productive life.[42] It might also be that he found in this slightly embarrassingly happy story by Norris, known for his much more serious and somber tales, an ironic statement about his own sentimentality, his desire to hold on to these pictures.

That my father is drawn to Crane and Norris is striking. Both wrote at the turn of the century, and both were innovators, writers with a new vision, a very masculine and quintessentially American vision for the new century. My father owns first editions of these writers and of some of their contemporaries with similar inclinations. (Here I am thinking of my father's shelf filled with all of the works of Jack London. I would have expected to see Henry Roth, whose novels evoke the atmosphere of my father's childhood home.) For my father, the otherness of these American writers was both alluring and compelling.

By reading the words of these writers and collecting various editions of their work, my father was also making space for a different future, his future as an American, as an intellectual, a reader who could appreciate and savor the production of a new American literary tradition at the turn of the last century. Again I need to say that reading these texts, going to the library and taking out long-out-of-circulation volumes on Norris and the standard version of *Blix,* I felt a certain distance from this tradition. Unlike Crane's poem, this work felt dated, old, of a very different time. My father was right—this is definitely not a volume I would ever have considered opening. It is not a place I would have expected to find anything of personal meaning or value, and again, my father said that this was his intention.

Looking at the Pictures

For a while I thought that there were more pictures hidden than there actually are. Somehow the closer I got to writing about them, the more I seemed to think that I had lost track of them, that although I knew what was there, there still had to be more. I must have forgotten something. And as I checked and rechecked my files and even called my parents to ask, yet again, for them to send me copies, I realized that my desire for more speaks to my longing for more information, more representations, more memories of Lena, and more memories of this time in my father's life, his life before his mother died.

Part of what strikes me most powerfully about these images is their ordinariness. Although the children are clearly cleaned up and the men are wearing ties, these are not formal portraits. They are cheap snapshots, most likely taken with an inexpensive, mass-produced Brownie camera. All the images are overexposed and poorly framed. In one, my father and his father on the right side of the picture are elided. In another, both his father and his brother are cut off. In yet another, an uncle is also cut out of the right side of the picture. This makes me think that the person who took these shots had a problem with one of his or her eyes. Whoever was shooting them was uneasy with a camera or felt awkward about shooting them, or the family was not cooperating. Yet, however ineptly shot, these photographs are the best we have, and so for my extended family these pictures are powerful and compelling. I

Single image from the Stash, enlarged. "The Family Portrait," Lena, Sol, Irving, Aaron, and Muriel Levitt. From Levitt family collection.

include part of the full set here but will only discuss the single photograph of my father with both of his parents and his siblings, the only photograph of all of them together in a single frame.

This is the image that my parents enlarged, framed, made copies of, and sent to my aunt and all of my first cousins. The family, two parents, and all three children are together. They are all seated on the grass in front of an unwieldy bush. The father is a young bald man in a shirt and tie. He sits in the back on the left. We can see his light trousers and even his shoes; his legs extend toward the photographer. The little girl is leaning on her father's left side, to his right in the picture. Her legs are extended and she is wearing a short dress. She has a big smile on her face. Her hair is cropped around her face in a kind of bob. Next to her is the middle child, he is playing with his shoe and not looking at the camera. Behind him is the children's mother. We can only see her light-colored top, she is squinting but there is a smile on her face. In front of her on her left is the oldest son, my father. Like his brother he, too, is in

Single image from the Stash, enlarged. Levitt children Irving, Muriel, and Aaron with their uncle, Hyman Levitt, on grass. From Levitt family collection.

short pants but his legs are fully extended. He is not playing with his shoe; he is smiling, laughing it seems. His eyes are closed. He is animated and happy.

On the color-copied page of these black-and-white photographs I had with me as I wrote about them, I was constantly reminded of what comes after. The single page of images anticipates what will happen later in the lives of these children. To try to read the earlier images without already anticipating Lena's death is nearly impossible. And yet I at least want to acknowledge that in those pictures, no one knew what the future would be. We do know what comes after, and this knowledge makes it hard not to see a profound change registered in the faces and bodies of these same children only a few years later.

In the center of the 8½ × 11-inch page is another photograph, this one clearly labeled. On the top white rim of the picture is written, "Schenectady Summer 1939" and on the bottom, the three figures in the picture are each identified, "Irving, Muriel, Aaron." Here the chil-

Single image from the Stash, enlarged. Lena Levitt and her
children, Irving, Muriel, and Aaron on step; others cut off.
From Levitt family collection.

dren are older, taller. They are also strikingly less animated. No one is
laughing. They are barely smiling. The little girl is trying very hard to
make this a nice moment. She is carefully dressed, and just as carefully,
she holds a small bunch of flowers in her hands. They are perfectly sym-
metrical. She holds the flowers close to her chest; they line up with her
chin as if they're on the same plane. The boys are scrawny. Irving, my
father, is the oldest and the tallest. He stands just behind his sister on
the left. Aaron stands behind her on the right. In contrast to the other
photographs, those from the stash hidden in Norris's *Blix*, this photograph is perfectly square. And unlike the person who took the other pictures, this photographer knew how to center an image. No one is cut
off or out of this picture. Despite these obvious differences, what really
concerns me about the juxtaposition of this later image with the earlier
ones is how much this photocopied page replicates the problem of hind-

sight or what literary scholar Michael André Bernstein describes as backshadowing.[43]

Let me take a step back here just to be sure we have not lost the chronology. What we know now is that the family depicted in these images will not be together much longer, that the children's mother will die not long after these pictures are taken. Although the images are not dated, it seems quite clear that they were made around 1935 in the summer or spring; perhaps it was as late as the spring of 1936. Lena died in July 1936. It is hard not to read with hindsight, not to read what we already know and what those who posed for these snapshots could not have known then—that Lena was going to die so soon, that these children were about to lose their mother.[44] I read into my father's expression and postures signs of a before and after. I overread his giddiness, his playful lightheartedness in the earlier pictures, and I read a somberness into his expression in the later one. And even knowing that this is overdetermined, I cannot stop myself from seeing his big laughing smile in another of these pictures, the one on the stoop, or his smile in the single family portrait. For me these postures and expressions embody what I imagine my father lost when his mother died. But even if in the other

"Schenectady 1939." Levitt children, Irving, Aaron, and Muriel. From Levitt family collection.

two photographs he is less clearly elated, there is something relaxed about his expressions in these pictures, despite what they say to me about what he lost. I am touched by his simple smile in the shot with his grandmother and the family and the fact that he is caught looking away in yet another one, an image with his uncle and the three children.

Mediating Grief

I do not see my father ever writing a book like Jane Lazarre's *Wet Earth Dreams,* but I do think that his ability to take these pictures out of hiding is a sign that he, like Lazarre, has come to a different place in his grief. With a certain astonishment, Lazarre writes, "How did I get to this place after so long a time, to be able to retrieve my mother's photograph from the bottom of a hutch drawer, frame it, and hang it on the wall?" (103). Like my father, Lazarre reclaims a photograph of her mother she had hidden away and finally is able to look at it out in the open, frame it and display it, sharing it with her friends and family. This is precisely what my father was able to do. The gesture is the same. For both my father and for Lazarre there is a kind of reckoning. And like me, I suspect Lazarre's son has also benefited from this reclaiming. The haunting has not gone away for me, but I feel less urgency knowing that Lena is a part of our family, no longer banished.[45] And I would like to believe that she is less restless, more at peace because she is no longer hidden away, literally out of view.

Having looked closely at these issues as they play out in the lives of individual families, we can better see what happens when the stakes of these losses and recoveries are exponentially larger. Nowhere are these questions more urgent than in efforts to recover all of the losses that make up the communal trauma of the Holocaust. When scholars and writers like Yaffa Eliach or Ann Weiss try to recover the images of Jewish life before the Holocaust, the stakes are that much higher. In these instances, our longing to remember and to recover the stories of those whose lives were destroyed intensifies our tendency to see these efforts as redemptive. And yet, even on such a grand scale, these efforts, like my own or Lazarre's, remain incomplete. These labors of remembrance are only partial, and given that there are few left to verify or confirm our findings, recovery, or any kind of salvage, is that much more difficult. And yet our desires for answers are that much greater. Remembering our more quotidian efforts and the problems involved reminds us how fraught these efforts at Holocaust memorialization can be.

Impossible Albums[46]

> We see babies; parents with their children; groups of teenagers; people at work, at school, at home, on vacation—normal people leading normal lives.
>
> —Ann Weiss, *The Last Album: Eyes from the Ashes of Auschwitz-Birkenau,* 2001, jacket cover

> The pictures left behind by people who were gassed and burned in Birkenau are cut off from their own time and the life that has produced them. The wish for continuity and meaning in one's life with which we look at them and hope that the nameless were given names, that at least some of the people fallen silent found their language once again and told us what had happened, is as insatiable as it is powerless. In order to avoid approaching these pictures in a voyeuristic manner, we have to be conscious about our powerlessness while pursuing our wish for continuity.
>
> —Hanno Loewy, " 'The Scandal of Their Silence,' About the private photographs of the murdered people of Auschwitz-Birkenau," *Before They Perished* . . . , Supplement, 12

I came to these issues and these precious photographs through an extended engagement with the first edition of Ann Weiss's book. I relied on her account. I read the discovery of the 2,400 family photographs at Auschwitz-Birkenau through Weiss's reports. I only learned of *Before They Perished* . . . , the two-volume official publication of all 2,400 photographs sponsored by the State Museum at Auschwitz-Birkenau (also published in 2001), much later.[47] There are no references to the museum's work in either the original edition of Weiss's book or her updated and expanded 2005 edition. And, I should also note that there is no reference to Weiss's work in *Before They Perished* . . .

I was jarred to learn that there was another book about these 2,400 photographs, and the fact that both volumes were published virtually simultaneously in 2001 made the lack of collaboration harder to believe. Although neither the Museum nor Weiss was willing to talk to me during the summer of 2006 about the relationship between their books or their ongoing efforts to identify those pictured, I was curious and disturbed by these silences.[48] As I have already said, even Weiss's expanded and updated 2005 second edition does not mention the existence of this parallel project.[49] From what I can gather, Weiss's text has circulated widely in North America. This can be seen in the long list of venues where she has spoken and where her exhibit has been mounted, as well as in the various media appearances she has made.[50] The museum's two-volume tome seems to have had more circulation in Europe, where it was published.[51]

In what follows, I retrace my initial close reading of the first edition of Weiss's book in relation to both her updated 2005 edition and *Before They Perished . . .* I then turn to *Before They Perished . . .* , the volume of photographs and the smaller narrative supplement published by the Auschwitz-Birkenau State Museum, to discuss what this work does and how its efforts relate to and differ from Weiss's work. Although both of these texts share a similar and powerful strategy to identify those in the photographs, neither is definitive. At their best, as Loewy insists, they offer partial recoveries, small acts of redemption. Each project is very much conscious of its inability ever to fully attain continuity with the world depicted in these images. And yet, despite the similarities between these two books, I conclude by highlighting some of the differences that separate these projects from one another and by marking the need for vigilance and caution in any of our efforts to engage in acts of recovery. In other words, by explaining how the discovery of the museum volume changed and nuanced my reading of Weiss's text, I make connections between these quests for continuity and my own. In this way, I insist on resisting redemptive narratives in acts of recovery both large and small.

Opening The Last Album

On first reading, taking the text at face value, it was difficult for me to know how even to begin to write about Ann Weiss's book, *The Last Album,* much less the photographs collected in it. The story of Weiss's chance encounter/discovery of these photographs at Auschwitz-Birkenau, her painstaking efforts to rephotograph the entire collection of 2,400 images (only 400 of which are included in her book), and her remarkable labors to identify these pictures makes this an extraordinary project. Weiss's identification efforts have involved determining where the people depicted in these photographs came from and who the individual images might have belonged to, and therefore, who might have brought each of them to Auschwitz-Birkenau. And yet the story of Weiss's labors is just part of what is remarkable about this book. In addition to all this, Weiss's larger project has also had an amazing reception that is itself bound to Weiss's research.[52] Seeing these pictures either in the pages of Weiss's book or in the various exhibitions she has launched to display them around the globe, is an extraordinary experience; it is humbling and daunting. For, like the photographs in the Tower of Faces, these images offer access to what came before. They reveal, in Leon Wieseltier's words, the "voluptuously quotidian universe" (Weiss, 2001, 14) of Jewish life before the Holocaust, the everyday lives lost whose very existence mark part of what is so excruciatingly difficult to recover in the present. James Young gets at this problem, powerfully writing, "The photographs in Ann Weiss's precious collection are a little like survivors themselves—not of the Holocaust, however, but of a pre-war era nearly blotted from memory by the Holocaust. For part of the tragedy of the Holocaust is the way it has tainted the memory of lives lived before with their terrible end, the way it has blinded a post-war generation to the richness of the lives destroyed" (Weiss, 2001, 19). As Young reminds us in this book, part of the tragedy of the Holocaust is that it taints our ability to see that universe as it existed before. Those of us attempting to see this world are blinded by our knowledge of what came after. Hindsight makes it almost impossible for us to see the riches, and also, I would add, the sorrows, the everyday sorrows of the lives that were destroyed.[53] The Holocaust casts its shadow over all of this and we can see hardly anything else.

Part of the power of the photographs in Weiss's book and those in the Tower of Faces is that they are strangely familiar. Their ordinariness is what enables us to remember, to imagine the prewar worlds and everyday lives of European Jews. The connections we make to our own family albums, to pictures of relatives from that time if not necessarily from those places, are what move us even if we quickly turn away from these connections in horror, remembering the collective fate of these Jews and these whole communities.[54] And yet James Young reminds us in his introduction to Weiss's book that making these connections, these ordinary connections, enables us to resist containing the lives of those depicted in the photographs and those for whom these images were precious objects up until their deaths. Unlike the debris collected by the Nazis, stored and on display at places like Auschwitz-Birkenau, "floor to ceiling piles of prosthetic limbs, eyeglasses, toothbrushes, suitcases, and the shorn hair of women," these pictures do not recall the "brokenness of lives, now scattered in pieces" (17). For Young, this is itself a tragedy of the Holocaust, "that their lives should be recalled primarily through the images of their death." For Young this "may be the ultimate travesty" (18). By contrast, as he suggests, the pictures in Weiss's book offer us a way of resisting this pervasive impulse. They offer us all-too-rare glimpses into the textures of these people's once ordinary lives. They restore "the humanity of the victims" by showing us "the contingency of daily lives as lived and perceived then—not only as they are retrospectively freighted with the pathos and portent we assign them now" (19). I cite James Young here at length in order to help frame my own reading of this powerful text and its haunting images because I, too, worry about this freighting, the retrospective fallacy that makes it almost impossible to appreciate the contingency of Jewish lives lived in Europe before the Holocaust, lives that are in fact familiar, much like our own, or better still, like those of our own families who lived their lives at the same time albeit in other places like the United States.[55]

The normalness of these pictures, of those depicted, is part of what makes them so excruciating. It is what makes it difficult to reconcile what we know about what happened after and what we see before us now, the remnants of life before. The tension I speak of, the importance of not freighting these images with the knowledge that comes after, and at the same time our desire to value these images, to appreciate what they have come to mean for us now, is very much in evidence in the framing of Weiss's text.

Framing and Seeing: Ambivalent Visions

Weiss's book was first published in 2001 by W. W. Norton, and again in 2005 by the Jewish Publication Society, as a high-end trade-press book. It is oversized and published on thick glossy paper. It looks much like a coffee-table book, a collection of black-and-white photographs.[56] It is beautiful and was conceived to be so. And yet, it is hard to imagine that those purchasing this book would be quite comfortable placing this book on their coffee tables. One imagines this book being donated to a synagogue or a public library, another copy on a shelf of other books about the Holocaust, books about Israel, or books about Judaism, taken down to share with children, family members, and friends in solemn tones. But these may be just my fantasies about what those who buy this book do with their copies. Or what they do with other similar books: Yaffa Eliach's book about Eishyshok, the shtetl whose Jewish population makes up the Tower of Faces; Serge Klarsfeld's book on the deportation of French Jewish children, a tome that includes over 2,500 family photographs of these children; or even James Young's own books on Holocaust memorials and monuments.[57] I am still not sure what to make of the book-buying public's fascination with these volumes. In this instance, I only want to make a small intervention into a broader understanding of this phenomenon. I want to suggest that this fascination has a lot to do with the issues at the center of this book—the ghostly pasts that both animate and discomfort us as we engage with the legacy of the Holocaust, our desires to identify with both those who died and those who survived, and our simultaneous desire to distance ourselves from them and how they connect us to that past and to our own unmourned pasts. We want it both ways and neither way. And it is precisely this ambivalence that marks the opening of Weiss's text.

There are four distinct introductory pieces to this book that include both words and images. The first is an epigraph from Elie Wiesel, perhaps the most famous contemporary survivor of the Holocaust; the second is a long narrative dedication written by Weiss, herself a child of survivors; the third is a foreword by Leon Wieseltier, a famous Jewish public intellectual perhaps best known for his book about mourning his father's death, *Kaddish*;[58] and finally, there is James Young's introduction. Seeing these short pieces together along with the images that accompany most of them, I am taken by the tensions among and between these narratives—much less within some of them—about how readers should engage with this book. The passage from Wiesel is accompanied by a full-page facing image of an observant Jewish man. His head is covered and he has a long gray beard; perhaps he is a rabbi. This image clearly pays homage to Wiesel. It is a way of signaling and reinforcing his stature and authority in matters of the Holocaust. He is here depicted as the face of this lost world, an iconic image of a learned Jewish man.[59] Wiesel's passage reads as follows:

Let us tell tales—all the rest can wait, all the rest must wait.
Let us tell tales—that is our primary obligation.
Commentaries will have to come later,
    lest they replace or becloud what they mean to reveal.

Let us tell tales so as to remember how vulnerable man is
    When faced with overwhelming evil.
Let us tell tales so as not to allow the executioner to have the last word.
The last word belongs to the victim.
It is up to the witness to capture it, shape it, transmit it.[60]

In Wiesel's words, we are led to believe that there is a contrast between tales and commentaries, but although "the last word belongs to the victim," it is the responsibility of the witness to "capture," to "shape," and to "transmit" these very words. Stories must be told that are somehow direct, immediate, unmediated. And yet, the victims cannot speak, which leaves the witness in the position of having to craft tales that are not his or her own. He or she must not yet write commentaries. And for Wiesel as witness, this makes some sense even as he struggles in all of his work, especially his fiction, to make vivid and compelling the tales of the victims. But is Weiss, the child of survivors, in the position of those who must, with all due honesty, write commentary? What about the rest of us who were not there and cannot claim the status of witness? And what are the fantasies that animate our desires to be there, to bear witness belatedly?

These are haunting questions crucial to contemporary Holocaust scholarship and at the heart of literary critic Gary Weissman's *Fantasies of Witnessing*.[61] Weissman makes clear the disturbing implications of these desires for a kind of vicarious witnessing. This is all a part of what Weiss is trying to negotiate by using Wiesel to frame her own efforts. And it becomes complicated because, according to Wiesel, it is the witness who must craft his or her narrative in order to transmit it. In this way he or she becomes oddly more like those of us who come later and must write commentary. Both personal stories and commentary are crafted and composed. In other words, we are all in danger of replacing or beclouding what we hope to convey by the very act of our writing or even in our rephotographing and reframing.[62] There is no unmediated access to these legacies. Wiesel's words remind us of the contradictory legacy of what it means to remember, much less to witness, the Holocaust. These efforts are always fraught, impossible. Even pictures cannot offer us unmediated access to the words of the victims.

Turning the page from Wiesel's cautionary words, readers come to Weiss's dedication. There are no images accompanying these words. Weiss begins with her mother's death and her dying wish, a wish the author hopes to fulfill through the creation of this book. Weiss writes "BEFORE SHE DIED, my mother left a note asking my sister and me to remember the *yarzheits* (memorial dates) of her family. She listed the dates and explained, 'My family has no tombstone. I am their tombstone'" (9). This is, in part, Weiss's reason for compiling this book. As she goes on to state,

> I dedicate this book as a grave maker and final resting place,
> to the millions whose stories we will never know,
> to the thousands whose name[s] are recorded nowhere else,
> to the hundreds whose photos appear in this book,
> and to the blessed memory of my mother,
>
> Lunia (née Athaliee Backenroth Gartner Schaffer) Weiss (1922–1995),
> who, despite experiencing life's worst, chose to emphasize—and teach—
> life's best. (9)

Weiss then goes on to offer a partial list of the names of those members of her mother's family who were murdered by the Nazis, those without grave markers for whom this book, she hopes, will serve as memorial. The list goes on for two more pages and includes names and brief biographical sketches for many of these lost maternal relatives as well as a note that refers to some of those who survived and their families. There are also references to a few other survivors, friends of the family, including one friend who survived the Warsaw Ghetto and helped save Weiss's mother's life. In her updated and expanded 2005 edition, Weiss extends this account to include one of the survivors pictured in the book who helped her in her research efforts, Cvi Cukierman (1927–2004).[63]

In the 2005 edition of her book, Weiss also adds a photograph. The photograph on the final page of the dedications is from the author's own family. It is a picture of Chana Backenroth Gartner and Naftali Schaffer Gartner. The image is accompanied by an extended narrative about this couple and their family, all of whom died in Poland. Although a powerful addition, what is striking about this photograph is that it is clearly not from the collection found at Auschwitz. It is, instead, a family image from the author's own family. The inclusion of this image is instructive. It further illustrates Weiss's desire, in the final words of her dedication, for her book to "serve as a tombstone and final kaddish for those who have no one to remember them, and as an additional memory for those who do" (11). It is a loving gesture, but it is also complicated because it blurs certain distinctions. In this case, it blurs the differences between the specific people depicted in the collection of images found at Auschwitz and all of the millions of others who were murdered by the Nazis for whom there is so little evidence of the lives they once lived, including the stories of the author's own lost family. This book is not Weiss's family album, although her longing for such an intimate album is utterly understandable. This is part of what Loewy cautions viewers about. We need to watch our desires for continuity and redemption because they can cause us to confuse what we do know with what we do not. In order to resist this confusion, I think it might have been helpful for Weiss to have more fully clarified the status of this photograph, to have explained how it is both related to and different from those found in the rest of this book. She might have done this by noting how this particular image was preserved and how she obtained it. And then perhaps she could have explained how this narrative relates to the story of the other photographs because it is different.

I understand these impulses to draw these tales together. We make connections between losses. This is very much what this book is about. But making these connections is risky when we lose sight of how different narratives of loss touch one another but at the same time cannot be made into one and the same single story. What concerns me about Weiss's book is that, in the process of making connections, she seems to lose the distinctions between what is hers and what is not hers. She blurs the lines between her own tragic family story and the narratives of all of those who are depicted in the Auschwitz-Birkenau photographs. This is understandable. Both are stories of Polish Jews killed by the Nazis. The connections are very close, perhaps too close, but in the end, *The Last Album* is not Weiss's lost family album.

The album she has created is of and about other Polish Jews. In working with the photographs found at Auschwitz-Birkenau and seeing the connections, Weiss seems to forget whose photographs belong to whom. She confuses the familiar with the familial. Although her relatives resemble those depicted in the 2,400 photographs, these are not her family's pictures. Thus, although her book is dedicated to the memory of her lost family, it is *not* their family album. Rather it is a compilation of the shards of lots of other lost Polish Jewish family albums otherwise destroyed by the Nazis. Weiss's inclusion of a photograph from her precious family collection without marking it clearly as such, without making this distinction, blurs the boundaries. This takes away from both the story of her family photograph whose tale we are never told, and the stories at the heart of her book.[64] These are the kinds of distinctions I insist must be recognized as we bring our own ghosts with us to places like the Tower of Faces or in reading a book like Weiss's.[65]

Returning to her text, the Wiesel passage and the dedications together provide weight and authority as well as an intimacy to this work. For Weiss, this book is a familial obligation, a sacred task, and it connects her to the obligation of the telling that Wiesel describes. These words place readers in relation to survivors and their heirs. First and foremost, we are invited into their worlds. And having just entered this space, readers are offered words of commentary, the words of those who write from a distance, first the public intellectual Wieseltier and then the scholar Young.

Wieseltier's words are accompanied by an amazingly beautiful image of a dapper young man, a staged and indeed professional image, a portrait of this young man seated before a mirror.[66] He sits in front of the mirror with his hand on the table below it, his fingers on the rim of his hat. His white gloves are draped over the top of the hat. There is a vase with flowers next to the hand, but in the mirror we see the man's face as well as two more partial views. The photographer captures the seated man in profile as well as the mirrored images of his face. I cannot help but wonder if Wieseltier chose the image himself, if he identified with this young man. I wish I knew more, but reading Wieseltier's foreword, I kept thinking about this photograph and the man in the picture. He is so polished, so poised, so seemingly self-assured. Like him, in many ways Wieseltier more than any of the other contributors to this volume writes in a similarly self-assured manner. His language is bold. He writes of suffering and pain and the tensions between these visceral experiences and abstraction. He then goes on to write, "There are times when the most significant service that the mind can perform is to say: look, and then to say nothing more. The sign of lucidity is sometimes silence" (Weiss, 2001, 13). He then reinforces this sense that there is nothing to say, by telling us that these photographs "make discourse of any kind seem impertinent. Even mourning would be too knowing" (13). Coming from the author of a book all about the power of Jewish mourning practices, this is a powerful statement. And having said this, one would think that he would say no more. But his foreword continues. This is only part of his response to the images Weiss has collected.[67]

Wieseltier demands that we look at these images and take them in, and then he goes on to tell us exactly what we should see.[68] These images make stark the contrast between good and evil. Because the images themselves do not supply the "evil," it is our task as viewers who come later, who know the ending, to take the next step. "We must complete the story of every picture. We adhere these families to their fate" (14). In sharp contrast to what James Young suggests, Wieseltier asks us to complete the stories, to move from the contingencies of the lives they illustrate and instead to remember their ending retrospectively. Although I want to resist this demand and am more sympathetic to Young's perspective, I am struck by the inclusion of both these opening invectives precisely because, again, I am not sure we can escape either. We need to remember the contingencies, as difficult as that might be, and we are also always already remembering their terrible ending.

Nevertheless, I align myself with James Young and Michael André Bernstein, mostly because I think that few of us need to be reminded of where these pictures were found and the "fate" of the vast majority of those depicted. What is needed instead is a fuller appreciation of the ordinary and prosaic nature of these images and what these things have to teach us about what was lost. As Bernstein explains in another context,

> Prosaics . . . would stress that in our culture it is not the attractiveness of extreme risk or the darkest teachings of violence and domination that are repressed. Exactly these issues have long constituted an enormous, if not actively the major, portion of our intellectual conversation about history as well as about the human psyche. What is repressed, though, is the value of the quotidian, the counter-authenticity of the texture and rhythm of our daily routines and decisions, the myriad of minute and careful adjustments that we are ready to offer in the interest of a habitable social world.[69]

In other words, we need to resist backshadowing and overreading the ending, and instead we need to allow for the contingencies of the lives of those depicted. The danger is the arrogance of hindsight, of our knowledge taking over and making all that came before adhere to a notion of "fate"—the belief that it was all inevitable. With Young and Bernstein, I want to insist on recognizing that part of what we lose in "completing these stories" in this way is the prosaic ordinariness of these lives. We blot out the normal, everyday character of Jewish life before the Holocaust. Instead of doing this, I want to try to see the richness of the lives destroyed, the familiarity of the quotidian, and the contingencies of everyday life outside the framework of extremity that reduces everything to itself. I want to resist that arrogance and the narcissism of the photograph that accompanies Wieseltier's foreword.

I find myself more comfortable with the brokenness of the smaller ripped image that accompanies Young's introduction.[70] This incomplete picture of what appears to be a couple at their wedding reminds me that none of us who come after can ever fully know what any of these images meant to those who carried them with them into Auschwitz-Birkenau. We must try to find out as much as we can. Weiss's project, among others, attests to this. But what these efforts also teach us is that the results of such labor are always necessarily partial, contingent, and incomplete. It is, in part, for this reason that Weiss's calling her book an "album" is so effective. Like family photograph albums, the text is a hodgepodge of images, narratives, some brief, some quite elaborate, and lots of blank pages, lots of silences literally signaled by the lack of commentary. The text does not fit together neatly. Its organization falls apart time and time again. For me, following Young, this fractured, inconsistent, broken character of the book is its strength. And although I suspect that many come to the book to see triumph, to complete the pictures through our knowledge of the ending, this is not the only way of reading this or other such books or of appreciating the excruciating labors of their authors and editors.

James Young's introduction follows Wieseltier's foreword, and as I have already indicated, it contrasts sharply with Wieseltier's approach. For Young, the power and significance of Weiss's project is that it resists the ways that readers generally approach the Holocaust. Instead of dwelling on the ending, the terrible ending of the lives and communities of the vast majority of eastern European Jews, Young argues that Weiss offers us a way of remembering the rich and diverse lives and communities of eastern European Jews before the Holocaust. He does this by contrasting the family photographs that Weiss presents with the all-too-common debris, the broken traces that viewers generally associate with these communities, the evidence of their destruction. Like Bernstein, Young suggests that this knowledge of endings and only endings is a travesty. He writes,

> But here we must ask: "What precisely do these artifacts teach us about the history of the people who once animated them?" Beyond affect, what does our knowledge of these objects—a bent spoon, children's shoes, crusty old striped uniforms—have to do with our knowledge of historical events? In a perversely ironic twist, these artifacts—collected as evidence of the crimes—were forcing us to recall the victims as the Nazis have remembered them to us: in the collected debris of a destroyed civilization. Armless sleeves, eyeless lenses, headless caps, footless shoes: victims known only by their absence, by the moment of their destruction. In great loose piles, these remnants remind us not of the lives once animating them, so much as the brokenness of lives, now scattered in pieces. (Weiss, 2001, 17)

I quote Young at length here to offer a sense of the urgency of his appeal. Instead of asking us to "complete" the stories of these pictures knowing their ending, Young insists that the real challenge is to try to see the photographs Weiss has collected in her volume, or those same images collected and displayed by the State Museum at Auschwitz-Birkenau, or those collected at places like the Tower of Faces, as counternarratives to the story of destruction, evidence of the lives, communities, families, and worlds that existed before the war, evidence of what was destroyed and not simply or only of the destruction itself.

With this in mind, the ripped wedding photograph that accompanies Young's introduction echoes precisely these sentiments. Here we catch a glimpse of the promise of that other time already knowing that the evidence is partial and incomplete. The image cannot take up a full page; the picture is no longer whole. Nevertheless, what such an approach offers is, in Young's words, "an invaluable corrective" to the tendency to see and engage only with the ending, to miss remembering all that was destroyed (18). What Weiss does in her book, according to Young, is to restore some semblance of Jewish life before the Holocaust, lives as they were "portrayed in their own times and places" (19). This is in sharp contrast, Young contends, with the tendency to see these lives only "as they are retrospectively freighted with the pathos and portent we assign them now" (19). What Weiss does is "not only restore a measure of the victim's humanity . . . , she preserves the contingency of daily lives as lived and perceived then" (19). As will become clear, my reading builds of these insights.

Young's reflections lead directly into Weiss's own text, her essay "Eyes from the Ashes." In this narrative, Weiss offers an overview of the book: its purpose; how it came about; some general background about the photographs and their history, as well as the history of those depicted; and information about the Jewish communities and families of Bendin and Sosnowiecz, Poland, what those communities were before the Nazis invaded Poland, the ghettos they became, and, finally, how they were liquidated in August 1943. She ends her essay with a brief statement about her methodology—her approach to the pictures and her efforts to learn about those depicted in these photographs.

In this narrative, only somewhat revised in the second edition, Weiss punctuates her account not only with photographs from the collection, but with a few other Holocaust-era photographs as well. The second page, for example, opens with a photograph of "suitcases confiscated from Jews at Auschwitz-Birkenau." As she explains in her note about the photograph: "Many photos were found in such suitcases" (21).[71] The other photograph included in this section is an iconic image of the gates of Auschwitz-I taken by the author.[72] These two photographs graphically bring readers into an already familiar representation of the visual landscape of the Holocaust. The seemingly familiar images we are about to see were found in Auschwitz-Birkenau. These more recognizable images help set the stage for Weiss's account.

Another photograph not from the collection included in Weiss's narrative makes clear her role in this project. It is a photograph of the author rephotographing the images found in the camp. She is depicted in control, looking through a camera using elaborate lighting and, perhaps, magnifying apparatus focused on images in an album. Her focus is on the images she is reproducing. The note reads, "The author copying photographs at Auschwitz. It took several trips to copy the twenty-four hundred photographs in the collection. The process began in 1988 and continued until the early 1990s" (25). In this way, Weiss makes clear her role in this project.[73] Her focused labor is a crucial part of these efforts to preserve and bring these images to light. Her role is critical.

The story Weiss tells is very much a narrative of rescue and recovery, how she found these pictures and began this project. Like my own story about my father's stash of hidden photographs, Weiss's story is also accidental. It begins in 1986 when Weiss was on a special diplomatic mission to Poland to visit Auschwitz-Birkenau with a group of American Jewish communal leaders. She was chosen to participate in this trip because of her work as an investigative reporter who had written about "Operation Moses," the Israeli effort to rescue Eritrean Jews in 1984.[74] Weiss heightens the drama of her story by explaining that the very guide she had to escape while on the tour ended up ushering her and a few others in the group into a locked room where the photographs were kept. "I entered a corridor just as my group was gathering for the bus. I heard the guide say, 'Maybe you'd like to see what's in this room?' 'Yes,' was the reply. In the dimly lit corridor, en route to the bus, the guide paused and unlocked the door. We walked into the room" (25). Weiss then goes on to describe her overwhelming reaction to seeing the photographs, and one image in particular, before she returns to the narrative of that day. "Almost as soon as we were allowed to step into the room, we were, in the words of Miriam Bisk, one of the participants, 'immediately pushed out.' It was as if the tour guide realized she had made a mistake by unlocking the door" (26). After this, Weiss explains that she returned to Auschwitz-Birkenau over and over again in order to document and rephotograph these pictures. This became her calling.

In terms of the pictures, Weiss writes about a single image that moved her, that compelled her to return.[75] The photograph, reproduced and included in her essay, becomes the model for what she does throughout the book. The picture is a portrait of a little boy. Weiss begins by describing how she first imagined the context of this picture only to go on to challenge her own assumptions by learning more from any and all who might help her. In the process, she tries again and again to capture a more accurate account of what is in any and all of these individual images.

> I looked at the photo of a beautiful child with adult eyes, and imagined the child was giving flowers to his mother or grandmother in honor of the Sabbath. Later I learned that the bouquet was not in fact flowers, but rather a cone filled with candy, called a *Schultüte* in German, to signify the first day of school. Candy-filled cones were a ritual on the first day of school to link the sweetness of learning with the sweetness of candy. (26)

In the new edition, the note at the bottom of the page is expanded. It says, as does the original, that the author "could not bear to have this child's face covered in darkness again" and that "It was this child's portrait that first compelled me to bring these photographs to light" (26). It then goes on to provide more information about the photograph presumably not available when the first edition was published. "From the German inscription on the back,[76] we learn that this child is Adolf Landon on his first day of school, September 1928, and the photo was sent from his father to his cousin, who, most likely, carried it to Auschwitz-Birkenau. The inscription reads: 'This picture is a token of memory for my niece Blimche to remember how my son made his way to school for the first time. From your uncle, J. Landon May 10, 1928. Adolf Landon was born on May 26, 1922.'"[77]

Like me, Weiss begins with her desire to know and her imagined knowing as a starting point. From here her task is to fill in what she can. Sometimes it is a name or an elaborate family story; at other times it is a once common ritual, an insignia on a shirt, a photographic technique. She provides what she can. This means that the text is not neat. Labels are inconsistent, and their content ranges from the mundane to the profound. And still, many, perhaps most, of the pictures in this book are not labeled at all; little or nothing may be known about them. Despite this, as promised, Weiss's efforts continue; in the second edition, she adds new information wherever she can.

As Weiss explains, although she cares "deeply about accuracy, and [has] taken great pains to insure that what is printed about these photographs is as accurate as [she knows] it to be . . . there will inevitably be mistakes, since many who knew the truth are already dead, and people remember events in different ways" (38). Given this, Weiss shows us the process, her efforts and movement from one interpretation to another echoing the move from the Sabbath flowers to the candy-filled cone in her interpretation of that initial photograph. And she makes clear that she anticipates ongoing revisions. As the book circulates and the images continue to be displayed, she hopes that readers and viewers will continue to come forward and tell her what they know about any of these individual images. In the body of the text, she often includes these stories again to make clear her commitment to this process.[78]

Despite this powerful statement, I was disappointed to see that Weiss does not let readers know what changes she has made between the first and second editions of her book. Such an account would have been in keeping with the language of her methodological promise.[79] Although that statement remains more or less the same in the new edition, there is no acknowledgment of any of the specific changes made on this page, or anywhere else in the book, between the first and second editions.[80]

Again, the passion, dedication, and vision that drive Weiss's project are familiar to me, but I am struck by what is left unacknowledged. In the second expanded edition, there is no clear account of all that has changed. Without marking these distinctions, other differences are also effaced. Distinctions between us and them, ours and theirs, and then and now are all lost, despite Weiss's good intentions. The book cannot do justice to the individual tragedies collected in this volume that make up a part of the catastrophic communal loss that is the Holocaust. For me, Weiss's project is again a cautionary tale. It shows what can happen if we overidentify and blur these boundaries.

Different losses touch one another, inform one another, but in so doing they cannot efface or replace one another. The challenge of commemoration is to recognize these distinctions over and over again. This means appreciating how different legacies of loss illuminate one another and make each loss distinct. This is the kind of touching I long for in bringing together my own family stories and the stories of these 2,400 family photographs.

2,400 *Pictures in a Locked Room at Auschwitz-Birkenau in 1986*

As Weiss explains, she returned to Poland over and over again, negotiating with the Polish government, with authorities at Auschwitz-Birkenau and with the archivists on site to learn as much as she could about how this storeroom of photographs got to this place—first how they survived liberation and what happened after that, and then how they might have been hidden and preserved during the war. Although the postwar story is seemingly more straightforward, what Weiss describes is a series of contradictions. It is not clear how the Soviet liberators learned about the pictures or when. It is also not clear if the pictures remained in Poland at the camp or if they were moved to the Soviet Union and then returned to the archives years later. According to Weiss, preserving anything from the camp was extremely difficult. There were no supplies in the town, and former prisoners who tried to collect records had to compete with cold, hungry, and desperate townsfolk who needed these same supplies to keep warm, to wrap food, and to burn so that they could cook for their families. According to the archivist Weiss initially met,

> The photographs were hidden in the camp during the war, somewhere in Birkenau. After the war, most of the prisoners were taken out of the camp on a Death March, but some remained. When the liberating Russian army came to Auschwitz and Birkenau, the photos were turned over by one or more of the Jewish inmates. The photographs were then taken to the Soviet Union for some years. When the Museum was opened, someone in the Soviet Union sent the photographs back to Auschwitz in the latter 1950s. (Weiss, 2001, 2005, 28)

After citing this account, Weiss explains that not all agree. The official story is that the pictures never left Auschwitz. Here Weiss offers both accounts and asks her readers to decide or, more likely, to struggle for ourselves about what to believe. As Weiss explains, even after finding a Russian Jewish liberator of the camps, she was unable to get the verification she longed for. This man knew nothing about the photographs despite having been there. The narrative Weiss tells is stark and dramatic. It is her story. She is at its center.

I spend a lot of time carefully reading Weiss's text because it illustrates the power and the dangers involved in recognizing the connections between different losses. My close reading expresses both my attraction to the promise of Weiss's text as well as my disappointment. Having taken her at her word when reading the first edition of her book, I had hoped that the second expanded edition would enact her method of revision overtly, explicitly. By not acknowledging even some of the largest revisions, Weiss missed an important opportunity to show readers the labor of remembrance in process,[81] how she had inevitably made mistakes in the first edition but was able to correct at least a few of them here in this new edition. And, connected to all of this, Weiss also seems unable to fully express the power of collaboration, the ways that her revisions are marked by the work of many others, including those at the museum at Auschwitz and all of their collaborators.[82]

The Pictures: Surviving Auschwitz-Birkenau

Part of what is striking about Weiss's text is that she insists on the contingency of all of her explanations. She seems to want to offer accuracy but also knows how impossible it is to corroborate so much of what she has learned.[83] She tells readers up front what she does not know and why she includes the information she does, even if it is only partial. In explaining how the photographs were preserved in the camps during the war, she offers the account of a single survivor. "I have not been able to independently substantiate this testimony, but I include it because of the important facts it discloses and the high likelihood that the story is true" (36). She uses the authority of this survivor to verify the position she takes. According to this survivor, this was the work of the underground, an elaborate network of inmates who smuggled, hid, and moved the pictures into safe places. These were dangerous endeavors for all involved. The story Weiss presents is that when it became known that the last transport of Polish Jews was coming to Auschwitz, many decided that it was crucial to try to salvage whatever they could from these people, "pictures, documents, any evidence of their lives" (36).

Jewish Life in Bendin and Sosnowiecz

In spite of all these acknowledged limitations on her project, Weiss goes on to offer pieces of everyday life, an effort very much in keeping with what the State Museum did in its publication and display of these same photographs.[84] Echoing child survivor and poet Irena Klepfisz's powerful plea in her 1988 commemoration of the Warsaw Ghetto Uprising,[85] what both books show us are the textures of quotidian life that *der khurbn,* or the destruction, took from these people. For survivors, it is the loss of these ordinary lives, the lives they led before the Holocaust, that they mourn. As Klepfisz explains,

> *Der khurbn* that survivors experience is not general but very specific. It is reflected in precious sepia photographs pasted into incomplete family albums. It consists of identifiable names, of familiar faces of family members, of named streets, stores, and schools, teammates, friends, libraries, doctors, hospitals, lectures, marches, strikes, political allies and enemies—the people, places, and institutions that make up the fabric of

any human being's ordinary, everyday life. It is these specifics and the loss of that ordinary life that survivors remember and mourn. (42)

In many ways, these works piece together these found images in order to create incomplete and all-the-more-precious family albums in the face of those that were destroyed. They offer images of schools, stores and marches, allies and enemies, friends and teammates, and many, many pictures of family members; they try to capture some semblance of the lives of those who were a part of these Jewish communities, especially before the war. They also include images from life in these ghettos, family photographs of Jews with armbands and yellow stars.

In both Weiss's introduction and the narrative text from the State Museum, readers are presented with brief overviews of Jewish life in these Polish cities before the war as a way of contextualizing the images. As Weiss explains, although the Zaglembia region of south-central Poland was one of the first regions to be invaded by the Nazis in 1939, the Jewish communities of Bendin and Sosnowiecz were among the last to be liquidated. Before 1939 Bendin (also known as Bendzin and Bedzin) (31), had a Jewish population of around 30,000. Sosnowiecz had a Jewish population of about 28,000. "Jews in both cities comprised a significant portion of the total population, which was principally Catholic" (31). By 1942, unlike other Polish Jewish communities, the Jews of Bendin and Sosnowiecz were not "trapped in Nazi-controlled ghettos" (32). This is more or less the story told in the supplement to *Before They Perished* . . . The Jewish populations swelled with Jews from nearby communities, and conditions were difficult. Jews lost their homes and were crowded into narrowly confined portions of the city subject to sporadic deportations and killings until August 1943, when the ghettos were liquidated.

Despite all of this, what these books offer is not so much a look at the end of these communities but the fullness of Jewish life before the war, before the Holocaust. As noted earlier, in this respect both of these books are albums. Both offer their readers bits and pieces. As in most family albums, there are numerous pages filled with images of children; the whole first section of Weiss's book is devoted to the children. The section opens with an enlarged image of a man holding a baby. It is a haunting image in dark shades and shadows. The man is wearing a dark suit and the lighting is dark. The focus is on the child, a baby whose clothing, knitted sweater and pants, are light, virtually white, in the otherwise dark photograph. The man holds the child close to his cheeks, the baby stares at the camera while the man looks out toward the baby's left. The picture bleeds over the edges of the page and in white script over the bottom of the page we read,

> Photographs are the markers of their time. Even more so with these photos that in all too many cases are the only tangible evidence that an individual existed. When there is no one left who still remembers, these photos remain a silent sentinel of who once lived, and what once existed. (39)[86]

These words are a heavy burden but again echo the tragic cast of the image. When we turn the page, we see a man and a woman holding their newborn baby. Here again the adults are dark haired and the background is very dark, in sharp contrast to the baby in the foreground who is wrapped in an excessively large blanket extending up over the baby's head. Here the copy reads,

> Children represent the future. When one wants to destroy a group, it is not enough to destroy the people, the culture, the books, the ideas. One must destroy the society's most vulnerable members, the children who point toward the future, and the elders in whose memories the past resides. By killing the youngest and the oldest first, the Nazi's ensured almost a complete destruction of the Jews. Over one million children were killed. (40)

With these words in mind, Weiss introduces readers to numerous images of babies and young children. These include individual photographs of single children as well as group shots, photographs from the Bendin Orphanage, and numerous Jewish schools, girls' schools, boys' schools, religious and secular schools, and gymnasiums. There are pictures of classes, teams, and events at these schools as well as pictures of individual children in or out of the uniform that attach them to these institutions of learning.

In this section, Weiss moves from pictures of infants and young children to pictures of older children and teens. The section ends with images of courtship and marriage, happy couples embarking on their lives together. She then presents images of specific Jewish communities, with a large section devoted to life in the vibrant Hasidic communities in

Bendin and Sosnowiecz, as well as images from the growing Zionist organizations, sporting clubs and societies and political and cultural Zionist groups.

Organization is never neat, as in an album. Following these images
are pictures of Jewish soldiers presumably in Polish uniforms, group
shots, and individual soldiers. And then there are just various images
that do not and cannot fit together neatly. So, for example, in the first
edition of her book, Weiss devotes two pages to Robert Desnos, the
French poet and member of the resistance, whose image was also alleg-
edly among those collected in this archive of salvaged photographs. As
Weiss explains, after Desnos was arrested by the Nazis, he was sent
to Buchenwald, then to Auschwitz, and finally to Terezin, where he
died. She tells this story and also includes one of Desnos' poems (112–
113). When, it seems, she learned that this picture was misidentified as
Desnos, Weiss removed this entire section in the second edition. The
photo that had been identified as Desnos is included elsewhere: Weiss
is no longer clear about the identity of the man in this photograph.[87]
Again, I wish that there were an overt acknowledgment and explanation of this change in the second edition.

This entire section of the first edition ends with a series of individual
images, pictures of Jewish town folk with the Sosnowiecz "bear," the
city's mascot, pictures of commuters en route to work on the train, and
more individual images of mothers and grandmothers, pictures from va-
cations and holiday celebrations.

Weiss then offers another large section, which, like the first, opens
with a single picture that takes up an entire page, an image that bleeds
over the edges of the full page. This time a general text about families
and their importance is printed in white script over the bottom portion
of a group portrait. This is a formal portrait of a family taken around
the turn of the century. The parents, a woman in a fur stole and a man
in a day coat and tie, stand behind their two young daughters who are
seated on wooden outdoor chairs or benches. The whole family stands
before a lush garden. The copy reads, "Family is the foundation for the
rest of one's life. Shared experiences continue to have an impact long after family members are separated" (119).[88] This section is devoted to
longer family stories and the images that have carried them. In many
ways, this section can be viewed/read as a series of smaller albums. It
includes pages devoted to individual families and their narratives. These
are all presented as the fruits of Weiss's labors, the family stories she has

been able to recover. In its first edition, her album ends with these larger stories and the images that occasioned them. In the revised edition, Weiss adds an addendum at this point to what she presented in the first edition, demonstrating how her work continues. Here additional photographs and text are included.[89] Thus even more than in the first edition, these stories of recovery are offered as evidence of and as the culmination of Weiss's research. She tells readers as much as she can about the provenance of all these pictures, who is depicted in specific images, and overall, what the lives of these particular families were like before 1939 and after. When she can, she also tells us what became of both these individuals and their families after the war. In this way, the power of these incomplete stories is most evident. We catch glimpses—fleeting glances, at some of these once ordinary lives, something that also happens in reading *Before They Perished* . . .

Weiss ends her book with a brief afterword. In this way, she completes the frame with which she began by making explicit her adherence to Wiesel's counsel and her own role as witness. And as Wiesel demands, Weiss gives the last word to a victim. She cites the last testimony of Zalmen Gradowski, one of the *Sonderkommando* who "tried to deter the killing by bombing the crematorium" at Auschwitz (216). Knowing that he will not survive, Gradowski writes to those who will come after, the "free citizens of the world" who might find his writings. As he tells us, he wants them/us to know what happened in this terrible place, but he also wants us to remember something else:

> I ask also a personal favor, dear finder and publisher of these writings. . . . Find out who I am. . . . Then ask my relatives for the portrait of my family, as well as that of my wife and me and, using your discretion, print them in this book. In this way I hope to immortalize the dear, beloved names of those for whom, at this moment, I cannot even expend a tear! (217)

This is clearly what Weiss has tried to do, an impossible and necessary undertaking. And, in the end, having "captured, shaped, and transmitted the words, the images of the victims" as Wiesel commands, Weiss makes explicit her role as witness in putting together this album, and then she asks us, her readers, to join her in this ongoing labor. She wants us to become witnesses as well by engaging with her and this particular ongoing project.

Before They Perished . . . *A Collaboration of a Different Order*

Before They Perished . . . Photographs Found in Auschwitz is an over-sized, almost five-hundred-page picture book with virtually no copy. The only words included in the book are the names of individual sections, sections named for specific families, schools, or communal organizations. These pages are translucent velum. They are in stark tactile and visual contrast to the rest of the book. Glossy, hard-stock color pages make up the rest of the book. Although most of the photographs are in black and white, the color reproduction enables readers to see both those images that were found color enhanced and those originally produced in sepia tones. Many of the pictures are in shades of sepia. Unlike Weiss, who carefully selected 400 images from the full collection of 2,400, this book reproduces all of the images.[90] Surrounding the photographs, the glossy pages are a pale sage, echoing the color of the cover of both the big book and the supplement. The supplement offers information on each of the photographs, a virtual guide to the picture book. The haphazard grid is punctuated by the named sections. These sections open with extended narratives about the families, institutions, or organizations depicted within them. The references are orderly and carefully organized. There are longer framing narratives about the project that form the opening section of the supplement. Here the collaborative nature of this project is most evident. No individual contributors are singled out as central to this effort.

In the opening essays and acknowledgments, readers learn the extent of this collaboration. The editors/researchers who put together this book are not named on the cover of the book or in its supplement. Readers learn their names only on the title page of each volume. The supplement opens with a page of acknowledgments printed in two columns. The first reads, "Our special thanks go to those who have survived. We would like to thank them for the several hours of discussions and many pieces of advice. Their invaluable support was a great contribution to this publication" (3). The column then lists approximately fifty names of individual survivors who were consulted. The second column explains that this publication "serves as a catalogue to the exhibition presenting in a symbolic way the world of European Jews before the Holocaust." It goes on to explain that the book is part of the "Interior Design for the Former Sauna Building in Birkenau project" (3). The editors then offer special thanks to those private and public funders, "individuals, companies and institutions," who made these efforts possible. These include the German Federal States and the jury members who chose this project, and finally the various researchers from around the world who contributed to this work.

There are then a series of interrelated essays by the editors. Loewy's words at the opening of this section come from one of these essays. The first essay is "The World of the Photographs," written by Krystyna Olesky. I want to focus on this particular piece because the story of the pictures Olesky tells contrasts sharply with the narrative Weiss presents. Here there is no drama. Olesky opens her essay by acknowledging that "the origin of this collection is not precisely known; no one can say who found the photographs or where they were found" (4). She then goes on to explain that the most likely explanation is that "they were found after liberation on or near the grounds of the camp, in the barracks of 'Kanada' where the belongings stolen from murdered Jews were sorted" (4). Asking how these photographs survived, Olesky suggests that it is "rather likely that chance was responsible" (4). She goes on to explain where they came from, Zaglębie, Będzin, Sosnowiec, and vicinity, and that the vast majority of them seem to be clustered in family groupings and came to the camps with members of these families. "Most probably the workers in 'Kanada' threw them into some box or other, or a suitcase, and simply forgot about them, and that they survived to the liberation in this way."

Olesky's account is chronological. She goes on to explain that "a protocol written in the Auschwitz Museum on March 6, 1951, seems to indicate that for a time they were indeed kept in a suitcase. Perhaps the same one in which they were discovered?" (4). I focus on this opening essay precisely because it is so different from the personal narrative of discovery Weiss tells.

Olesky's essay continues by explaining some of the postwar history of the photographs. She explains that sometime after 1951, the photographs were glued into "account books" by an unknown staff member at the museum. It seems that this is how Weiss initially encountered the photographs. The picture of her rephotographing the collection shows her with such an album.[91] Olesky then explains how the photographs circulated over the interim years. She informs readers that they were on display numerous times in Poland. In 1980, some of the pictures were displayed in exhibits in Great Britain, and in 1985 in the United States. "Some of them appeared in books, and Jerzy Ziarnik used them in a moving film called 'Patrzę na twoją fotogrię' ('I Am Looking at Your Photograph'—1974)" (4).

As she explains, they could not be shown all together because they were glued in the ledger books and needed first to be carefully separated from these pages. These efforts seem to have begun in the early 1990s at the museum. Once the State Museum had removed the photographs from these albums, they were able to see the backs of the photographs.[92]

Olesky continues her account of the history of the collection by explaining that once the photographs were removed from the albums, the museum was able to enlist a team of international researchers to work with them to identify those depicted in each of the photographs leading to both this publication and the museum's exhibition.[93] As one of the researchers, Olesky then discusses some of the various trips she and others made to Israel and around the world to meet with survivors to help identify those depicted. She concludes by highlighting a meeting with the former students of the Fürstenberg High School in Będzin, which took place in 1997 in Tel Aviv.

Kersten Brandt, Hanno Loewy, and Marek Pelc's essay in pieces, "Photographs . . . So Many Photographs," follows Olesky's account of this history. These pieces were first published in German beginning in 1995.[94] The first, written by Brandt, is entitled "2400 Moments. Photographs of Deportees from the Archives of the Auschwitz Memorial" (6–8). It is followed by Pelc's "Conversations with the Survivors" (8–10). The last of these is Loewy's haunting and informative " 'The Scandal of Their Silence.' About the Private Photographs of the Murdered People of Auschwitz-Birkenau" (10–15).

These lyrical and scholarly pieces are followed by an essay by Avihu Ronen on the Jews of Będzin. Ronen's essay moves back and forth between historical materials about the community, the world of the photographs, and the author's own trip to Będzin in 1996. Each historical section is devoted to a particular theme that then resonates with the impressions of the author from specific locations and moments in time from within the town in 1996.[95] Ronen's essay, like those before it, is both lyrical and informative.

The final section of this opening portion of the supplement is "a note from the publisher." Like Weiss in her note about her method, here, too, the publisher explains his logic. He writes that "the most important criterion considered while choosing and ordering these pictures was the identity of the people presented and their belonging to a specific group (family, circle of friends, or acquaintances, school, organization, etc.)" (28). The publisher then describes how the pictures are ordered, chronologically in separate chapters, and when the identities were not known, the images are arranged thematically. And like the editors, the publisher also thanks all of those whose labors made this publication possible. From here the supplement follows the order of the first volume, explaining what is known about each and every image in the collection, page by page.

No Redemption: Resisting Heroism

When I first decided to write about Weiss's book, I worried that it would only confirm my suspicions about redemptive narratives. I was afraid that those coming to this book would not be able to resist seeing Weiss's efforts as redemptive. When I finally began my close reading of the book, I found myself attracted to the various ways in which it remained incomplete. I honed in on this aspect of Weiss's album. This approach still informs my reading of the book, but as I returned to Weiss's text, seeing it alongside the museum's project and the new edition of her own book, I was struck by how much her album is just that, hers. Weiss's vision is beautiful and haunting. It is carefully constructed as such. But it is also very much a triumphant story, a redemptive narrative with Weiss at its center. Weiss's fingerprints are all over her text, for better and for worse shaping the partial story she tells.[96] The museum has its own blind spots;[97] nevertheless, I find their efforts more compelling. The self-effacement of the editors in each of their individual essays and the fact that they do this project collectively helps make this a less triumphant narrative. These strategies seem to help these editors resist the desire for continuity that Loewy so powerfully identifies as a danger in this kind of project.

Although, as I have suggested elsewhere in this book, becoming a witness is not a simple matter, our own desires for continuity and for redemption are difficult to resist. Given this, I hear Wiesel's plea for caution. The task of remembering is not easy and it is never complete. There is an urgency to this labor. Although I am not sure what it means to be a "witness" or, for that matter, to engage in what Marianne Hirsch has called "postmemory," the recovery of once hidden, now precious objects and images demands our attention. These efforts in the present are necessarily partial and incomplete, but the task is not about finality or completion. It is about doing what can be done mindful of the limitations of the distances of time and space that separate so many of us from the world of these photographs. For those of us who were born after the war, to remember a past we have never known means to acknowledge the sediments of time and space that separate us from those we come to remember. It means not mistaking hindsight with actual knowledge. This is a commitment I share with those at the State Museum even as I resist the notion that this labor can ever really be redemptive. There are things we can never know even as we devote ourselves to learning more. The task is never done. These images are never complete, and this is why redemption is the wrong metaphor. For me the task is much more humbling.

There is a danger in remaking these legacies into our own in the present. We can too easily slip into the position of the hero or heroine even when we know these efforts at recovery are necessarily incomplete, and therefore, remain simply undone. For those of us who come to these stories belatedly, our labor requires a profound humility, a clear appreciation of how the past will always elude us. We also need to think of our labors as collaborative. For me, this does not mean that we should not try. There are things that we can learn about the past. These things may not be what we thought we were going to find or what we thought we were looking for. There are no answers. In this way, like Weiss and those at the State Museum, we can *never* "complete the story of every picture" as Wieseltier suggests. By starting with the fact that completion is neither possible nor desirable, I believe we just might learn some of what the past can teach us, and this is what I believe, together, these two books attest to. Although not redemptive, there is some solace here, something has been salvaged.[98]

Incommensurable Losses: Some Conclusions

Comparison is not the point. I do not want to try to measure suffering or loss or to make claims about which stories are more important. Instead, I want to simply say that it is important to see these stories next to each other, my father's stash and the 2,400 photographs from Auschwitz. I do this, not to fold them in on each other, but to see them in conversation, touching each other but not necessarily overlapping. Given this, I have tried to offer a reading of Weiss's book and the broader collection depicted in *Before They Perished* . . . that is counter to the way most readers might engage with these texts. Instead of reading these books as a story of salvation, a redemptive tale about the recovery of a trove of images that should have been destroyed but were somehow saved in the past and then recovered—whether they were recovered by Weiss, a daughter of survivors almost fifty years after the war, or by the dedicated staff and researchers at the Auschwitz-Birkenau State Museum—I have tried to show the contingencies, the partial and unfinished aspects of these extraordinary labors. I want to remember this uncertainty and contingency as a way of valuing and respecting the specificity of these stories, all 2,400 of them.

I do not want to use the grand narrative of redemption or salvation to collapse these distinctions. In other words, unlike Wieseltier, I do not see these images as individual instantiations of a single inevitable narrative of destruction. I vehemently refuse that stance. I do not believe that even our knowledge of what happened afterwards allows us to "complete" these images and the stories they tell. Such attempts at completion take away the agency of those depicted, of those who hid these pictures, and of those to whom they once belonged. This is what hindsight or backshadowing does. I resist this stance because it gives us credit for somehow being smarter than those who came before us. It also fundamentally denies the possibility of our seeing that history is always contingent, that things work out in all kinds of ways, and that nothing that happened, especially the Holocaust, was or is inevitable.[99] Only after having acknowledged this, it seems to me, can we begin to see these photographs from Auschwitz-Birkenau or those in the Tower of Faces in relation to other Jewish pictures and other Jewish stories.

The reading I have offered of these photographic collections allows us to begin to make connections between Weiss's project and that of the museum and our own. By not reading any of these efforts as redemptive in any simple way, we begin to see, for example, how all of our projects share a kind of contingency. And, given this, we might appreciate on a much less grand scale the ways that our everyday lives are precious even in relation to the Holocaust. We might come to see how even a single solitary image can be utterly powerful precisely in all the ways we cannot fully know its meaning. It is this dynamic that makes Abraham Ravett's film *Half-Sister* so moving. His is, after all, a filmic meditation on a single ordinary family image that, in so doing, raises a myriad of desires and longings for a past that is otherwise totally inaccessible.

We need not flatten out the past and everything that must remain inscrutable about it in order to appreciate how the past continues to shape our lives in the present. In this way I believe all of these photographs remind us that ordinary life, even when it has been destroyed in grand terms, need not be appreciated completely otherwise. On the other hand, we need not dismiss the stuff of our more common and everyday pasts just because our losses are not catastrophic. Even in everyday life, there are losses that transform individual lives and families. It is the loss of these ordinary sufferings, broken hearts, illnesses, that has been so poignantly lost after the Holocaust.

Obviously, there is something absolutely amazing about the recovery of so many family photographs from Auschwitz-Birkenau, and I do not want us to lose sight of that. But I also don't want us to get lost in it. Although it is hard to keep these 2,400 pictures in perspective, I want to try by keeping in mind that this trove of images is made up of thousands of precious individual photographs, pictures that belonged to men, women, and children, families and friends who carried them with them into the camps.

"Incommensurable" means lacking a common measure or standard of comparison, conspicuously disproportionate, inadequate. All of these things are true about the contrast between the stories I have told about my father's efforts to hide things and these other projects. There is no common measure. These are conspicuously disproportionate stories. And yet there are formal connections. In both, there are hidden ordinary images, images of early 20th-century lives. Both offer stories about family photographs of eastern European Jews that have been recently brought to light. Both ask questions about what it means to revisit these images belatedly, already knowing what happened to those depicted or at least partially knowing some of their stories. Both of these projects ask what it means to be the witness, the one who recirculates these images, who frames them and makes them public. In this way, my task is not that different from those at the museum and Weiss.

For me it is the partialness, the tentativeness we read in these works, that allows me to see my efforts next to theirs and, in so doing, to resist the kind of comparison that makes such connections impossible —the notion that ordinary losses can never be seen in relation to the

Holocaust. In my readings of both *The Last Album* and *Before They Perished . . . ,* I have insisted that the most powerful aspect of what each has done is that they have made clear how much we can never know about the pictures they have so carefully collected, researched, and brought to a broader public.

Let me explain this in a slightly different way. I want to resist the strange and disturbing thrill and power that many readers might expect to find in these works. Although, in some ways, these books do offer a triumph over oblivion, a grand reading loses sight of precisely the tragedy they depict. Only by reading more partially can we appreciate the fact that this trauma can never be overcome.

These books bring to light what were once hidden and presumably lost images. They put these images back into circulation; they let eager publics participate in this act of belated redemption. But not to see the gaps, the unfinished character of these works, is to follow Wieseltier's command to complete these stories and, in so doing, to take away their specificity. It is to reduce these stories, the thousands of stories collected in these books, and make them all into simply versions of a single inevitable tale of destruction. It is to take our knowledge of what happened next, and read these images only and inevitably in that light. As terrible as that story might be, there is something reassuring about reading and seeing these images in this way with hindsight. It allows us to become all knowing and from this position to fix the past, to redeem it, when in fact, such redemption is impossible.[100]

Even more than this, such knowing demands the inevitability of what happened, as if these stories might not have had other endings. This neat, clear, and devastating narrative trajectory might be a cautionary tale, but I do not believe it does justice to those depicted, those to whom these images once belonged, or all those who helped preserve them. It tells us that they should have known better, and that we can and must know better in the future. This is not a stance I can take. I do not believe in the inevitability of history. And I want to insist on resisting the ease that comes with assuming such a position even as we confront our various pasts. Life is just not so simple.[101] By reading these two books as incomplete, as partial, I have tried instead to open up the past and resist foregone conclusions. I have done this in the hope of imaging other futures and remembering other pasts.

4

Mary, Irena, and Me
Keepers of Accounts

Embodied Conflicts: A Return to the Problem of Incommensurability

> I cannot say I know how to fit my own private ghosts into the terrible tally of the twentieth century, when whole populations and whole belief systems perished. But I do understand now that my own life is part of that aftermath.
>
> —Jonathan Rosen, *The Talmud and the Internet*, 110

It is difficult to image where to go after writing about family photographs found at Auschwitz. What can come after the rediscovery of 2,400 hidden photographs from the final Polish transport to Auschwitz-Birkenau? As I began this chapter with a different argument in mind, I found myself stumbling. I did not know how to move from my discussion of the two photographic collections of those images back to the seemingly more quotidian concerns of this final chapter, a chapter about ongoing legacies, of life after the Holocaust. This time, instead of the Dutch cultural critic Ernst van Alphen,[1] I found myself in the company of contemporary American Jewish writers, the eloquent scholar of classics and beautiful writer Daniel Mendelsohn and the talented novelist and essayist Jonathan Rosen. I thought about the relationship between Mendelsohn's memoir *The Elusive Embrace: Desire and the Riddle of Identity* and Rosen's essay *The Talmud and the Internet*[2] as well as how both of these works echo many of the concerns at the heart of this book. In different ways, we all struggle with "private ghosts," even in the aftermath of the Holocaust.[3]

Like Ernst van Alphen, we were all born well after the war and struggle with what it means to understand our own lives as "a part of the aftermath," but Mendelsohn, Rosen, and I struggle with these issues as

American Jews. Each of us longs to appreciate our relationships to both ancient and more contemporary ancestors, and, in different ways, we struggle with our identities as Jews. In a sense, we all write about legacies much closer to home. Even given the proximity, the familiarity of these authors and their struggles with their familial inheritances, there are, of course, differences among us. Each of us struggles to make sense of what was bequeathed to us, and although our particular legacies differ, we engage with them in similar ways. What interests me is how these writers deal with the tensions, ambivalences, and contradictions that mark these inheritances. In both Mendelsohn's *The Elusive Embrace* and Rosen's *The Talmud and the Internet,* the authors struggle with sharply contrasting family legacies. For Mendelsohn the tension is staged between two father figures, his father and his maternal grandfather, two men with very different ways of being in the world and with very different histories: his excessively colorful European Jewish grandfather, and his understated American Jewish father. For Rosen the tension is between his two grandmothers: the haunting legacy of his paternal grandmother who died in the Holocaust, and the maternal American Jewish grandmother he knew while growing up in the United States. In both books, the authors struggle to come to terms with incommensurable family histories and each tries to relate how he has been shaped by these haunting and conflicting inheritances.

Part of what attracts me to these books is this reckoning. Like me, both of these writers want to be able to appreciate the powerful allure of European Jewish history, a history that for our generation always shapes our identities in more or less direct ways. Like me, both Mendelsohn and Rosen are committed to addressing "private ghosts," the stories of ancestors who were already in this country before the Holocaust, haunting legacies not overtly bound to that traumatic past. In many ways, given that each of these writers looks at the legacies of his two parents, it might be said, that each is, in Adrienne Rich's resonant phrase, "split at the root."[4] They literally embody these conflicting inheritances. While my concerns in this book are with the tensions and complexities within my father's family, I cannot so easily lay claim to a notion of being split in two;[5] splintered might be a more apt metaphor for me. And, for Mendelsohn, the idea that the tensions and contradictions are only between two things is also not quite right. Although he addresses the legacies of his two fathers, what he offers is a way of dealing with incommensurability without reconciling the contradictions or smoothing out the differences. Mendelsohn turns to classical Greek language and literature in order to do this. He brings this cultural legacy to bear on his own family stories.

A Classical Interlude

As a scholar trained in classical Greek culture, Daniel Mendelsohn uses the familiar and culturally powerful images of the classics to build his argument about identity—its movements back and forth between often contradictory desires.[6] For Mendelsohn, this quality is best understood in terms of "the ancient Greek tendency to bipolar thinking—on the one hand x, but on the other hand y" (25). He goes on to explain that this quality is found in the very structure of the language itself in terms of "the existence of two untranslatable monosyllables—particles, they are called, not really full-fledged words at all—whose presence in any given sentence tells you about the balance of that sentence, what its rhythm and, ultimately, its meaning will be" (25). Mendelsohn continues,

> What is interesting about this peculiarity of Greek, though, is that the *men . . . de* sequence is not always necessarily oppositional. Sometimes —often—it can merely link two notions or qualities or names, connecting rather than separating, multiplying rather than dividing. . . . Inherent in this language, then, is an acknowledgment of the rich conflictedness of things. It is a tongue that sees how x and y, which look to be opposites, can be part of a sequence, can inhere, somehow, in a whole. (26–27)

This classically inflected notion, that it is possible to hold together two often competing things, shapes the whole of Mendelsohn's narrative, his movements between the gay male world of Chelsea and his seemingly straight suburban life in New Jersey, as well as his ability to hold onto the flamboyant legacy of his maternal grandfather and the stark simplicity of his father, the mathematician.

As his narrative unfolds, Mendelsohn confronts the mythic dimensions of his grandfather's legacy, contrasting the records he finds in the archives with the monumental legacy of the family plot in a cemetery in Queens, New York. As a part of all of this, he reflects on the allures of tragedy, reconsidering the legacy of Ismene, Antigone's sister. In this way, he uses the Greek tragedy to shed light on his own ghosts.

As he explains in the opening paragraph of his chapter entitled "Mythologies": "Nobody has ever written a tragedy about Ismene, Antigone's sister—the one who counseled caution, the one who lived. How could you? Tragedy loves extremity. It celebrates the vertiginous beauty of total destruction" (157). He goes on to explain that what makes tragedy so gripping is not the way it enacts the clash between "Right and Wrong," but rather between two Rights (157), and this helps him explain the tension between Antigone and her sister. Contrary to the trajectory of the play, in other words, he argues that both sisters may be right. Instead of simply making the claim that one is more right than the other, Mendelsohn uses the notion of the *men . . . de* to figure a universe where these two positions are continuous and not implacably opposed (158). He does this by rereading the play, highlighting Ismene's position. According to Mendelsohn, "In this quintessential tragedy, the only character who counsels compromise—and, therefore, life—is Ismene. 'You have a warm heart for cold matters,' Ismene tells her death-obsessed sister at the beginning of the play when she, Ismene, declines to assist in the forbidden burial. But it is she, ultimately, who leaves her sister, and us, cold" (158).

What concerns Mendelsohn is why Ismene's plea for life falls on deaf ears. He wants us to reconsider with him why life is so much less compelling than death, why "The everyday is anathema to tragedy" (159). He wants to know why compromise is so unattractive, even at the cost of death. And this leads him to reflect on why the tragedies still hold so much power over us in the present. According to Mendelsohn, part of the allure is that we are ashamed of our own compromises, our own everyday lives.

Given this, in tragedies like *Antigone,* we find "the pure beauty of absolutes, a beauty you cannot have if you choose to live" (159). For many of us, after the Holocaust, this is an especially disturbing claim. It is part of what literary critic Terrance Des Pres attempted radically to reconsider in his now classic study of the writings of Holocaust survivors, *The Survivor: The Anatomy of Life in the Death Camps.*[7] In his study, Des Pres argues that in the context of utter destruction, in extremity, survival becomes heroic. In other words, in extremity, the structure of tragedy can no longer be figured solely in terms of heroic death. When dying is the norm, survival becomes a profound act of resistance.

It becomes tragic in and of itself. And yet, as Mendelsohn makes clear, Des Pres's critique is not the norm, the allures of the tragic death continue to engage our imaginations. Despite Des Pres's efforts to resist the notion that death is heroic, in 1999, twenty years after Des Pres's study was published, Mendelsohn writes, "You can't make a tragedy out of survival. You can't write a tragedy about Ismene" (159). Although Mendelsohn makes this overt claim, his account of Ismene nevertheless offers readers a way to reconsider this notion. He calls our attention to the merits of Ismene's position. In this respect, Mendelsohn does offer us a way of reconsidering the power and importance of survival after the Holocaust. His reading for Ismene echoes other efforts to reconsider what it has meant for Jews to live after the Holocaust, to carry on ordinary lives even in the aftermath of this most horrible historic and communal trauma.

And so, we return to where we began. In the face of those 2,400 collected photographs, what might it look like to hold together, to place next to each other, "the legacies of two continents,"[8] Europe and America? This is, in a sense, what Mendelsohn does as he claims the legacies of both his father and his grandfather, Ismene and Antigone. Instead of claiming only the high drama of his maternal grandfather and his European family, the legacy of Antigone, in the end Mendelsohn comes to appreciate as well the more ordinary legacy of his father and Ismene. He reconsiders the power of compromise, what it means to choose life in all of its messiness, the *men* and the *de,* even as he continues to appreciate the allures of the tragic. He holds onto both the ordinary and the traumatic and their various reverberations.

The Legacies of Two Grandmothers

In *The Talmud and the Internet,* Jonathan Rosen attempts to reclaim the legacy of the Talmud alongside the contemporary Internet. He also claims, in more intimate terms, the inheritances of his two grandmothers. Part of Rosen's struggle is to deal with some of the ways in which he has always seen these legacies in oppositional terms, unable to fully appreciate these women's lives in their fullness and complexity. As he explains, "When I think about my two grandmothers, I find myself thinking symbolically. Worse, I find myself fearing that these two grandmothers cannot exist simultaneously in the same world, even though I am equally a product of both of them" (58). Rosen grapples with how to accept the inheritances of both of these women as his own without collapsing one into the other. As he goes on to explain, "The world of European calamity that my paternal grandmother represents seems irreconcilable with the lucky life of American ease that my maternal grandmother embodied" (58). He contrasts these two distinct legacies in search of some reconciliation. In some ways, like me, he looks at his two grandmothers and tries to understand what each has come to teach him about who he is in the present. And like Mendelsohn and I, he struggles with what it means to deal with very different inheritances without folding one into the other. But unlike us, for Rosen the Holocaust is literally a part of the home in which he grew up. His father survived the war because he was one of the precious few children who were sent to Scotland on a *Kindertransport*.[9] His father lost his parents in the Holocaust, and it is his father's mother's haunting presence that colors Rosen's relationship to this past. As he questions, "How do I inhabit my murdered grandmother's world without losing myself in a tragedy I did not experience? How do I live inside the comfortable life my American-born grandmother bequeathed to me without feeling I am somehow betraying history, ignoring the larger voices of suffering outside?" (58).

Rosen longs for something complex but, perhaps, a bit neater, a way of living with contrasts, with opposites. He is not looking for reconciliation or integration, but rather for the possibility of putting these two inheritances next to each other. "Why can't the two live together in my mind—if not integrated, then at least, in the manner of the Talmud, side by side, a point and a counterpoint?" (108) In other words, he finds this possibility in rabbinic literature. Rosen wants, as he explains in his final chapter, what he imagines Proust offers his readers at the end of *Remembrance of Things Past*, an in-between position. He writes that at the end of Proust's opus, "Marcel, grown old, revisits Combray and discovers a shortcut that in fact unites the two paths. The two 'ways,' it turns out, are connected after all" (124). This is the promise Rosen longs for. He wants to discover that the two alternative paths through life he has inherited are, in fact, connected. Although he confesses, "I have yet to discover the path that links what seem to be the two emblematically divergent 'ways' I have inherited. I know that the lives—and the deaths—of my two grandmothers may be ultimately irreconcilable. But since I am literally a product of both of them, I owe it to myself, and to them, to try" (124). In other words, Rosen longs to bridge this gap. And although he has not found a secret pathway, like the "disjointed harmony" of the Internet, the Talmud has offered him a way to live with these contradictions. The Talmud "devised a culture intended to be a kind of middle term between extremes—between destruction and new creation, between the dead and the living, between God and man, between home and exile, between doubt and faith, between outward behavior and inner inclination" (131), a side-by-side, a point/ counterpoint. The textual tradition of the Talmud is a culture well suited to Rosen's own ambidextrous disposition.[10] When in the end, he imagines passing on these legacies to his first child, Rosen writes, "I can only wish for her a world that, chastened by the tragedies of the last century, manages to keep its contrary impulses in healthy Talmudic balance" (132). Although I am less sure that any of these legacies can be so easily summed up as a series of binary oppositions that can ultimately be balanced, I appreciate Rosen's struggle and identify with his powerful concerns for the future, but I am also troubled by the compromises he makes.

With the death of his beloved American grandmother, Rosen finds himself returning to these issues with an urgency he had not expected. Her death shifts the symbolic landscape that he had inhabited. The neat categories of "comfortable America" versus "the murdered world of Europe" begin to unravel. As he explains in his preface, "This book began as an elegy for my grandmother. . . . In writing this book I realized that what interests me is learning to embrace contradictory forces: ancient tradition and contemporary chaos, doubt and faith, the living and the dead, tragedy and hope" (1). To do this, he "set down stories—ancient and modern, private and public—that help [him] make sense of the multiple worlds [he has] inherited." Given this, although Rosen powerfully illustrates these contradictions, in the end, for him the Talmud offers an answer. It allows him to keep these oppositions together. As he explains, in the Talmud they can exist side-by-side. For Rosen, the Talmud provides a vision of faith that resists absolutes and enables a kind of middle position (85).

Unraveling: The Labor of Remembrance[11]

For me, the places where Rosen's narrative is most powerful is in the final chapter, where he begins to address the complexities within each of his grandmothers' stories and what he can and cannot ever know about their lives. In the case of his maternal grandmother, it is the moment when Rosen begins to admit that her life might not be so easily figured in terms of luck, ease, and prosperity that interests me. And to get to this complicated truth, he needs help. His wife intervenes. She asks his grandmother an intimate question, something not easily done in his family. She asks his grandmother why she only had one child. In answer to this question, the veneer of Rosen's grandmother's idyllic life begins to crack, and we begin to see more clearly the often invisible textures of her everyday life, which included sorrows that animated each and every one of those days. We learn that this woman did not intend to have only one child and that she had another child who did not live. Astonished, Rosen listens as his grandmother explains what happened. "The child, she told us, had been stillborn. This was news to me. Nobody had ever told me that story" (126). He is left speechless. It is his wife who encourages his grandmother to say more. His wife asks his grandmother if she had known the gender of the child. "Yes, she said. It was a boy. And then she asked my grandmother if she still thought about that boy" (126). In answer to this question, his grandmother explains that she thought about this child every day. The lost child, the son who did not survive his entry into the world, was missed for the rest of her life. She never stopped thinking about him.

In response to this powerful and haunting story, Rosen explains that he came to learn that "hidden beneath the surface of her [his grandmother's] seeming contentedness was a seed of perpetual sadness" (126). This is the story that captured my heart. I longed to hear more about this sadness and how his grandmother masked it, what it meant for her finally to speak this story and what happened when Rosen discussed this revelation with his mother. I also want to know if, having learned about the existence of this child, he and his wife traveled through the Jewish cemeteries of New York in search of this baby's grave and what happened when and if they found it. Rosen's text does not answer these questions. We do not know what he did with this revelation. I regret this because it is here that my own writing begins. Like my family story, Rosen's is a tale of everyday loss and I long to know what one of my contemporaries did with it, how it has reverberated in his life into the present. When I think about why Rosen does not address this story more fully, I want to say that perhaps it has something to do with gender, about what kinds of questions a grandson might ask his grandmother in contrast to the kinds of questions a granddaughter might ask. But that feels too easy. Rosen seems to suggest such a reading by attributing this discussion to his wife, but again I do not find this particularly satisfying. I still think that he might have done more with this revelation. And here I find myself returning to Mendelsohn, who, albeit serendipitously, ends up revisiting and reconfiguring a perhaps more dramatic story from his own family.

Mendelsohn's family story begins with his great-aunt's grave and winds its way back to the story of her short life. Mendelsohn unravels a very public narrative from his mother's family only to appreciate its more complicated intimate dimensions and ultimately its reverberations in the present. He moves from his own preoccupations with the tragic tale of his great-aunt's death, his family's story, to the less dramatic story found outside of his grandfather's telling and the grandeur of her gravesite. He reveals a more quotidian tale, evidence of which is found in the archives and among those banished and dismissed family members in his grandfather's stories. This new story both challenges and contradicts the family legend but does not, in Mendelsohn's hands, replace it.

Mendelsohn brings readers with him into the messy terrain of family lore as he begins to unravel the story of his great-aunt's life and her death, one of his grandfather's most treasured family stories. What impresses me about this retelling is that, even eighty years after his great-aunt's death, Mendelsohn is able to convey his loyalty to his grandfather and the narratives he told while also challenging the veracity of these same tales. Mendelsohn shares his rich and complicated journey into this familial past, and in the process he makes clear why these stories matter, not only to his family and himself, but to other readers as well.

By contrast, in Rosen's final chapter, the story of his grandmother's grief is quickly folded into other known losses in his grandmother's life. "I may not have known about her child, but I certainly knew about her husband" (126). Rosen uses this memory of his grandfather to leave his grandmother and her various sadnesses altogether. Instead of staying with them, he describes some of his own memories of his grandfather. He never does allow himself, much less his readers, to get any closer to his grandmother's grief and what it might mean for him and his family in the present, after her death.

Family Plots Revisited

The image of Mendelsohn's great-aunt's grave is so vivid in my mind that I can hardly believe I have never seen it. He writes, "The cemetery where three generations of my mother's family lie buried is on the southern part of a necropolis that spreads east from Brooklyn through Queens" (159–160). Having carried us with him from Manhattan to the cemetery, Mendelsohn goes on to describe his family's burial place and the monument at its center.

> The largest and most grandiose plot . . . is my family's plot. In the center of this expanse of ground stands an imposing gray slab, like a headstone but much larger, fitted with delicately wrought bronze Art Nouveau mountings, that bears bronze letters spelling out my great-grandmother's maiden name. This is the name—it would have been the girl's married name, had she lived another week (or so we were told)—this is the name of her first cousins, who paid for her funeral and who, according to my grandfather, were responsible for her death. (161)

Here we find in both Hebrew and in English the tale of Ray Jager, beloved daughter, dear sister who died on September 3, 1923 at the age of twenty-six. In the Hebrew, she is figured hauntingly as "an unmarried girl, *Ha'betulah.*" It is this unmarried figure and the various tragic tales his grandfather told about his sister's untimely death that animate Mendelsohn's imagination. According to his grandfather, this unfortunate, beautiful young girl was fated to a terrible marriage to an ugly cousin in payment for her family's safe passage to America,[12] but before this wedding was ever able to take place, the bride became very ill. According to his grandfather, the wedding, whose invitation Mendelsohn has seen in his family's records, never happened; it was postponed. And before the ceremony could finally take place, the bride was dead. The tragic heroine was laid to rest, forever at the center of this family plot. This is only the beginning. Mendelsohn goes on to offer a richly detailed account of this perpetually cared-for grave, its sculpted monument, its carefully manicured plantings, the haunting photograph of the young woman who will remain here in perpetuity as well as the story told about her life at this very site, literally on her gravestone.

As Mendelsohn explains, this was the story he grew up with, the grave he visited again and again, but this was not the end of the story. It continues. Mendelsohn writes, "There is one more text apart from the inscriptions on my great-aunt's tombstone that is relevant to her death. I found it only recently, almost by accident, while doing some research on my father's family at City Hall" (183). Like Rosen, the contrast between the two sides of Mendelsohn's family is great. His parents' family histories are entirely different kinds of stories. "The History of my mother's family, vain, meticulous, garrulous, had always been well documented. We know little, by comparison, of my father's uncles and aunts and grandparents" (183). And so in 1996, Mendelsohn set out to find some information about his father's family in the Municipal Archives. Finding little—no tragic tales, no dramatic, stories—he went in search of Ray Jager's death certificate under the pretext of determining, for sure, the cause of her death. What he assumed would be an easy task became strangely difficult. Despite the fact that he knew the date of her death, he could not find her. "At first I was unperturbed, accustomed as I was to the strange things that can happen to very old texts. So I set to work, using, to find this dead Jewish girl, the techniques of philology and paleology I'd learned to study the Greeks" (184).

Slowly, after checking various spellings of his great-aunt's name, Mendelsohn finally decided to see what happened when he looked up what her married name would have been. It was this formulation that worked. "The Manhattan Death Index 1923 does list a death certificate, #22—, for a Ray M——, who died 3 September 1923" (185). And even more strangely, under the heading "occupation" the form read "Housewife."

Finding this record challenged profoundly the story that Mendelsohn had always heard about his great-aunt. One document led to another. Mendelsohn found not only his aunt's death certificate but also her marriage listed in the city's "Bride Registry."[13] When Mendelsohn cross-referenced this listing with the city's marriage certificate records, he discovered that his aunt had, in fact, married her cousin well before September 1923. The date on the marriage certificate is February 1922. The records show clearly the names of both the couple and the witnesses at this wedding. And here again Mendelsohn is surprised. One of the witnesses is his grandfather, the very man who denied so fiercely that this marriage had ever taken place. Mendelsohn even recognized his grandfather's familiar handwriting.

Undeterred, Mendelsohn tried to find out more about the now-distant relatives his grandfather so despised, his great-aunt's husband (the cousin) and their family.[14] He traveled to Tennessee to meet those who were still alive and to hear what they could tell him about their family's past. Meeting the woman who was the cousin's now-adult daughter, he discovered a radically different person. The man whom Mendelsohn had always known as gruff and ugly had been, according to his daughter, "a great reader . . . [and] in this he had had much in common with the long-dead Ray; during their engagement, they had enjoyed talking about books" (189). Moreover, Mendelsohn learned that this long-ago marriage was understood by members of that branch of the extended family as "a real love match" (189). Having learned these things, Mendelsohn does not move on to other concerns. He stays with the contradictions he has unearthed and the discomfort that comes from learning that what you thought you knew about the past, the stories passed down to you, are not quite what you thought they were. As he makes clear, the truth is more elusive.

This entire tale is extraordinary. Long after the death of his great-aunt and the official story of her death, the narrative becomes something else entirely. The once tragic virgin bride becomes a happily married woman. Far removed from the tale his grandfather had told him and the story engraved on this woman's tombstone, Mendelsohn is able to narrate a different past. In his new telling, we begin to see many conflicting stories existing side by side. Among these newly revealed stories is a tale of two contrasting visions of Jewish identity, that of Ray's brother and that of her husband/cousin. Part of her story is what it meant for her to love both her Orthodox Jewish brother and her free-thinking cousin/husband. As Mendelsohn explains, his grandfather had tried to bury this contradiction, remaking his beloved sister in death into something less conflicted. By seeing his nice Orthodox Jewish sister as a tragic virgin bride, he made invisible the free-thinking, happily married modern Jewish woman she also was.

What I find so compelling about Mendelsohn's narration of this story is the way he insists on holding on to his grandfather's beautiful stories even in the face of very different tales about these same people and this same event. For Mendelsohn, truths and lies are profoundly intertwined. He can admire both the man his grandfather loathed and his family, even as he continues to love his grandfather and the dramatic stories that animated his life for better and for worse. In a sense, Mendelsohn comes to appreciate the power of the myth his grandfather and so many of his siblings had created about the death of their sister. As he explains, they needed this story for themselves. They needed it to help the family go on.

> Maybe they had erected a virgin's monument over a married woman because they wanted to maintain in her death what they could not maintain during her life, which was the myth of their distinctness from ugliness, their aloofness from a squalor so terrible that it could force you to sell your own child, sacrifice your beautiful eldest daughter, your rose, to your need to survive. (199)

In this way, Mendelsohn knowingly preserves the myth. Even as he takes it apart, he perpetuates this necessary family fiction.

Like the ancient Penelope, Mendelsohn both weaves and unweaves these stories as an act of loyalty to his mother's family. In this new configuration, as he tells us, his relatives are made into "the authors of their own histories, the scribes of their own myths" (199). And like them, he too tells stories, creating new narratives out of the stuff of their lives and their imaginations as well as other traces, other evidence, and other stories. But even this does not end the story. Mendelsohn continues to surmise, to reason, to figure out answers to the mystery. Nevertheless, the secret remains even as he adds new layers of conjecture; he wonders, for example, whether immigration quotas and the need to help relatives get into the country before new quotas were enacted might have played a part in his great-aunt's story. By refusing to pin down the past, Mendelsohn lends new life to the family myth.

All we can ever know about even our private ghosts is partial. We can find evidence, learn stories, and build explanations. And the more we do these things, the more richly textured out families' pasts become, not because we know for sure, but because these multiplying tales help animate what we can never know for sure. They strangely provide us with the illusion that these lives, now long gone, are still bristling with life, still somehow in motion. The new and now contradictory stories seem to breathe new life into these long-dead relatives. The proliferation of narratives challenges the ossification of the past.

Children and the Future: For Whom Do We Write?

Rosen ends his book with the promise of inheritance. Although his book begins with the death of his grandmother, he ends it with the birth of his first child, a child he will name in honor of this grandmother, signaling that her legacy will live on along with her name. "I can only wish for her a world that, chastened by the tragedies of the last century, manages to keep its contrary impulses in healthy balance" (132). For Rosen, "balance" is the healthy way of the Talmud, a way for him and his daughter to hold on to the contradictory legacies they embody. He says this even as he asks this child to be his answer to this same legacy. "My child will not redeem those terrible events. . . . But she is perhaps the only answer I can make in the face of such terrible extremes" (132). In other words, bringing this child into the world and naming her for the beloved grandmother he knew so well is his answer. His daughter cannot redeem the world she enters, a world already marked by the horrors of the twentieth century, nor can she ignore these horrors. Instead, what Rosen hopes for her is a balance between these "terrible extremes." Closing his book in this way, despite his protestations to the contrary, makes this a redemptive ending. Death is responded to with a renewed commitment to life. It is in the end, "a light, invisible thread, a fragment of the beloved past" that Rosen hopes his child "will carry with her safely into the unknown future" (132).

Despite this hopeful wish, I am left uncomfortable. I am startled by the sharp contrast between this vision of a "beloved past," and the "terrible extremes" that Rosen also insists that his daughter be able to keep in balance. I am not so sure that his young daughter will find what she needs to make all of this work in either the Talmud or the Internet. I wonder what might have happened had Rosen dug deeper into the more complicated legacy of his American grandmother, especially her grief. What might the story of her lost child have taught him about the future? And here I find myself returning to Mendelsohn who shows that it is possible to tell new stories about once familiar pasts without denying the necessity or the power of those older stories.

For Mendelsohn, the future is also, at least in part, in the hands of a child he is raising, but for him, inheritances can be messy and they need not be biological. As a gay man, Mendelsohn shares parenting responsibilities with his son's birth mother, a woman he is not married to. Here there is no simple line of inheritance. Mendelsohn does not choose parenting over his life in Chelsea; he insists on both and the power of compromise. And so, he writes toward the very end of his book about his other life, his life as a kind of parent in the suburbs:

In this place you may teach classics, which allows you to remember your Greeks, with their precise grammars and their statues that even when broken are beautiful and whole, even as you live the life of your Hebrews, a life with children and holidays and messes, a life in which you know that one day the child whose birth you witness will be there when you are not, will bury you, will watch as you disappear into the same Jewish earth that already holds the man who told you beautiful stories and the girl he told stories about. (205)

When Mendelsohn considers his own death, he insists on his Jewishness and in so doing makes explicit something that separates him from his child.

For this child there is no simple father figure. Mendelsohn's fathering is complicated. This father and son do not even share the same rituals. The son is baptized a Christian in his mother's tradition. And even so, Mendelsohn sees his future in relation to this child. I am moved by this account, this wonderfully messy and complicated vision of attachment, of parenting and inheritance that cannot be contained within a family plot.

And yet, I am struck that in the end, both Mendelsohn and Rosen envision the future in terms of raising children. In the pages of these two widely acclaimed books, it is not writing that assures a future but children. Even as each of these authors write about the promise of children, I wonder about this literary conceit. After all, both of these men are professional writers who spend their days producing books and articles. Both of these writers have chosen to share their intimate family stories, not only with their children, but also with a broader reading public. Both of these books were well received and sold well. So, although these writers self-consciously craft their books as if they were written for their children, the truth is that these are very public enactments. A broad readership is invited to share these legacies with them.

I am fascinated by this conceit and the tension it seems to smooth over. Is it really all right to publish family stories, especially if there are no children to whom they might be said to ultimately belong? I find it important to reflect on this point because this conceit is what separates me from these writers, these two men of my generation. Although I, too, am writing about intimate family legacies and making them public, I do not have a child to whom I can address my writing. I have no children. There is no single child to whom I offer my family stories. Although I love Mendelsohn's complicated reckoning—his two lives and the compromises he has made—these are not my options. As a woman without children, a woman who has chosen to teach and to write and not to bear or adopt children, I struggle with the meaning of my family stories and their audience. To whom am I addressing my writing? Without the fact of children, is it possible to still tell these kinds of stories? In other words, what does it mean for me to somehow be disloyal to the very narrative of family inheritance that makes this conceit so powerful? And even so, what does it mean for me to both embrace and reject this whole notion of family inheritance simultaneously? Put another way, what does it mean for me to choose not to "mother" and instead to teach and to write about my family for others?

Just putting these words down on paper makes me uncomfortable. Even the voices in my own head are agitated; how could I not have children? And yet, I find myself stumbling. As much as we have in common in terms of the kinds of stories we are engaging with in relation to this issue, Rosen and Mendelsohn cannot help me. In the end, despite the fact that they tell their family stories in public for a broader audience than I might ever hope for, they can address their work to their children. They can justify these efforts because they are also fulfilling, more or less, a family plot; they pass their inheritance on to another generation as parents.

Without children, I address my family stories to my students, my colleagues, my friends, and my extended family, and, through them, perhaps to a broader audience. I do not know if this form of address will be effective. I am not sure that I can bridge the gap created by my decision not to pass these family stories on to children of my own. Without that guarantee, can these stories still be meaningful? These are some of the questions that haunt my writing. My fear is that my decision not to have children will somehow make me an unreliable narrator. After all, this is what my narrative lacks. It is what separates me even from my male contemporaries.

In order for me to better get at these questions, I need to take a few steps back and explain why not having children seems to be such an affront and why, in turn, it is so hard for me to write about these issues in this context. Of course, we all know that women and mothers are not synonymous terms. Women have a great deal of agency. But the sedimentation of the expectations that all women should have children is so powerfully pervasive that it is hard to remember that these are not necessarily natural or normal assumptions. And it is still quite difficult to make other choices.

The conceit of children to justify one's more public writing as deployed by men is quite different when considered from the point of view of a woman writer, whether or not she becomes a mother. Still, for the mothers, these labors are much more than a conceit.[15] There is little or no time for women with children to read and write. . . . But if women don't have children, we find ourselves unable to deploy the trope of inheritance as a way of justifying our writing.

The expectation that I would become a mother when I grew up was central to how I was raised, and in this, I know that I was not alone. For women of my generation, the notion that we would be mothers was learned early on. For me, playing at mothering was central to some of my earliest memories.[16] I grew up playing with dolls. Playing with dolls was not the only thing I learned about what it meant to be a grown-up woman, but it was important and telling.

Despite this powerful message, my own mother modeled something a bit different. She taught me about teaching and mentoring, roles that were very close to her heart. These labors were an alternative to the kind of play I did with my baby dolls. And all of this was complicated. Even as I grew to admire my mother's work with her students, I was often jealous of her students, wanting my mother's attention all for myself.

In part, I am afraid that in not having become a mother, I have been disloyal to my dolls and maybe to my mother as well. I have not played out the lessons they taught me. And yet this is only partially true, I still hold on to some of these lessons. In what follows, I want to look again at my dolls and in so doing to return to the legacy of my grandmother Mary Levitt and to the work of Irena Klepfisz. Through them I hope to complicate this story of disloyalty. Having done this, I will then look more carefully at what I learned from my mother, the English teacher, watching her with her students, her other children. Having done this, I will conclude by turning to a different genealogy of Jewish women writers and their inheritance as women without children.[17] And so I find myself parting company with both Mendelsohn and Rosen. When it comes to these issues, neither of them can help me, I need to look to the legacy of other women, especially those without children, and what they have to tell me.

Playing with Dolls

We will soon return briefly to Abraham Ravett's film *Half-Sister* in order to think a bit more about dolls, the dolls at the beginning of the film
and those throughout, and all that they signify. But first, I want simply
to explore some of the many resonances that dolls have for me. I was a
little girl who loved dolls. There were the baby dolls and the Barbie
dolls that I played with, and then there were other dolls. In particular
there was a large formal doll who sat on a rocking chair in my childhood bedroom. She was an especially complicated doll in that she was
less a doll than a stand-in, my way of playing out my loyalty to the
poor and distant grandparents who gave her to me. She came all the
way from Albany as a sign of my grandparents' love for me. She was especially tied to my loyalty to Mary, my frail little grandmother. I knew
that Mary loved me and this doll signified that love.[18] Among all my
dolls—and again, there were a lot of them—she was both embarrassing
and important. Although I rarely played with her, she was always present, and she sat in a place of honor even as my dislike of her was a reminder of something else that I could hardly name. She was unreal,
clunky. She had pink hair and a matching dress. She was neither a baby
doll nor a grown up doll and she carried no brand name. I never found
her pretty.

Even now as I write about her, I feel guilty admitting to these complicated childhood feelings. It is as if the doll was always a signal of something else, something unspoken in my family. Like the dolls in the opening segment of Ravett's film, this doll has always triggered inchoate, unnamed things, things I felt well before I learned about my father's other
mother or about Mary's unusual role as a mother. These feelings are not
unlike those Abraham Ravett felt well before he learned about the existence of his half sister.

I need to say a bit more about my love of dolls. I continue to have
them around. They are a part of my life, even if their role is now less
emotionally charged. There is a Groovy Girl hanging from the closet
door in my office connecting me to some of my closest friends; groovy
girls, like me, with little symbolic figures of their own. There is also a
famous doll from the 1930s that I had always wanted to own and was
finally able to purchase because the dealer in an antique shop didn't realize that she was a real Shirley Temple doll. Admittedly she has never
been in very good shape, but I wanted her and bought her for $25 in

my early twenties. Shirley connects me to my father and his childhood. He and I spent many weekend afternoons watching Shirley Temple movies on TV when I was a little girl. She was a pleasure from his past that we shared. My Shirley Temple doll has bad hair, a soiled dress, and hollowed-out eyes. The pin that signifies her authenticity, the pin that places her specific outfit in a particular film, is rusted. Friends from graduate school were often horrified to find her atop a shelf in my bedroom; some asked how I could sleep with her looking at me. And years later, when I had students from a feminist theory class over for an end-of-the-semester party, they were especially horrified because we had read Toni Morrison's *The Bluest Eye*[19] together and discussed Pecola's tragic fascination with this iconic doll. I showed them the doll because I had mentioned her in class. She and the doll with the pink hair, a doll who never had a name, are actually about the same size and body type, if one can talk about dolls in terms of body types. And this, too, I find confusing. I so wanted the Shirley Temple doll but found the form of the pink-haired doll troubling despite their being so similar.

These are some of the dolls that haunt me even now. Of course, they are different from the dolls in Ravett's opening sequence and throughout his film, but there is much that they have in common. In both instances, the dolls are reminders of certain relationships with a specific past. Both my Shirley Temple doll and the dolls in the opening sequence of Ravett's film date from around the same historical period, circa 1935. They are also emotionally charged. For Ravett, the dolls link him to his mother at a time he did not know her, a time before he was born. My pink-haired doll links me to Mary and the fragility I associated with her for so much of my life, a fragility I could not acknowledge or own in other ways. As a child, I could not play this out with this doll because I would not play with her.

Ravett's film begins with little girls and dolls. And like me, initially, he does not know why. Although this becomes clearer as his film continues, dolls remain elusive, as does his more immediate fascination with images of women and girls, mothers and daughters. Throughout his film, Ravett juxtaposes and repeatedly shows these images in different orders. He includes various images of women and girls over time, and together these images capture his particular experience of uncertainty, a kind of frail fascination that seems to signify a loss that has remained unconscious. Ravett's dreamlike desire to eventually imagine who his sister was or could have been after he finally learns of her existence is still bound to an older and less conscious fascination with dolls. In the film, we see these desires intermingling. There are images of girls and women, aging, not aging, stilted, and alive. And there are the less than animate images of dolls, baby dolls, rag dolls, and sophisticated grown-up dolls. I, too, have such dolls carefully packed away and on display, not on film, but in my home. Part of what is odd about all of this for me is that I am not sure what it is that I am still doing with these dolls. Most women save such precious childhood possessions to pass them on to their own children. Others hold on to them because they are of some special value, collectors' items. This may be part of the allure of my Barbie collection, but the emotional resonances for me are not so much with the Barbies but rather with the baby dolls, the clearly less commercially valuable dolls, the ones I have been writing about.

Sometimes I fantasize about donating all of these things to an archive, the dolls as well as my grade school notebooks, the art projects and the gossipy notes I passed in class that meant so much to me at the time and that, because they once meant so much, I have not had the energy to sort through and throw away.[20] I think about this stash as an archival treasure for a future historian interested in mid-twentieth-century American Jewish girlhood.[21] This is a recent fantasy. As a middle-aged woman without children, I have begun to realize that I need to figure out what I am going to do with all of this stuff, the kinds of things a woman might otherwise pass on to her children. This is part of what Mendelsohn and Rosen need not worry about with the children in their lives. And now I find myself wanting a place for at least my dolls to live on in the context of my work, not so much because they are my things, commodified possessions, but because they continue to have an emotional hold on me even in the present, and I want to understand that hold more fully.

In this respect I know that I am not alone. Aside from Abraham Ravett, I also find myself in the company of Irena Klepfisz for whom the figure of a childhood doll also carries meaning. As she explains in the final paragraph of her 1977 essay "Women without Children/Women without Families/Women Alone,"[22]

> While writing this article I visited my mother who had just discovered, stuck away somewhere in a closet, my favorite doll. I was surprised by my instant sadness at seeing and then holding it. The sweetness of the face, the smallness of the head against the palm of my hand. I felt as if I

wanted to cry. But in touching it, it was not a baby I envisioned, but rather myself, five or six years old, cradling the doll in her arms and rocking it gently to sleep. (14)

I am struck by Klepfisz's distance from her doll. Unlike me, she seems to feel perfectly comfortable referring to her doll as "it," while I cannot help but personify my own dolls even now. They are "shes" or sometimes "hes," often named, and never "its"—even the doll with the pink hair is not an "it" for me. She is, after all, "the doll with the pink hair." And yet what Klepfisz has to say about the rediscovery of her doll resonates for me. For Klepfisz, the doll triggers a sadness, and not the sadness she might have expected, especially in the context of her essay. For her, the once beloved doll did not come to stand in for a child, for a baby she did not have, but instead for the child she herself once was, the child who once clung to this same doll soothing herself, rocking herself to sleep, holding tightly to this small, sweet-faced doll.

For me, the pink-haired doll connected me to my grandmother. When I saw the doll again last summer, when I took her soiled body out of the box in the basement and washed her off, I was reminded of how I had had for so long intuitively understood my relationship with Mary. I remembered what it felt like, the painful ambivalence that I felt, the confusion. I remembered what it was like not to have language for those feelings, and now I am struck by the role this doll has played in my imagination and the ways she physically allowed me to act out these feelings in my everyday life.

For little girls, dolls are safe. They are socially acceptable ways to play with all kinds of emotions. For me, baby dolls and childlike dolls were especially powerful. They were literally transitional objects that helped me enact what I was otherwise unable to express. Dolls automatically placed these emotionally latent engagements into a socially sanctioned narrative. For me, and I suspect for many other women of my age, doll babies contained these emotions within a broad narrative of motherhood. They were the children we would someday have. They contained our perhaps more complicated emotions within a normative framework. They helped reinforce that someday we would conform, we would be prepared to take on our highly gendered biological destinies. We knew even then that we would become mothers and that, ultimately, in motherhood, all of our emotions would find a place. Motherhood would enable us to deal with these things when we were finally adults.

In many ways, had I known when I was five or six that my grand-mother was my step-grandmother, that my father had had another mother who died when he was still a little boy, and that Mary, the woman I knew as my grandmother, had never given birth to children, I don't know if my relationship to the pink-haired doll would have been so fraught. I think it was the inchoate sense that something, actually many things, didn't quite fit together neatly in my relationship with Mary that troubled my interactions with the doll she gave me. And, oddly, all of this left me unable to ever really play with this doll. Per-haps knowing more might have made it easier for me to play with her and to play out or imagine other ways of sorting through the estrange-ment and shame I experienced then.

Object relations theory[23] posits that transitional objects like dolls have the potential to help us work through our emotions, but they do not always function so neatly. "Working through" may be a possibility, but for many people dolls have been stand-ins for other things, other people and relationships. They have helped us externalize some of our feelings and hold them in place. There is often no easy resolution, no fixing of the discomforts held by these often intimate but ultimately inanimate objects.

And so, I find myself playing again with my dolls, thinking about what it has meant for me to learn more about the complicated family history that marked my childhood relationship to my grandmother Mary Levitt and surprised by the ways I am now claiming her and the company I want us to keep. As a woman without children, I return to Mary through my dolls to think about how Mary and I are similar and what we both share with Irena Klepfisz. I also find myself more keenly aware of how Irena and I are different from Mary. Although we have all played house, taking on the role of mother, albeit in very different ways, each of us is also a woman without children of our own, trying to figure out what possibilities are open to us, what ways we might pass on lega-cies of our own to future generations. By looking more closely at Mary in her role as wife and mother, I hope to make clear what has remained barely legible to me in thinking about Mary and what she has left me. I also want to think about what it means to reassess this self-conscious legacy of mothering having decided not to become a mother. How can I hold onto Mary's legacy even as I turn to Irena Klepfisz and other women to find alternative ways to imagine contributing to a different future?

Following my account of Mary's legacy, I will return to the writing of Irena Klepfisz and especially her notion of what it means to be a "keeper of accounts," the promise as well as some of the dangers in taking on this role. And finally, having looked carefully at these two inheritances, I turn to the legacy of my own mother and her role as both teacher and mother, connecting some of what she has taught me to a legacy of German Jewish women of letters.[24] I do this to reconsider my role as a Jewish feminist scholar writing in America, at the beginning of the twenty-first century, a woman without children but with many students, colleagues, friends, and extended family to whom I address my words.

"Mother Mary"[25]

Given my father's fascination with Christian imagery, it may not seem quite so odd to title this section "Mother Mary," but I do so with some trepidation. Despite the fact that my grandmother and that other Mary share some things in common, I don't want to make my grandmother into a saint. That would not be helpful. Rather, I am interested in the excessively charged resonances of this configuration for my grandmother, a woman who did not, and perhaps could not, bear children of her own.

Mary Levitt wanted to be a mother. Marrying my grandfather, she immediately became wife and mother all at the same time. Yet this is not quite accurate. Prior to marrying my grandfather in the summer of 1939, Mary had already spent over ten years mothering her youngest sister Paula after their mother's death, taking on this role, the responsibilities, and the obligations that entailed. She was in her early thirties by the time she married my grandfather, at which point she become mother to the Levitt children as well. None of this was easy on her young sister who both did and did not gain new siblings in the process. Although the Levitt children were Paula's contemporaries, she did not simply enter into their family once her oldest sister married. She found herself on the road, unsettled. During those first few years after her sister Mary married, Paula spent periods of time visiting with various other older siblings and their families. She moved between their households. And although she grew to love the Levitt children, especially Irving, my father, and Muriel, his young sister, there was always a sense that they had taken her mother away from her.

These arrangements were never simple or straightforward. The reasons behind these various negotiations may have been more about economic necessity than any emotional considerations. My sense is that these moves had a lot to do with the precarious financial position of my father's family and of Mary's extended family. Although the Depression was coming to an end, it had left its mark on all of these households. By 1940, my grandfather had lost his business as well as the family's home in Schenectady. These losses led the family to move to Albany, where they lived in close proximity to Mary's family, especially her sister Rose. At various points my father lived with Rose and her young family to help everyone make ends meet. Times were difficult and this extended family worked hard to take care of one another. They did the best they could.

I have only been able to find a single snapshot from Mary and my grandfather Sol's wedding. Unlike the elaborate weddings I am familiar with in more recent generations of my family, theirs was a very simple ceremony, or so it seems. Here my knowledge is quite limited. My father has no memory of attending this wedding, nor does anyone else who is still alive.

As I began working on this project, I went in search of family pictures, grave sites, and whatever else I could gather from my various relatives. Mary's youngest sister, Paula, offered me letters—the ones my father sent her from Europe when he served in the United States Army. She was one of the people to whom he wrote regularly. My father's sister had albums and scattered pictures. It was among these incomplete pages that I came across the one photograph I have found of Mary and Sol's wedding in the summer of 1939. It is an informal snapshot, and like those in my father's secret stash, it is another overexposed black and white image. What distinguishes it, in part, from the other images are the dimensions of the actual print. This picture is rectangular, not a neat square, which suggests to me that it was taken by a different inexperienced photographer. I know that it was not taken by Rose or her husband because they figure prominently in the picture. The other person I think I can identify from the extended family is Mary's father. We know it is a Jewish wedding because there is a clearly visible *huppah*, or wedding canopy, under which the couple is standing. The groom is clearly visible. He is on the right side of the image, and if you don't look carefully, it almost looks as if Rose, the tall dark-haired woman standing behind the huppah, might in fact be the bride. But if you look more closely, you will see in the foreground a very tiny figure in a white suit and a mesh veil. This is Mary, the bride. The men are all wearing hats, and, like my grandfather, most of the men also appear to be dressed in suit and tie. Aside from Mary and Rose, we see no other women in the photograph. The rabbi or cantor we see from the back is in a dark suit. His back takes up much of the right foreground. His hands hold a large-sized document, very white in the overexposure, and this paper separates the bride and groom and is in line with Rose, who stands behind it in the middle of the space defined by the huppah. No one is smiling. This adds to the difficulty one might have in realizing this is a wedding picture. It does not resemble the kinds of formal and informal wedding pictures I am most familiar with. And yet, I find myself needing to look again at this snapshot alongside the professional photographs taken at my parents' wedding twenty years later.

These formal pictures are lush. They are the fruits of my maternal grandparents' financial success. The wedding they created for their daughter celebrated all they had been able to accomplish. Here the men of the wedding party are in morning coats. The women are in elaborate formal dresses. They are sequined and bedecked with jewelry on their wrists, necks, ears, and hands. In these photographs Mary is appropriately dressed. She, too, appears in sequins and chiffon. She is often smiling, clearly enjoying all of the fuss around her oldest son, the groom. She is a proud mother. In one photograph my parents are surrounded by my father's immediate family. Mary and Sol are on their left, and Muriel and Aaron, my father's siblings, are on the right. Harold, Muriel's husband is not there. He was unable to attend the wedding.

This is a familiar photograph. It looks exactly like many others taken at middle-class Jewish weddings on Long Island in the late 1950s. The couple is central, and in this shot, the groom looks adoringly at his bride while she looks out toward the camera. Her dress and flowers are clearly the main attraction; the groom and his family are all overshadowed by her presence. She is not quite smiling; her look is more a smirk. The others are smiling. The women stand closest to the couple and the two Levitt men, my father's brother and his father, round out the edges of the photograph in their top hats and tails. My father is not wearing his hat for this picture. In others he is figured in his full regalia. In another picture my father, his father, and his brother are all in top

Irving and Phyllis Levitt, Muriel Wilson, Aaron Levitt, and Mary and Sol Levitt. From Irving and Phyllis Levitt wedding album.

hats and tails, and here my grandfather takes center stage with his sons both captured in profile looking at him and at each other. He is smiling.

It is hard for me to imagine a more stark contrast than the one I see between the snapshot taken at Mary and Sol's wedding and the formal professional photographs taken at my parents' wedding. For Mary this contrast is a celebration, a victory signifying how much her family was able to accomplish. Who would have believed that the couple pictured in the 1939 snapshot would, twenty years later, celebrate their oldest son's wedding in such opulence? That just did not seem imaginable in 1939. And my guess is that Mary appreciated this.

In almost every picture taken of her after Mary entered the Levitt family, she is depicted with children, always with children. Aside from the formal professional photographs taken at family celebrations, weddings and bar and bat mitzvahs, this is how Mary appears in virtually all of the scattered images I have seen. I only want to look at one of these pictures here, and that is an image of Mary as grandmother taken in the early 1950s. It is a good example of these pictures. This is a picture of both of my grandparents with their first grandchild, my cousin Linda. In the photograph Linda is a toddler. She is relaxed and seemingly content seated in a child's swing. The swing is set up on an outdoor porch. Linda and her swing take up most of the left-hand side of the photograph. On the right, almost lined up, are her grandparents, our grandparents, Sol and Mary. Sol is crouched behind Mary and Linda. He is wearing a sleeveless man's undershirt, arms and chest clearly visible. He is smiling brightly. In front of him, seated on what might be a step, is Mary. She is smiling proudly. Mary's hair is tousled and her large black framed glasses make it hard to see her eyes, but even still she looks comfortable, satisfied. She is wearing a floral short-sleeved dress with a different floral patterned apron over it. Like most of my father's family pictures, this one is also overexposed, but unlike many of the others, it is clearly in focus and the grouping has a kind of

Irving, Aaron, and Sol Levitt. From Irving and Phyllis Levitt wedding album.

Mary and Sol Levitt and Linda Wilson. From Levitt family collection.

symmetry. I suspect it was taken by my uncle Harold, the same man who filmed my father's movie. He always had a good eye.

The elated grandparents are captured with their first grandchild. They are comfortable and contented in this role. What strikes me is the satisfaction I see in Mary's face. Although there are lots of other images of her with children, unlike in those older pictures here Mary is easy and natural in her stance. It reminds me of the kind of normalcy my father and his siblings longed for as Mary entered their lives. It seems to say that these efforts, all of their efforts, were successful. This is who Mary wanted to be and what her stepchildren wanted for both her and for themselves. This was not a "natural" occurrence. It took work, but it was what Mary wanted, and she was able to make it happen through her own volition. Although our desires are different, part of what Mary has taught me is that I, too, can choose to make a life perhaps different from what might have been expected of me.

I need to say something else about Mary's role in my father's life. For a long time my father wandered. He was drafted into the army just after graduating from high school in 1944, which led him to Europe, where he fought in the Second World War. After the war, on the GI bill, my father moved from one college to another, never settling in just one place. He attended Union College in Schenectady, New York; Syracuse University; the New School for Social Research in New York City; and Russell Sage College in Troy, New York. It was only when he got seriously ill with a case of pleurisy that he came home so that Mary could take care of him. But during most of this time, he did not live in Mary's home. Nevertheless, it was in many ways still his home. It was his base. It was where Mary kept account of my father's things, his most prized possessions—his books, paintings, and writings—while he was on the move. Until my father married my mother, his things all lived in Mary's house. She was the one who watched over them in ways that might have seemed impossible when my father was still a boy hiding things.

In all of these ways, Mary was a wonderful mother. She brought order, comfort, and new life to my father and his family. She also offered the promise of a kind of continuity. It was not exactly smooth, but Mary and her family tried hard to make it seem that way. I might wish that there had been ways for all of them to be able to signal this lack of fit, but that was not what they wanted at the time. I would like to imagine that they could have more overtly acknowledged Lena's existence and her death or the fact that Mary could not give birth to children of her own, but these are desires of a different time; they are mine and not theirs. My father and his family longed for a semblance of normality, and this was something they shared with Mary, who also simply wanted to be a wife and mother. This is part of what the marriage between Sol and Mary accomplished. Even more distant relatives marveled at how Mary brought the household together again, how she straightened out the literal and emotional messes left in the wake of Lena's death. She also brought with her a rich and vibrant new extended family, the families of her various siblings. In all of these ways, Mary was of another generation. She was different from Irena Klepfisz and me. She was a part of a generation where motherhood was much more defining. Motherhood was the role that Mary was expected to embody, and the fact that she could not bear children of her own meant that she had to work that much harder to fulfill this desire and cultural expectation. In her case, I suspect that these were one and the same thing. As a woman who could not bear children of her own but who very much wanted to be a mother, Mary's marriage to my grandfather made a great deal of sense. It fulfilled these promises. And although she might not have appreciated my efforts to show the seams in this enactment, I have read her legacy against the grain for what it has taught me about her agency, her ability to make possible the seemingly impossible. Although her desires were conventional, her efforts to fulfill them were extraordinary, and again, for this I am grateful.

Keeper of Accounts

Irena Klepfisz not only used the figure of "the keeper of accounts" in the title of the final prose section of her poem *Bashert,* but she also used it as the title of the book of poems in which it first appeared.[26] In many ways, this trope aptly captures a central motif in Klepfisz's career as a poet, teacher, and activist. It illuminates how she operates in the world. She keeps track. She remembers and passes on what needs to be passed on. She conveys what others might forget, and she acts. And unlike the doll she once cradled, this labor has not been maternal. As she explains even as early as in her 1977 essay "Women without Children," there are other ways for women to contribute to the future that need not be enacted solely through the labor of mothering, of bearing, adopting, or otherwise nurturing children. And although this essay was written almost thirty years ago, its claims remain all the more true today. Even in the interim years, despite all the gains that have been made by feminist movement, the issue of women who choose not to have children remains an underexplored area of critical inquiry and public discussion. In the opening section of her essay, Klepfisz writes:

> This article has grown out of my need to express some of my feelings and conflicts about being a woman who has chosen to remain childless, as well as to break the silence surrounding the general issue of women without children.
>
> That the silence has persisted despite the presence of the women's movement is both appalling and enigmatic, since the decision not to

have a child shapes both a woman's view of herself and society's view of her. I have read a great deal about woman as mother, but virtually nothing about woman as nonmother, as if her choice should be taken for granted and her life were not an issue. And though I have heard strong support of the right of women to have choices and options, I have not seen any exploration of how the decision to remain childless is to be made, how one is to come to terms with it, how one is to learn to live with its consequences. If what follows seems at moments somewhat bleak, it is because I feel very strongly that in celebrating a woman's liberation from compulsory motherhood, we have neither recognized nor dealt with the pain that often accompanies such a decision.(3)

I cite this passage in full because, as I experience it, these words still ring true today.[27] It still remains difficult for women to define ourselves outside of the norms of motherhood. We remain "women without children," "childless women," women who lack something still seemingly essential to who we are. This lack still needs explanation.

In addition to this, Klepfisz goes on to address the special status of childbearing in the Jewish community after the Holocaust, which only adds to the broader cultural compulsion she describes. And in Klepfisz's voice, these are especially powerful claims. As an only child and child survivor of the Holocaust, the sole heir to her father's family, to choose not to have children remains a brave act, a decision that stands in sharp contrast to the urgency, post-Holocaust, for Jews to repopulate the Jewish world.[28] As she explains:

It has been extremely difficult as well as painful for me to live with the knowledge that I deliberately never produced the child who could have continued "my father's line"; that I never provided my mother with the new family and the grandchildren she was sure would appear, which she thought were her right to expect. (11)

Although for Klepfisz there is a direct and immediate urgency to this demand, the need to repopulate the Jewish world continues to burden subsequent generations of Jews.

This burden is especially haunting and daunting for Jewish women, those most immediately compelled to address this problem quite literally through the act of bearing children. Even in the late 1980s when I was in graduate school, the director of the Jewish Studies program I was enrolled in, a deeply thoughtful man, once told me that I might make a more significant contribution to the Jewish future by becoming a mother than I would by completing my doctoral program and becoming a professor of Jewish Studies. I don't mean to disparage my teacher. In part, I believe he simply said more directly than most what many others in less overt ways also believed and perhaps still believe about the obligation of contemporary Jewish women to have children.[29]

In other words, Jewish women are strongly encouraged to have children by Jewish communities that, at the same time, give them little or no resources to help them do just this.[30] Despite all of this, it still is not necessarily acceptable for Jewish women like me and like Irena Klepfisz to choose not to have children, to make other choices, to imagine other ways of contributing to a Jewish future.

And yet this is precisely what Klepfisz has argued for in much of her writing, not only in her 1977 essay, but again ten years later in her essay "Jewish Lesbians, the Jewish Community, Jewish Survival." In this essay she insists that Jewish survival is not only a matter of having children. And, although lesbians were already having children in 1988, Klepfisz insists on calling attention to all of the other kinds of contributions Jewish women, both lesbian and straight, including women without children, were making toward Jewish survival. She writes:

> And though I understand the emotions and concerns which lie behind that pressure [for Jewish women to bear children], I feel it is imperative for us to resist this specific form of sexism which reduces a Jewish woman's value simply to a biological function. We have to resist the view that the most significant contribution a Jewish woman can make to *undzer folk* [our people], is to give birth to a Jewish child. (76)

Again, Klepfisz does not mince words; she insists that this putative claim be challenged again and again. In this essay, she argues that such an acknowledgment would help bring together all Jewish women. And then she goes on to offer numerous examples of lesbian Jewish women, many of whom were not mothers, who contribute to Jewish continuity in the work they do as educators and artists, librarians and historians, rabbis and activists.[31] Here again I am grateful to Klepfisz for paving the way toward an acknowledgment of these issues. In all of these ways, she works toward a more expansive vision of what it means to imagine contributing to the future, even the Jewish future, as a woman without children. She helps envision a sense of what it is we do, and in so doing, she validates and affirms these other labors. And she does this in ways that still affirm the power and importance of the work of mothering.

In a sense, as I have already suggested, Klepfisz's notion of becoming a "keeper of accounts," in its widest application, is a way of figuring such an alternative vision. In her various prose writings, Klepfisz suggests some of the many crucial ways that scholars, teachers, social workers, rabbis, poets, and artists all contribute powerfully to various Jewish futures. We do this by keeping account, seeing where we have been and where we might be going, by not forgetting the past, by keeping cultural legacies and languages alive, and by transforming them in the present. These are some of the deepest commitments at the heart of Klepfisz's essays and speeches. But to see the notion of "keeping accounts" within such a broad political and cultural vision in some ways forgets the roots of this trope in Klepfisz's poetry, more specifically in her poem *Bashert* where its meaning is much more specific.

In her poetry, Klepfisz complicates this notion of keeping account. She allows us to see the contradictions and the tensions built into this vision, including the antisemitic aspects of this trope. Jews "keeping account," after all, has marked them as misers. It has been a way to disparage their labors as bookkeepers, petty merchants, and of course as money lenders who care more about ledgers than they do about lives, more about ducats than they do about human flesh. Given this, for Klepfisz, becoming a keeper of accounts is not simply an affirming gesture, but it is also an act of defiance. In *Bashert*, the narrator, a child survivor of the Holocaust, concludes this long prose poem in 1981 still marked by the legacy of antisemitism. She is haunted by its specter. These are some of the resonances that haunt the narrator when she says that she becomes a keeper of accounts.

In 1981, she is living in the rural American town of "Cherry Plain," but even here she proclaims that she must remain vigilant, always alert to contemporary manifestations of antisemitism. She keeps track of even minor infractions as they are enacted in this innocuous place. In Cherry Plain in 1981, the narrator insists on her alliance with all of those despised Jews, both past and present, whose lives were forged by an ancient and ongoing legacy of hatred. In this final section of the poem, she embraces a full panoply of stereotypical Jews, embarrassing, shameful, ugly and despised Jews, and claims them all as her own.

Like the patriarchs, the shabby scholars who only lived for
what was written and studied it all their lives

Like the inhuman usurers and dusty pawnbrokers who were
quarantined within precisely prescribed limits of every European town and who were as accurate as the magistrates that
drew the boundaries of their lives and declared them diseased

Like those men of stone who insisted that the *goyim* fulfill the
Contracts they had signed and who responded to the tearful
Pleas of illness, weakness, sudden calamity and poverty, with
The words: "What are these to me? You have made me a keeper
of accounts. Give me my pound of flesh!" (85)

All of these stereotypically despised Jewish men are embraced, as are
their female counterparts. These women include:

> . . . all of the matriarchs, the wives and daughters, the sisters
> and aunts, the nieces, the keepers of button shops, milliners,
> seamstresses, peddlers of foul fish, of matches, of rotten apples,
> laundresses, midwives, floor washers and street cleaners, who
> rushed, exhausted all week so that *shabes* could be observed
> with fresh *challah* on the table, who argued in the common
> tongue.
>
> and begged for the daughter run off to the revolution
> and the daughter run off with a *shegetz*
> who refused to sit *shiva* and say *kaddish* for a living child
> who always begged for life
> who understood the accounts but saw them differently
> who knew the power of human law, knew they always counted
> no matter what the revolution or the party or the state
> who knew the power of the words *Zyd, Juif, Jude.* (86)

In this instance, becoming a "keeper of accounts" is something quite
specific. It includes both the doing of a stereotypical Jewish act, keeping
accounts, and a broader insistence on remembering and embodying all
that has been despised about Jews both in the past and in the present.
For this narrator, these stereotypes are both enumerated and affirmed.
And she does this in the present of the poem whenever she feels threat-

ened as a Jew. "At those moments, the myths that propel our history, that turn fiction into fact, emerge in full force in me, as I stare into the eyes of strangers or someone suddenly grown alien. And when I see their eyes become pinpoints of judgement, become cold and indifferent, or simply distanced with curiosity . . ." (85)—in these moments, she becomes a keeper of accounts.

And yet, despite this quite specific function within the poem *Bashert,* as the title of Klepfisz's 1982 book of poetry entitled *Keeper of Accounts* indicates, to be a "keeper of accounts" has broader implications. As the description on the back cover of that book explains:

> Born in Warsaw, Poland in 1941, Irena Klepfisz views America as alien country where safety can never be assumed by the outsider. In *Keeper of Accounts,* she writes of the connections between historical events and the individual, of common entrapments, and of the erosion of identity to meet daily needs. These themes emerge in a variety of settings: a cage in a zoo, a country road in Poland, a Xerox room, a flower pot on a fire escape, the Jewish cemetery in Warsaw. Her poems reveal the fragility of the soul as well as its tenacious will to live, not just survive, on inhospitable, even hostile, soil. Acutely aware that the past cannot be undone and that the present holds new dangers, Irena Klepfisz nevertheless expresses the necessity and the possibility of hope in our lives.

In part, this description echoes the broader vision I began with. Here the book *Keeper of Accounts* offers an expansive vision of outsiderness. It is both historical and quotidian. It can be experienced anywhere and for all kinds of reasons. Strikingly, this back-cover text does not explicitly address one of the major themes of this collection, Klepfisz's lesbian desire and the many poems devoted to this theme. This outsider position goes unnamed.

During one of the first times I ever heard Irena Klepfisz discuss her work, she described the reception of this first book of poems. On the one hand, she explained, Jewish readers focused only on the Holocaust poems, while lesbian feminist readers seemed only to notice the lesbian poems. In part, what Klepfisz longed for was a broader accounting, a more expansive reading that could include all of the poems without denying the specificity of any particular poem or theme. Perhaps the back-cover copy was an attempt to do just that. Given that the book was circulated in feminist bookstores where lesbian readers would already have been familiar with Klepfisz's lesbian works, it offered a broader thematic. And yet it is not clear that all of these legacies can be seen together.

Keeping account goes only so far. The trope remains fraught. It is tainted by antisemitic assumptions about what Jews do, it boldly defies these same negative connotations, and it continues to offer a strangely compelling vision of what various kinds of outsiders, including often invisible lesbian feminists, must do to become visible. And, finally, in addition to all of this, it may provide a vision of what those of us without children can offer to a more expansive notion of the future. In a sense, we too are keepers of accounts.

On Being Phyllis's Daughter

As I have already indicated, being my mother's daughter complicates these dichotomies as well. On the one hand, my mother adhered to the norms of mothering that defined her generation. Although she was educated and worked before she had children, she left her job when my brother and I were very young and stayed at home. She did not go back to teaching for almost five years, but this is not exactly where I wanted to begin. I wanted to start by saying that my mother, like me, played with dolls. Her favorites, so she tells me, were paper dolls. She spent long days as a little girl cutting out various outfits, experimenting with how each looked on her paper dolls. Given this, I suspect that my mother would have enjoyed playing with Barbie dolls. Like her paper dolls, Barbies are also all about dressing up. Crucial to playing with Barbies are the fantasies of what to wear and what might transpire if one is dressed in any given outfit. They were made to dress up in elaborate and changing costumes. Nevertheless, Barbie is not of my mother's vintage. And, unlike her paper dolls, Barbies never offered the challenge and physical labor of cutting. Part of the fun of paper dolls is that they require work. The little girls who play with them must become skilled at using scissors in order to dress their dolls. Here the fantasies are anticipatory; they are part of what animate the labor of cutting.

I think about my mother playing with her paper dolls when I think about her accounts of what she did during her long days at home with me as a young child. For my mother, staying at home was not easy. She loved teaching and regretted giving up her job when I was born.

In the early 1960s, it was still expected that middle-class women like my mother would leave their jobs to be at home with their young children. My father felt strongly that my mother should do this as well. It was not easy for my parents to lose my mother's income. In the first few years of their marriage they both made relatively small salaries and needed both of them to cover their expenses. In order to compensate for this loss of income, for the first few years of my life my father worked a second job just to make ends meet. And yet, for my mother, the thought of going back to work was not imaginable. It was just not done. Women like my mother could not consider going back to work until their children were in school. In the fall of 1965, my mother was offered a position teaching junior high school and wanted it badly. I had just started kindergarten and my younger brother was still at home. My mother insisted on going back to work, but in order to make this possible, we both had to be in school. So my mother enrolled me and my brother in a private kindergarten and nursery school. Part of the reason for this private school was that my public kindergarten offered students only a half-day program. It had no mechanism in place to accommodate students who needed to be in school for the entire day. The private school was different. It made it possible for my brother and me to be in school all day so that our mother could work. As it turned out, the vast majority of my mother's salary went to pay for our private schooling, but for her it was well worth it. My memories of that school are still vivid. It was a magical place. The following year, I began first grade, and our family moved to Dover, Delaware, where things were to change even more radically.

I have little or no memories of my mother at home with my brother and me. I have memories of playing with friends and a spattering of memories of other adults, but I do not have any clear memories of my mother. What my mother tells me is that she spent a lot of this time cleaning and ironing my various outfits and dressing me up in them. I cannot help but imagine that, in part, my role was quite similar to that of her paper dolls. She did the labor in order to get my clothes ready for me to wear and then spent her days putting them on and taking them off me. Again, my own memories of these early acts of dressing up are few. What I do recall are itchy crinolines and a longing to take them off, and short lacy socks that needed to be pulled up over my heels again and again. I think I sensed even then that my mother was not particularly happy staying at home.

In the fall of 1967, my mother began teaching senior English at Dover High School. This job was transformative. My mother came into her own as a teacher. She fell in love with her work and especially her students. Senior English was my mother's calling. And, not surprisingly, it was with this job that my memories of my mother began. My mother's passion for her work was contagious. I imbibed it. I fell in love with her students and her colleagues, their stories, their intrigues, and always my mother at the center of all of this storytelling. To this day, I still remember more about the class of 1969, for example, than I do about all of the German verbs I learned in years of study at college. The stories about my mother's students mattered to me, and strangely, they still do. Over the years, I have maintained this specialized knowledge. It has enabled a kind of intimacy between my mother and me. It allows me to easily confer with my mother about her former students and to share this part of her life with her even now.

My mother taught at Dover High School for over twenty-five years.[32] For most of those years, she was the chair of the English department. This meant that she worked on an eleven-month schedule and spent much more time at school. As it turned out, so did we. My bother and I were often recruited to help her inventory books over the summer. We would stamp them and number them and then cart them off to either specific classrooms or back to the book storage rooms. We loved being at school with our mother, where we were part of the behind-the-scene processes that made the English department work.

Eventually, my brother and I became our mother's students, literally. Dover was a small town and as such it was common for teachers to teach their own children. And so it happened that both my brother and I were students in our mother's classroom. Here again, we came to see our mother in her element. We watched her perform as a teacher. We learned to navigate complicated boundaries, to make distinctions between our interactions, deciding when our mother was our mother and when she was our teacher. These efforts were complicated in different ways for my brother and me, but this is not what interests me here. What I want to focus on is how well my mother taught, how much she loved this work, and how I came to learn those skills from her. In other words, what interests me is how I learned to teach and mentor from my mother. These were roles my mother inhabited with unusual skill, talent, and passion.

What stands out the most for me is my mother's passion for her students. I knew this early on. She loved blurring these lines between home and school, bringing her passion for teaching into our home and into all of our lives. Students could turn in assignments until midnight. That was my mother's policy, and it worked. Individual students would come to our home regularly. Often there would be a knock on the door just around midnight. But students also came in groups. For almost the entire time that my mother taught at Dover High School, she held a Great Books class in our house. The class met once a week. Students read the green-boxed edition of the Adler series not only with my mother, but with my father as well. My parents loved to talk about books and literature with each other and with these students, and the students loved being a part of these discussions. Some students formed informal reading groups over the summer after they graduated, and others asked for reading lists whose titles they would dutifully read on their own, writing or returning to visit to discuss these works with my parents, especially my mother.

After having spent lots of time at our house, it seemed natural that students would return to visit after they had graduated. These visits were a regular part of my childhood. Like my parents, I loved these occasions. I loved how my mother's students came to catch up, to share their lives with her. Some would bring girlfriends and boyfriends, others children or friends, but they came, over and over again. Some would return from college, others from Vietnam, and still others from life adventures that took them to other places. Those who remained in Dover simply talked to her on the street or in store parking lots, still others at civic events or performances.

During the spring of 2005, while I was living in Williamstown, Massachusetts, as a visiting professor at Williams College, my parents came to visit. They stopped in Albany on the way up. Part of their trip included time with my father's family, but they also devoted time to one of my mother's former students, a poet who lives in the area.[33] Before their trip, my mother asked if it might be all right to invite this man to come and join us in Williamstown. This request was somewhat unusual. More often than not, my mother would just make these kinds of plans and then let me know about them. I think she was trying to be respectful in asking if her student could come to my house on this visit. I was touched that she asked but could not imagine saying no. Of course he could visit. At the designated time, the former student, now a man in his early fifties, drove in from Troy, New York, a relatively quick ride over the mountain. He came to see my parents, especially my mother. They are close. They write and phone and meet whenever they can. He sends her copies of his published work and they exchange holiday cards and letters. In part, I think I was startled to actually meet this former student again. The last time I had seen him was a very long time ago. Needless to say, we had both aged. I had a hard time reconciling my present and our pasts. Time felt confused.

Once everyone was settled, a very familiar pattern began to emerge even in this strange setting, my house in Williamstown. My mother sat down next to her student. They began to talk. He had her full attention. I became very quiet. I sat myself on the sidelines of this conversation, listening carefully. The role was familiar. It was my role since childhood. I had become the little girl I once was. It was as if I were nine or ten all over again, a little girl watching my mother engage with one of her students. I was strangely fascinated, enthralled. The grown-up me had disappeared. For a long time I thought that my response to this kind of engagement was all about my mother's amazing students. And in retrospect there were times in the more recent past that I have tried to explain this fascination in competitive terms, a kind of competition between me and her students, and I was jealous. I wanted the kind of attention my mother could give her students, but I think that this explanation misses much of what it is that still draws me into these occasions even in the present. Let me explain. As a child I was so excited about these visits that I would refuse to go out and play with my friends just to stay at home to be a part of them. I loved these occasions. I longed to be a part of them. They are still among the highlights of my childhood. This desire had little to do with jealousy. I loved the students and my mother when she was with them. I craved these encounters.

What I began to see sitting on the sidelines of this more recent conversation is something more about this allure. I began to appreciate that it was never just the students' stories that I loved hearing. It was who my mother became in these encounters that I found captivating. Part of what I had always loved was witnessing my mother as she gave her full attention to these students, the seeming effortlessness of her engagement. In these encounters, my mother became fully present in ways I had otherwise never seen her. She became someone I found extraordinarily compelling. I was mesmerized. It was in these encounters that I learned up close, from my mother's example, how to mentor and teach. I experienced her as completely comfortable and engaged in this role.

There was nothing awkward or uncomfortable about these encounters. In these moments I learned to idealize my mother. She became the mother I have always adored and admired. It isn't that I do not know my mother in other ways. I do. But unlike those other more complicated roles, in these situations my mother seemed most fully herself. This, perhaps more than anything else, is why I loved being with my mother in these moments. Given this, I guess it is not surprising that this is the part of my mother I have come to most fully embody in my own life as a teacher and perhaps most especially as a woman without children.[34] In my engagement with my students, I am most fully my mother's daughter. I know that my mother is the person who taught me how to perform this role.

I do not know who my mother might have become had she been born a decade or two later. I do not know what she might have done had she not stayed home with my brother and me when we were very young. There were times when she said she might have become a lawyer, but I no longer believe that would have been the case. I know that teaching was my mother's calling and that as a teacher she taught me to teach as well.

High school teachers are not often producers of knowledge of their own. They are not required or encouraged to publish in the same way that professors are. In this way, my teaching is different from my mother's. In order to work with graduate students, and even my undergraduates, I have needed to model what it means to be a writer, to be a producer of knowledge myself. For a long time, learning to privilege this aspect of my own work was a challenge. This was not the kind of thing my mother had done. And so, I have had to look elsewhere to imagine doing this kind of work. Here I am reminded of the ease with which both Rosen and Mendelsohn seem to write. For me, finding friends and colleagues with whom to share my work has been crucial, and yet this notion of a legacy of writing women remains for me a relatively recent phenomenon. Although there are more and more texts by women, we remain not that far removed from the Virginia Woolf of *A Room of One's Own*. Many of us continue to yearn for an inherence of writing women. We want evidence of intellectual women who were engaged with one another and with other intellectuals. We want to know that there were women producing knowledges both public and private, work that was of and about their lives and their passions, and that this work had readers.

Laying Claim to the Jewess Pallas Athena

In the spring of 2005, I stumbled upon Barbara Hahn's *The Jewess Pallas Athena* and was struck by the vision of intellectual Jewish women that she describes. According to Hahn, these German-speaking and writing Jewish women were a critical part of Modern German letters, and her book offers glimpses of not only their public writing but also of letters and journals, the intimacies behind these more public works. She shows readers, in other words, the relationships that nurtured and produced these intellectual women. As I read this book on a different register, I noticed how many of these women of letters were also women without children, women whose legacy is their writing.

In some ways, I come to these Jewish women very much as my mother's daughter. I am improvising, looking for ways to make my life choices make sense. I now realize that it is inconceivable to me that my mother, who came from a family of pharmacists, a household without books, a woman who had never had a mentor of her own, would became an English teacher. I suspect that, like me, my mother was able to give to her students part of what she came to imagine she would have wanted from her own teachers but had never gotten. In a sense this is another lesson I learned from her. But, in turning to the Jewesses of German letters, I am also engaging in a kind of imaginative enactment. I am laying claim to an inheritance I can only embrace through an act of imagination. In reading Hahn's work I find I am not alone. There is a history of intellectual Jewish women, modern Jewish women who write and whose writings reveal traces of a different kind of intimacy, a legacy of relationships that are generative, relationships that inspire writing that has both specific and broader audiences. Strangely, I find myself picking up a delicate and broken thread, the legacy of the Jewess Pallas Athena, and instead of trying to recreate it, I carry it forward as inspiration in a different language in a different time and a different place. As I wrote in a review of Hahn's book,[35] Hahn offers feminist scholars, especially contemporary Jewish feminist scholars and writers, insight into an earlier cultural constellation of intellectual and impassioned Jewish women and their writing. As I went on to explain, when Miriam Peskowitz and I edited *Judaism since Gender*[36] in order to address the state of contemporary Jewish feminist scholarship, we hoped that such a legacy already existed. At that time, we had little access to the women Hahn writes about. In fact, we fantasized about precisely such a rich tradition, bookshelves filled with books by intellectual Jewish women, not unlike the account offered decades earlier in Woolf's *A Room of One's Own*. Like Woolf, we wanted books that would have included insights into their relationships with other women, especially their impassioned intellectual relationships with one another. This is, in part, what Hahn offers.[37] She shows us that we are not alone, that there has already been such a thing that we can hold on to as we continue to read and write and teach, and either mother or not mother in the present.[38]

Teacher and Parent, Woman and Writer: Toward a Conclusion

In many ways, this chapter is about my attempts to imagine both an actual and an intended audience for my work. And in this way, I have tried to imagine how I contribute to a future through my writing. This chapter has asked how my often intimate but also quite public writing can contribute to a different future. While completing this chapter, I talked to a good friend and colleague about what I was writing. I told her about how I had found myself writing about my mother. In response to this, she reminded me of a rabbinic dictum, a position I had not fully known that addresses the relationship between teacher and parent.[39] As she explained, there is a tradition that says that when asked to choose between saving the life of one's parent or one's teacher, a man should choose to save his teacher. Of course, my use of the masculine here is deliberate, it is clear that this rabbinic dictum was a masculine fantasy if not an actual enactment; it was about fathers and male teachers. Nevertheless, I am struck that my friend thought of this dictum in relation to what I had told her about this chapter.

For me, the challenge is to resist such stark choices. These contrasts just do not ring true. After all, my mother was my teacher. And for me, part of the legacy of Hahn's German Jewish writers is that they offer a gendered alternative to the authority of ancient rabbis. The Jewesses Hahn writes about included women with and without children who lived rich lives of Jewish letters. For all of these Jewish women, relationships, intimacies and intellectual labors were intertwined. If asked to choose, they would have had to have chosen both or all of their identities, they could not have separated out the teachers and the parents. The identities of these German Jewish women, like those of contemporary

Jewish feminists who also refuse to choose or to split off pieces of them-selves,[40] are rich and complicated. This is, in part, what enabled them to write.

Over the past number of years, I have watched my best friend Miriam's daughter play with her dolls, jump on a trampoline, and fall in love with baseball. I do not want her or any of us to have to choose among these things. And I want to be able to write not knowing for whom my words will resonate. Unlike Mendelsohn, I am not at all sure who will bury me or in what ground I will find my final resting place. And I do not know who will say *Kaddish* for me.[41] What I have learned from my grandmother Mary, from Irena Klepfisz, and from my own mother is that I have some say about these things. However difficult these choices might sometimes feel, I do have some agency in these mat-ters. I need not become the idealized rabbinic teacher to justify my role as a woman writer, a woman without children. To do that would be to refuse to appreciate all of the labors of all of the women who came be-fore me, those with and those without children, as well as my contem-poraries. And I refuse to do that. Instead, I want to imagine more possi-bilities. I want us all to be able to write more and live more fully the lives we choose. In my case this means being able to read and write and teach and mentor, not always having to justify my choices.

Conclusion
Other Ghosts, Other Encounters, Other Communities

Returning to the Tower of Faces, we reconsider the allure of other people's family pictures knowing what we now know about what it means to look at disparate images and legacies next to one another, ordinary and extraordinary stories of loss, images marked by the horrors of the Holocaust and intimate family albums. With all of this in mind, I return to the Tower with my narratives and images of my two grandmothers, my father's stories, as well as the many tales of friends and colleagues who, in reading various sections of this book, have shared their stories with me.

Reentering the Tower, I hope that you, my reader, will also consider bringing your own pictures and stories with you. Instead of being ashamed or embarrassed about coming to this place encumbered with our own losses, we will affirm this practice and make clear how generative it can be. By sharing some of our family stories in a more public way, we will reaffirm the power of ordinary stories and show how they also change over time.

Before we go to the Tower of Faces, I want to think with you a bit more about what happens when we share intimate tales of loss in a more public way. In the process of writing this book, I have had the good fortune to have been able to show drafts of my work to colleagues and friends, including Tania Oldenhage and Michelle Friedman, my former students. And like our conversation in the car after Marianne Hirsch's talk about the Tower of Faces almost ten years ago, this more textual sharing has continued to teach me things about what it means to work collaboratively and what happens when we risk sharing intimate stories with one another through our work. My wager throughout this book has been that as we craft our family stories, as we remember them now, those who read and hear them, especially those who are not a part of our immediate families, make connections. Instead of feeling as if they are interlopers or intruders in someone else's narrative, these accounts bring them in, inviting them to engage with their own memories[1] and tell their own stories.

Intimate Engagements: Other Holocaust Lessons[2]

Early on, I shared much of my preliminary writing with Michelle Friedman. In part, these discussions became a bridge between our relationship as adviser and graduate student and what is now a more collegial engagement. After reading a big chunk of this early writing, parts of which have become the preface and introduction to this book, Michelle, whose mother is a child survivor of the Holocaust and whose dissertation was about next-generation writing by children of survivors, began to talk to me about her father. Michelle's father is not a survivor, and like my father, he grew up in this country. My father's family stories resonated with some of her own father's past. This led Michelle to begin to reconsider the importance of her American Jewish family and its past. In her case, these ordinary stories had been quite literally overshadowed by the Holocaust. In her family, the traumatic legacy of her mother's European Jewish childhood had been so overwhelming that it was hard to remember this other familial past. After she completed her dissertation, Michelle began to write more about the intermingling of different legacies of loss, including different Jewish pasts similar to those in her own family. She began to think about how different kinds of haunting have shaped American Jewish identity, and she wrote about what this looks and sounds like.[3]

By way of contrast, after reading a draft of "Looking Out from under a Long Shadow," Tania Oldenhage wrote to me about a discussion she subsequently had with her partner Markus about their German pasts. This time, my work led to a very different kind of engagement. Tania wrote to me about how she and Markus had discussed how difficult it is for them, as Germans, to relate to Holocaust narratives and yet how they found themselves identifying with some of what I had written.[4] My account touched them, not because what I had written was the same as their experience but rather because it triggered something different. It led them to memories of their own, German memories, the content of which were quite different from my American Jewish stories. As Tania explained, she and Markus talked to each other about how they related and did not relate to Holocaust narratives. She wrote, "I again got a sense that the process of identification that you are concerned with is something unfamiliar to me. I can just vaguely get a sense of the pain involved in this."[5] For Tania and Markus, this too was unfamiliar. As she went on to explain, "These differences should be obvious I guess, but to me they are not so."[6]

Part of what I had written had defamiliarized what Tania and Markus thought they already knew. This had a lot to do with my attempt to grapple with my American Jewish experience as someone without a direct connection to survivors and those who died, the distance between my experience and those of other Jews, including Lori Lefkovitz and Marianna Hirsch, who have more intimate connections to this European past. In light of these multiple American Jewish responses to the Holocaust as I described them, Tania and Markus began to consider the range of German positions they knew.

Quickly, Tania's account of this conversation with Markus moved from the theoretical, the confusion she experienced around the notion of identification as I had described it, and into the telling of a story of their own. Her email to me continued with a new paragraph. There was no transition. That paragraph begins as follows: "At the same time we were both thinking about Markus's father and I don't know if I told you the story before." She then proceeded to tell me the story. "Markus' father was sent to a children's camp during the last years of the war. When he came back he was 12 years old and his entire family had been killed; they lived in one of those cities that were bombed to the ground." She continues, "We thought how odd it is that we never would talk about him as a survivor, even though in some sense he is very much a survivor. I don't think that he ever saw himself in these terms." Groping for the right term, trying to figure out how to talk about this experience given its relation to the Holocaust as well as its difference, Tania went on to say that this had everything to do with their Germanness. According to Tania, Markus's father still understands what happened to him, the loss of his entire family, as a kind of punishment. This happened because they had not done enough to resist the Nazis. And this, in part, explains why Markus's father became, in Tania's terms, a "very rigid Christian" after the war and has remained a devout Christian ever since.

Reading my chapter brought Markus and Tania back to this family legacy. And by not conflating these tales—my American Jewish account of going to the Tower of Faces and wanting to see my family somehow on display there, and their particular German Christian story—Tania and Markus were able to look again at his father's story. They were able to do this not by assuming that Markus's father was a survivor but rather that he survived something traumatic that shaped his life in the context of Nazi Germany and its end. They began to appreciate this legacy of loss and its consequences. And even as Tania shared this story with me, she concluded by saying, "I am telling you this because the story is so different from the ones you are concerned with." As I read it, just telling this story feels risky. We are all-too-often so quick to judge the invocation of other losses in relation to the Holocaust. Somehow just telling another story seems to neutralize or relativize the Holocaust. It is as if simply telling another story, especially a story about a German non-Jewish loss, we are somehow letting the Germans off the hook, relinquishing them of responsibility.[7] But here again, what happens if, as Tania suggests, we are willing to acknowledge and take seriously that these narratives are of a different order and yet still allow ourselves to consider some of the ways that they are, nevertheless, connected? In Tania's most recent work, this has meant looking more carefully at how Christian commemoration of the Holocaust can happen in both Germany and in Switzerland with reference to the Cross without having to make these different traumatic narratives one and the same thing.[8]

It is precisely the acknowledgment of these kinds of differences that enables a form of sharing, that occasions the possibility of having quite different stories stand next to each other without having to make them into versions of the same. Again, I think that this is part of what can, and often does, happen when we view a film like Ravett's *Half-Sister* or look at a book like *Before They Perished . . .* , or even when we read texts such as Mendelsohn's and Rosen's. My hope is that by taking seriously these often private encounters with other people's stories of loss, we might be more able to visit public places of commemoration like the Tower of Faces without fearing what these memorials might evoke in our own memories. This means not knowing what such works might trigger for contemporary viewers and being open to even surprising responses. It also means embracing stories like my own that are not overtly authorized by the museum and the logic of its permanent exhibit. In contrast to that more static version of commemoration, this more intimate kind of engagement just might help us keep alive the memory of the Holocaust and its implications for future generations.

More Ordinary Losses, Other Intimate Lessons

On a different register, another friend and former student, Catherine Staples, read chapter 3, "Secret Stashes," and shared quite a different story. Like my father, Cathy had also lost her mother when she was a very young child. But unlike my father and his siblings, when her father remarried she and her siblings had a much more difficult time adjusting. In response to my puzzlement and confusion around my father's habit of hiding things, his secrecy, Cathy told me that these behaviors made perfect sense. She said that it was obvious. "Of course he hides things," she told me. "Children who lose their mothers hide things. It's about protection. We protect precious symbols of our lives "before" because we already know too well that what we love the most can be taken from us." And then she proceeded to tell me more about her own childhood, her siblings, and their beloved mother who had died. She also talked about the powerful role of hiding and about the stashes that are a part of the texture of her everyday life.

As a part of these conversations, Cathy eventually showed me a photograph of her own, a family picture she has kept hidden for almost forty years. It turned out that this was one of the only photographs she has of her mother. It is a picture of the two of them together, mother and daughter, taken before her mother died. After showing me this photograph, she told me that she was thinking about framing it and, like Jane Lazarre, finally hanging it on a wall in her home.[9] But, even so, there are secrets that continue to be a part of Cathy's life, connecting her and my father in ways that I can never fully fathom.

Another colleague, Marian Ronan, responded specifically to my account of having been named after a grandmother I never knew existed. She wrote and told me about "two disappeared women" from her own family, her father's mother who died when her father was nine and her father's sister who raised him and then died giving birth to her own first child while Marian's father was away serving his country as an American soldier in the Pacific during World War Two, far away from home.[10] These women were American Catholics, but, as with my father, Marian's father's engagement with his mothers was also fraught. As Marian explained, "I have never seen a photo of that grandmother and my father almost never mentioned her." She then went on to say that there were also no pictures of her aunt. In fact, she continued, "Once I was looking at a photo album I'd never seen before, and I turned over a page and the marker said 'Julia Ronan McGowan' but the picture was torn out." This account then led her to tell me a story about her own name. As she explained, she was supposed to have been named after this aunt but at the last minute her father could not go through with it. As she put it, "My father forbade my mother to do it because he thought it would bring me 'bad luck.'" For Marian's father, honoring his sister/mother was fraught, just repeating her name might harm his daughter, a daughter not so different from me. Marian is heir not to one, but to two disappeared women from her father's family, his two lost mothers. My story engendered her telling of this family story.

Returning to the Tower

In a sense, this book has become less and less about the Holocaust and the place of the Holocaust in accounts of contemporary American Jewish identity. By assuming that other losses matter and are part of what we bring with us to places like the Tower of Faces, I have asked other questions. Even so, I remain indebted to the works of Holocaust commemoration and memory. Again and again it has been works of Holocaust memory that have inspired these reflections. It is these works that have taught me the most about the labor of remembrance and the importance of telling stories about the past in the present. And so, we return to the Tower to reconsider more precisely the shifting role of this exhibit in shaping this project.

Before actually going to Washington, I tried to imagine what it would be like to reenter that space having lived with my own family pictures and my memories of that place for so long. I wondered if I could be there and not feel obligated to take on the strong normative stance demanded by the logic of the permanent exhibit and the very architecture of the museum. Could I resist that posture in this most powerful site of American public commemoration of the Holocaust? Could any of us really let our ordinary memories and the images of those of Eishyshok coexist in that space?

Part of my hope en route to the museum was that I would be able to look at the photographs that make up the Tower, images so lovingly gathered by Yaffa Eliach, in some of the ways that I had imagined looking at them when I initially tried to distinguish my readings from Marianne Hirsch's notion of postmemory. I wondered whether I would be able to see the images in the Tower in some of the ways that I could now view those collected by the State Museum at Auschwitz and by Weiss.[11] Although looking at a book alone in private is not the same thing as participating in a public memorial, part of me wanted to just write this ending and say it would be so. I wanted to make these claims metaphorically, but then I got stuck. I realized that I actually had to go back to the museum, something I had not done since my initial visit in 1994, and look at my family photographs—the ones I have written about—next to those in the Tower.[12]

Again, I wondered if one could do what I had been advocating. What if I failed? What if the Tower no longer moved me? I thought about these things as I gathered a few of my family photographs—an image from the secret stash, a copy of the portrait of Lena and Sol, and Mary's portrait—and placed them in a folder to take with me to Washington. I packed these things not being quite sure what I would actually do with them once I got to the museum.

Inside the Museum

In mid-October 2005, having secured a timed ticket into the permanent exhibit, I got on an early morning train from Philadelphia to Washington.[13] It was a beautiful day, unseasonably warm. The sky was clear. Once I arrived at the museum, I picked up my ticket and got into the elevator to begin my tour of the permanent exhibit, which starts on the fourth floor. As I walked out of the elevator's oversized metal doors, the sun was no longer visible. I began to retrace my steps through the museum in virtual darkness. This darkness was familiar. It was part of what I remembered about the museum. In addition to this, there is just something about being in a museum that demands a kind of quiet reverence and that is exacerbated in this place.[14] This day, people whispered, if they spoke at all. The tone was hushed, and this only added to the somber feeling of the place. I had quickly forgotten that it was a beautiful, sunny day.

I took this trip by myself, and the sense that there was no one to check in with, no one to talk to as I moved through the exhibit, was palpable. I wanted to break the aura by talking about it. At times, I satisfied this desire by opening up my notebook and writing down some of my impressions. At other times, I found myself swallowing comments I longed to make. By contrast, on my first trip to the museum I had been with a group, and all I had wanted then was to be by myself. Despite this new desire not to be there alone, a lot of what I experienced was familiar. I had remembered much of the permanent exhibit, its logic and its flow, moving from the Nazi rise to power on the fourth floor down toward the final solution on the third.

Of course, I was both eager and nervous about getting to the Tower of Faces. And it was as I got closer to the Tower that things began to feel different—actually radically different—from how I had remembered the permanent exhibit. I was startled by the room of photographs by Roman Vishniac, a High Modernist display of eight oversized photographs, that visitors enter right before they get to the Tower. I had not remembered this room although it had always been there. In part, I suspect that it was the radically different aesthetics of these two photographic exhibits—how I had remembered the Tower in contrast to this very different photographic display—that I found so jarring.

The room containing the Vishniac photographs is stark and minimalist. It could have been a gallery space in any contemporary art museum. There are so few photographs on display in this room compared to the hundreds that make up the Tower. The eight large images are symmetrically displayed, four on each wall. There are low benches on either side of the room to allow visitors to look more carefully at each of the photographs. At the center of the room is a glass case that draws our attention. In it is a scroll, which only heightens the feeling that this is a sacred Jewish space.[15]

As visitors enter this room, the panel on the wall explains that these are photographs taken by Roman Vishniac between 1935 and 1939 in Poland and Russia.[16] They are familiar images, beautiful, poignant. But what fascinated me more than the photographs was the scroll at the room's center. As I approached the glass case, I started to realize that this was not a Torah scroll as I had assumed. It seemed much too small. Instead, the panel on the case explained that this scroll, which had been rescued from Europe, was a Megillah Esther; it told the story of Purim, the story of how Queen Esther had saved her people from destruction at another historical moment. When such a scroll is read on Purim in an actual place of worship, the mood is neither somber nor reverent. Instead, congregants are often drunk, loud, and raucous—the scene is carnivalesque.

At first I found the placement of this scroll at the center of this room absurd. The invocation of Purim felt bizarre given the somber trappings of the space. Of course, the scroll does contain the story of another almost-destruction of the Jewish people, but that somehow did not solve my problem. The scroll complicated the whole sense of this room as a sacred space. This is why I thought that this room was a new addition to the permanent exhibit. I could not believe that I had not remembered this strange display.[17]

Inside the Tower

Leaving the Vishniac room, I immediately found myself inside the Tower, suspended on a glass bridge that cuts through its center. Despite the fact that the Tower is also comprised of photographs of Jewish life in eastern Europe before the war, there is little else that connects this display to the one I had just left. The space of the bridge is significantly brighter. Light streams in, and there is nothing closed in or contained about this display. The Tower extends up at least another floor above the bridge. This is the visitors' first encounter with the Tower. I remembered it well. Yaffa Eliach, the granddaughter of the town's Jewish photographers, Yitzak Uri Katz and Alte Katz, had created the Tower, designing it as a memorial for the museum. The panel explains that it consists of several hundred photographs of the shtetl of Eishyshok (Ejszyski) where she and her family had once lived.

Although the space felt larger than the room I had just left, it also felt much smaller than how I had remembered it. Over time, the Tower had grown in my imagination. Coming back to the museum this time, the Tower seemed significantly smaller. While on the bridge, I took my time. I tried to look at as many individual images as I could. I moved back and forth, getting closer to the railings on either side of the bridge, struggling to get a better view. I looked up and then down, turning around again and again. As I lingered, I realized that I was also waiting to hear what other people had to say. I wanted to hear the kinds of pronouncements of familiarity and identification that I had first experienced and written about. In these efforts, I was disappointed. Here

The Tower of Faces. Yaffa Eliach Collection, courtesy of the United States Holocaust Memorial Museum.

again, no one was talking. Other visitors seem simply to move through the Tower in silence. Some stopped for a short while, but then they left. Again, I was keenly aware of being alone.

I think that the high modernist aesthetics of the Vishniac display and my discomfort with the Megillah at its center shaped my impressions of the Tower this time around. I felt protective of the ordinary images that make up the Tower. Compared to the Vishniac images, these photographs seemed hardly able to get any attention. And I was newly aware of how difficult it is to see any of them individually. Few have any marks of identification on them, and none are officially labeled.[18] And yet I wanted to take notice of each individual picture. I wanted to compensate for this lack of specificity and to do justice, not to the collection as a whole, but to each photograph.

And, even as I found it difficult to make these distinctions, I kept thinking that the Tower was so much smaller than I had remembered it. I wanted there to be more, more specificity, and just more images, lots more. I longed for the Tower as I had remembered it, even as I realized that I wanted new things this time.

Leaving the bridge and the Tower, I entered the empty white space of the stairwell that takes visitors from the fourth to the third floor,[19] a brief reprieve before we get to the third floor devoted to the Final Solution. At the entrance to this floor, there is a small display focused on Anne Frank that includes a few iconic photographs. This, too, was not a display I had remembered. The otherwise ordinary snapshots of Anne Frank, despite their familiarity, linked her to the Tower. They echoed those family images. Exiting the Anne Frank display, I could not make any more connections between the ordinary images in the Tower and the Final Solution. The graphic photographs that illustrate the Final Solution are nothing like the images in the Tower. These terrible images show how radically different the final solution was from all that came before, the world on display in the Tower.

On this floor, the horrors of the Holocaust are signified by both horrible photographic images and literal objects of destruction. There are mounds of shoes and a case filled with aging hairbrushes and other personal objects; another case contains the mangled remains of eyeglasses once worn by those who were killed and tormented. There are life-sized photographs of mounds of human hair. There are pictures of tattooed flesh, the numbered arms of so many prisoners. There are also images of the tattooed chests of Soviet soldiers captured by the Nazis. These displays are the prelude to the most terrible portion of the museum that takes visitors through a Polish boxcar just like those used to transport millions of Jews to their deaths at places like Auschwitz and Birkenau.

Next to the boxcar is a glass room filled only with the voices of survivors describing life in the camps, a place I remembered well. Here visitors listen to accounts of medical experiments, and roll calls. These spaces are even darker and more hushed than the rest of the museum.

Only after having been through all of this do visitors find themselves reentering the Tower of Faces. This time, the panel on the wall tells us what happened to the Jews of Eishyshok. In September 1941, this town's Jewish community was systematically rounded up and murdered by Nazi mobile killing units. Virtually no one survived.

Marianne Hirsch describes this second entry into the Tower as darker, more contained; but on this visit, I did not experience it that way. Perhaps it was because there were not a lot of visitors and few people were standing above me on the bridge. The space felt brighter and less contained than I had remembered it. And again, the Tower felt much smaller than how I had remembered it. Although visitors can come closer here and even touch some of these pictures, few seemed to do so. Most visitors seemed to rush through this portion of the Tower. At one point, I overheard a little boy trying to find an image that had struck him when he first saw it on the bridge a floor above; he was looking for "a pirate," but he was an exception. Most people left quickly. Few visitors seemed interested in taking another look at these faces, especially not as I was doing.

This space at the bottom of the tower felt hollow to me. As I looked again and again at the images, getting up and sitting back down on the one bench along an outer wall, I did take out my folder and my notebook, trying to look at some of these photographs alongside my own family pictures. I did this discreetly, but quickly realized that the whole effort was not really necessary. It felt forced. Instead, I found myself continuing to try to differentiate between the separate images, longing to appreciate each individually. I became increasingly concerned about their anonymity. Hirsch argues that the anonymity of the Tower contributes to a kind of collective experience, a sense of the loss as a whole, but for me, this vision was difficult to hold on to. I wanted other things from the Tower, things that had not occurred to me the first time I visited the museum.

I began to wonder if Eliach or the museum had given any thought to shifting the display from time to time. Could some of the pictures way out of sight come down and be seen while others took their place? I had a hard time thinking that these images would remain static in this configuration, lifeless and anonymous. I longed for movement and change, precisely what both *Before They Perished . . .* and *The Last Album* attempt to do. And although Eliach offers those interested almost a thousand pages of documentation in her book about Eishyshok, *There Once Was a World: A 900-Year Chronicle of the Shtetl of Eishyshok*, the book does not reproduce the photographs. For those who only know of this place and these faces from their encounter with the Tower at the museum, I felt a keen sense of loss. The anonymity was alienating. It was neither a source of collective engagement nor a comfort. I was also disturbed by this definitive completion of the story of Eishyshok as if the story of the Nazis' destruction of this community was all there was to say.

Returning to the Tower after witnessing the museum's account of the Final Solution seemed overdetermined; it seemed to tell viewers the ending—as if there was a single ending to the narratives of any and all of those depicted in the Tower. Just as Weiss's book and *Before They Per-*

ished . . . try to resist this kind of logic by remaining incomplete, I wanted the Tower to open up. I wanted all of the photographs in the Tower to have stories of their own and for each and every one of them to become more visible.[20] I felt thwarted by the Tower's efforts to so easily complete and contain all of these diverse images within a single narrative of mass destruction. Disappointed, I left the Tower only to find myself entering another stark stairwell.

At the second-floor landing, visitors find an abstract painting, "Consequences," by Sol Lewitt, painted directly on the wall. The painting consists of a series of rectangles framed and reframed. The painting's colors echo those used by the museum in its floor plan, which is also on display in this entry space. As I read it, these two grids—the painting and the museum map—with their identical colors and seemingly different messages ask similar questions: Where are we as visitors, having gone through the first two floors of the permanent exhibit, and where are we in relation to the Holocaust these many years later? The Lewitt painting suggests a more careful consideration of the various frameworks that have shaped not only what we have just seen, but also our understanding of the Holocaust more generally. The painting makes us think about what these templates make visible and what they obscure, as well as the implications of these approaches. Even in abstract terms, Lewitt's painting suggests that he, too, asks viewers to figure out where we are, to make a map and place ourselves in this story and its aftermath; it is a good segue into the themes of the second floor devoted to the aftermath and consequences of the Holocaust.

Ten Years Later: First Encounters

As I left the museum, I thought a lot about how it felt to return and about how many of my first impressions of the Tower were informed by how unexpected those images had once been, how new the museum was then as opposed to now. These impressions were only reaffirmed by my encounter with "Deadly Medicine: Creating the Master Race," a special 10th-anniversary exhibit on display on the first floor. As I walked through this display, I was struck by the unexpected. There were images of the German Hygiene Museum that I had never before seen.[21] There were photographs and panels about the doctors who performed euthanasia and sterilizations on German citizens, especially children. I was horrified to learn that many of these doctors continued to practice medicine for decades after the war. But perhaps most startling for me was the video display that included the voices and faces of victims of these Nazi crimes. I was especially struck by those who had been sterilized as children for being somehow imperfect. Visitors listened as a deaf woman and a woman who had been a child with mental illness both told their stories. It was heartbreaking to hear these accounts.

Perhaps there will always be something about a first encounter that is striking, but in saying this, I do not want to suggest that only a first visit can be meaningful. I am still shaken that I had no memory of the Vishniac room. I also appreciate what it has meant to reconsider my initial impressions of the Tower and to place that story next to this new one. If I had not returned to the museum, I would never have known that I would find the anonymity and static nature of the display so upsetting. These were new impressions informed by my ongoing critical engagement with the power and allure of all kinds of ordinary family photographs and the Tower. As a result of these engagements, the Tower had become for me something else. My story had changed.

What Is It Like?[22]

I know that some of the most powerful ways we deal with loss individually and collectively is through our engagements with other people's sorrows, other people's losses and traumas. Works of Holocaust memory have taught me this lesson. And yet, even these encounters are themselves ephemeral. They, too, change over time. Like texts we read and reread, our ongoing encounters with monuments and memorials are also not static. Here we see and experience different things over time. Our interpretations and critical engagements change.

Again we are reminded that there are no single or definitive lessons to be learned or stories to be told. Instead, through the ongoing interplay between stories, we continue to learn new things about ourselves and others.

For American Jews, at least at this historical moment, coming to terms with loss may continue to be most powerfully articulated in our ongoing efforts to confront the legacies of the Holocaust. And yet, in acknowledging this, we need to be open to how even these narratives change over time. In other words, as I did in my return to the Tower of

Faces and the museum, we continue to learn new things from these encounters. We are forever reminded of the ongoing interplay between remembering and forgetting. In both forgetting and remembering, the
past continues to change. It becomes something dynamic. It changes
with us. Given this, efforts to commemorate the Holocaust must also
remain alive and capable of changing.

Commemoration is dynamic. In order for it to speak to us in the present and not once and for all time, it must not be reduced to any single
interpretation, lesson, or meaning. At their best, recent scholarship in
Holocaust studies, creative texts, and memorials such as the Tower of
Faces trigger such dynamic engagement. They do this because they
touch us in lots of ways, showing us all kinds of things about both the
past and the present. None of these engagements is predictable.

In the process of living with some of these works—the Tower of
Faces, Ravett's film, and the 2,400 photographs from Auschwitz—I
have begun to appreciate anew how memory works, what trauma looks
like, and how legacies of loss echo through time and across generations
in both grand and all-too-ordinary ways.

> Yet *der khurbn* [the disaster] that survivors experience is not general
> but very specific. It is reflected in precious sepia photographs pasted
> into incomplete family albums. It consists of identifiable names, of fa-
> miliar faces of family members, of named streets, stores and schools,
> teammates, friends, libraries, doctors, hospitals, lectures, marches,
> strikes, political allies and enemies—the people, places, and institutions
> that make up the fabric of any human being's ordinary, everyday life. It
> is these specifics and the loss of that ordinary life that survivors remem-
> ber and mourn.[23]

This is how child survivor, poet, and activist Irena Klepfisz describes
what it is that survivors mourn. And as she goes on to explain, they do
not just do this on those specific days officially designated for mourning
or remembrance, but "during all those frequent moments when memory
of childhood or ghettos or camps is triggered by something in the present—an angle of someone's jaw, a special shade of color, a faint smell
of a certain food, a dream. During those moments when the fabric of
our present life tears apart, survivors mourn and mourn again" (133).

Like survivors, all of us live with memories, especially memories of
loss that are triggered in the present not once and for all time, but again

and again in different and often contradictory ways. In this sense, like Klepfisz, we, too, make these kinds of connections and find ourselves transported to other times and other places. For me, family photographs and collections of family images like those that make up the Tower have been the most consistent of these triggers. This is why they have figured so prominently in each and every chapter of this book. These images, Abraham Ravett's photograph of his half sister, the 2,400 pictures from Auschwitz collected in those two incomplete and compelling albums, the photographic images described in Klepfisz's poem, and the faces of the Tower have been the formal connection between the legacy of the Holocaust and my own family. Intimate images have been the glue that holds each chapter together, connecting me to the Holocaust and then changing my relationship with it.

Although I was less impressed with the version of collective remembrance I experienced in the Tower this time, my return helped me clarify how slippery our grasp on the past continues to be. Memory is partial. As I complete this project I am increasingly drawn to the contingencies of memory, the specificity of individual images and stories. These multiplying tales hold out the promise of an ongoing critical and intimate engagement.

I left the museum this time wanting to imagine the Tower in motion, photographs changing place and the addition of labels—ever-expanding panels and explanations as a way of offering visitors more of a sense that there is still work for us to do in the present. This would show in more graphic terms that the work of remembering remains undone and needs our input and labor.[24]

Perhaps this dream of mobility, of the Tower in motion, is my way of giving new life to these pictures, but the more I reconsider the Tower now, the more I hope for such a revision. I want visitors to the museum to take another look at these pictures and not assume they already know their ending. I want them to take more seriously the fact that we have something to contribute to ongoing efforts at commemoration.

As I now see it, at their best, the Tower of Faces or books like *Before They Perished . . .* and *The Last Album* can cross boundaries of time and space and allow many of us with little or no connection to the legacy of the Holocaust to become engaged, to make connections and distinctions. I believe that more specificity, not less, can help make this happen, even if it is much more labor intensive. In this way, I believe that identification can continue to happen; stories can continue to come alive, and, in the process, new and different memories and other stories of loss can be more fully entertained. To really commemorate the Holocaust means to engage with all of these stories in an ever-shifting present. Even if what we learn is partial and incomplete, these efforts help us keep memories alive. Because there is no single authorized narrative, these are not passive encounters. Meanings get made over and over again. And, sometimes, if we are lucky, these efforts can help us forge new kinds of intimacies both within and outside of places like the Tower of Faces.

By unearthing all of these different stories and crafting new accounts in the present, we engage in the labor of remembrance, learning more about ourselves and about others. If we bring this knowledge with us into our relationships with all kinds of others, we might begin to imagine a different future where Michelle and Tania, Markus and Cathy, Marian and I are also somehow connected to you as well as to one another.

Notes

NOTES TO THE PREFACE

1. For a critical take on the use of the "we" in traditional scholarship, see Marianna Torgovnick, "The Politics of the 'We,'" in Marianna Torgovnick, ed., *Eloquent Obsessions: Writing Cultural Criticism* (Durham, NC: Duke University Press, 1994), 260–277. I thank Jennifer Hammer, my editor at NYU Press, for urging me to consider this strategy.

2. In eastern European Ashkenazi families, children are often named for the dead and share a Hebrew or Yiddish name. The child's English name often begins with the same first letter of the name of the dead relative for whom they were named, and is not always the same name. I am Laura and my grandmother was Lena. My first cousins, each also named for Lena Levitt, are Layne and Linda. For more on this see chapter 2, where I discuss this issue more fully.

3. *The American Heritage Dictionary*, 4th edition, s.v. "unravel" and "ravel." It is interesting that the word "ravel" is used both as a synonym for "unravel" and as its opposite. The first definition for "ravel" is presented as follows: "To separate the fibers or threads of (cloth, for example); unravel." The second definition continues, explaining that to ravel is also "to clarify by separating the aspects of." By way of contrast, the third definition offers the opposite meaning. It reads, "To tangle or complicate."

4. On the various Penelopes as a figure of both scorn and valor, see Miriam Peskowitz, *Spinning Fantasies: Rabbis, Gender, and History* (Berkeley: University of California Press, 1997), "Introduction: Stories about Spinners and Weavers," 1–25.

5. In order not to reify either the term "Shoah" or "Holocaust" and to acknowledge the use of both of these terms in the various sources I site, I will use both terms more or less interchangeably throughout this book. For more on the history of these terms and the nuances in their meanings, see James Young, *Writing and Rewriting the Holocaust: Narrative and the Consequences of Interpretation* (Bloomington: Indiana University Press, 1988), especially chapter 5, "Names of Holocaust: Meaning and Consequences," 83–98.

6. Between 1979 and 1989 both of my uncles, my father's brother and his brother-in-law, died, and so did my grandfather.

7. This was the first time I would consciously take his place, although, as I will suggest throughout this book, in many ways in this family I very much represent my father. I thank Michelle Friedman for calling my attention to this notion of "taking my father's place" and connecting this to the quite literal and powerful performative moves made by Deb Filler in her film "Punch Me in the Stomach" (Canada and New Zealand, 1997). Personal correspondence, Michelle Friedman, May 2005. For a powerful account of Filler's performance, see Michelle Friedman, "The Labor of Remembrance," in Laurence Silberstein, ed., *Mapping Jewish Identities* (New York: NYU Press, 2000), 97–121.

8. I am not sure that my father would have said it if he had been there; in fact, I suspect that he, too, would not have told the rabbi this part of Mary's story.

9. I don't want to use this space to detract from my more celebratory vision of Mary, but I do need to note that her generosity toward my mother was especially striking given my maternal grandmother's less enthusiastic response to my parents' marriage. It turned out that my maternal grandmother even went so far as to send a less than kind letter expressing her disappointment about this marriage to none other than Mary herself. Yet even this letter did not stop Mary from embracing my mother.

10. As my mother read a draft of this, she drew connections between her hopes for my brother and Mary's hopes for my father. May 2005.

11. Because we were not allowed to have such a service on campus, we had to meet in a student's apartment. And because the seminary would not allow us to borrow one of its Torahs for these services, we had to make complicated arrangements with the Conservative congregation in town to borrow one of their Torahs each month. Despite the fact that egalitarian prayer was a common practice in many, if not most, Conservative congregations in 1982, these practices were completely absent from the official practices of the seminary. Even a student-initiated egalitarian service could not take place anywhere on the Jerusalem campus. The irony in all of this was that only a year later, all of these gender policies changed. In 1983, the seminary began to accept women into their rabbinical program, and the institution implemented egalitarian practices at its various campuses, including its campus in Jerusalem. For me, these changes came too late.

12. *The American Heritage Dictionary*, 4th edition, s.v. "revelation."

13. George is the son of one of my grandfather's older brothers, who, unlike most of the family, spelled their last name with an "a." Recently, my father told me that on his birth certificate his last name was originally spelled "Leavitt" and that he had to have it changed when he went into the army. He had always spelled it without the "a." Conversation May 2005. My father's cousin Frances Levitt, the daughter of another of my grandfather's brothers, and her family always spelled their name "Levitt."

14. What I did not know until years later was that there is a penciled note on the back of the actual photograph that reads "Uncle Sol and Aunt Lena." The photograph seems to have been taken in the late 1920s or early 1930s. My father is unsure about whether it was taken before or after he was born in 1926.

15. The quality of the photocopy my father made was quite poor. At the time, there were no special technologies for copying photographs. Later copies made of other images in my father's stash were copied using these more sophisticated technologies in the late 1990s.

16. Oddly, it is only copies of copies of this image that circulate in my family. Over the past twenty years, my father has photocopied, color copied, photographed, and rephotographed this picture, especially the half of the picture with his mother, numerous times. When I ask to see the original, he all-too-often comes up with more and more copies of these photographs of the photograph. It was only when I turned over the image we think of now as the original that I came to wonder about its very originality. It, too, is a copy. Summer 2004.

NOTES TO THE INTRODUCTION

1. Michael S. Roth, "*Hiroshima Mon Amour*: You Must Remember This," in Robert A. Rosenstone, ed., *Reinventing History: Film and the Construction of a New Past* (Princeton, NJ: Princeton University Press, 1995), 91–101. All subsequent references to this essay will be in the text. I write about Roth's reading of the film because I got to the film by reading Roth. His work powerfully shaped my viewing of the film, helping me make the connections I draw between my father, myself, and the woman in the film.

2. For another reading of this important film in a different but related set of questions that explore memory and witnessing in other than visual terms, see Ariella Azoulay, "The [Blind] Gesture: Hiroshima," in *Death's Showcase: The Power of Image in Contemporary Democracy* (Cambridge, MA: MIT Press, 2001), 76–88. In this essay Azoulay connects Marie Ange Guilleminot's "Hiroshima Collection" to the film. Unlike the woman in the film, however, as Azoulay explains, Guilleminot insists on the fact that she saw nothing in Hiroshima and instead relies on the tactile; she draws on her body memory to remember.

3. Although there are alternate ways of reading this silence, I leave that to other critics to explore. I rely on Michael Roth's reading of the film precisely because it has helped me to appreciate this particular aspect of this silence.

4. This is an issue I deal with more intimately in chapter 2 and more fully in chapter 3 when I discuss my father's efforts to hide away the story of his mother's death and the kinds of enactments that he engaged in that may have allowed him to keep his mother's memory alive, at least in his own psyche. I

was also recently reminded of this problem and the power of this desire to keep the wound of loss alive by refusing to forget as I read one of the intertwining stories of traumatic loss that are at the heart of Kate Atkinson's novel, *Case Histories* (New York and Boston: Little, Brown, 2004). Contrasting the way a father and daughter deal with the death of another daughter, Atkinson writes, "and although they talked on the phone and e-mailed each other, they rarely talked about Laura. Jennifer had never liked the pain of remembering what had happened, but for Theo it was the pain that kept Laura alive in his memory. He was afraid that if it ever began to heal she would disappear" (89).

5. This is connected to Ernestine Schlant's notion of melancholy as ongoing and not somehow resolved by mourning, especially in relation to the Holocaust, in her discussion of the writing of W. G. Sebald. As Schlant explains, "Sebald defines melancholy not as *sui generis* but as a form of the labor of mourning (*Trauerarbeit*)." See Ernestine Schlant, *The Language of Silence: West German Literature and the Holocaust* (New York: Routledge, 1999), 233.

6. Given that the title of this poem is a Yiddish term, I have chosen to use italics and capitalization to signify that this is the title of a poem. The use of both italics and quotation marks seemed redundant. For a copy of the poem still in print, see Irena Klepfisz, *A Few Words in the Mother Tongue: Poems Selected and New (1971–1990)* (Portland, OR: Eighth Mountain Press, 1990), 183–200. In my reading of the poem I will be referring to the more accurate version of the poem first published in Irena Klepfisz, *Keeper of Accounts* (Watertown, MA: Persephone Press, 1982). See also Michelle Friedman, "Reckoning with Ghosts: Second Generation Holocaust Literature and the Labor of Remembrance," diss., Bryn Mawr College, 2001.

7. See either *Keeper of Accounts*, 85–87, or *A Few Words in the Mother Tongue*, 198–200, for the full text of this section of *Bashert*.

8. *Keeper of Accounts*, 85.

9. *Keeper of Accounts*, 87.

10. Klepfisz writes about this loss of self most profoundly in sections two and three. In section three, the narrator recalls what it was like for her as a child to have to stand in for all of the children who died in the Holocaust, especially at the annual commemoration of the Warsaw Ghetto Uprising that took place in the community of survivors where she grew up. In those moments, she would viscerally take on the legacies of all of these children, allowing their ghosts to inhabit her body.

11. I am indebted to Michelle Friedman for this notion of "reckoning with ghosts." It is a central argument in her dissertation.

12. Angelika Bammer offers a powerful account of what it means to make these kinds of connections between very different kinds of losses in her account of German war memories in Hamburg. She writes: "The language of public memory, I propose, is always inflected by the particular. It is the particular that

inscribes the communal memory space of a cemetery, both individual grave sites and collective memorials, with the specificity of personal loss; a name, the dates of a life, the lines of relationship, the signs of grief and love. The particular responses to a public memorial—a tribute of flowers, an angry graffiti, a site neglected or treated with care—casts collective memory sites within the idiom of personal significance. However it is not just in the details of a particular articulation that the specificity of a historical memory manifests itself. It is also in the weight given to a particular aspect of that memory, the emphasis added or taken away, that the cumulative press of individual memories as they converge shapes the collective memory of a given time and place" (355). Angelika Bammer, "Hamburg Memories," *German Quarterly Review,* 74.4 (Fall 2001), 355–367.

13. This is very much connected to Marianne Hirsch's notion of the aesthetics of what she calls "postmemory," and yet it also differs from Hirsch in the ways I suggest in chapter 1 of this book. See Hirsch, *Family Frames,* 241–268.

14. This dynamic is also something I will return to as I address Abraham Ravett's experimental film *Half-Sister* in chapter 2. In that case, I participated in this dynamic by not wanting to write about the film. Like Ravett, I kept the possibilities of animation alive by not pinning down the meaning of the film once and for all. In a sense, that animating spirit, that magic, enabled me to keep my own dead somehow potentially revivable.

15. Although for Klepfisz the connotations of the term *bashert* are decidedly ominous, it does have more positive connotations. Klepfisz's explanation of the term given on the very first page of the poem reads, "*Bashert* (Yiddish)—inevitable, (pre)destined." In sharp contrast to the meanings associated with *bashert* in Klepfisz's poem, there is a strong romantic tradition linked to this term as well that suggests that one's "*bashert*" is one's romantic partner in a cosmic pairing. The pair is inevitably fated to find each other. This is similar to the notion of soul mates.

16. Michael André Bernstein, *Foregone Conclusions: Against Apocalyptic History* (Berkeley: University of California Press, 1994), 124.

17. I am extremely moved by the work of scholars in Performance Studies who challenge this notion of text. I am increasingly convinced that they are right that the reduction of complex works to "texts" does not allow us to address crucial aspects of these works. At the moment I find myself caught at the crossroads. I began this work very much using the language of close reading to describe how I engage with the critical, imaginative, and commemorative works at the heart of this book, knowing full well that many of the ways I engage were not fully encompassed by the notion of reading, hence my equivocation. For a brilliant discussion of these issues see Marianne Hirsch, "What's Wrong with These Terms? A Conversation with Barbara Kirshenblatt-Gimblett and Diana Taylor," *PMLA* 120.5 (October 2005), 1497–1508. I am also especially grateful to Ann Pellegrini, Barbara Browning, and Barbara Kirshenblatt-Gimblett for

their thoughtful engagement with portions of chapter 3 of this manuscript when I presented some of this work at NYU. Laura Levitt, "Telling Stories Otherwise (or Revisiting My Father's Visual Archive)," Distinguished Lecture, Center for Religion and Media, New York University, New York, March 2006. I am also grateful to Ann Pellegrini and her students in her graduate seminar for reading and discussing with me chapter 4. Ann Pellegrini, "Getting Schooled: Performance, Politics, Pedagogy," Graduate Seminar, Performance Studies, New York University, New York, March 2006.

18. On this issue of sentimentality and the dangers involved when those whose relation to the Holocaust is indirect and mediated identify with the Holocaust, see the following essays included in Ruth-Ellen Boetcher Joeres and Marjorie Gelus, eds., *Women in German Yearbook 2003: Feminist Studies in German Literature and Culture,* Vol. 19 (Lincoln: University of Nebraska Press, 2004): Pascale Bos, "Positionality and Postmemory in Scholarship on the Holocaust," 50–74; Karyn Ball "Unspeakable Differences, Obscene Pleasures: The Holocaust as an Object of Desire," 20–49; Elizabeth R. Baer and Hester Baer, "Postmemory Envy?" 75–99; and Lisa Disch and Leslie Morris, "Departures: New Feminist Perspectives on the Holocaust," (9–19). I build on the work of Marianne Hirsch and her notion of postmemory because she risks precisely these kinds of identifications and I appreciate that. See Marianne Hirsch, *Family Frames: Photography, Narrative and Postmemory* (Cambridge, MA: Harvard University Press, 1997), especially chapter 8, "Past Lives," 241–270. I am weary of the cautions posed by some of these authors because I do not think it possible to dictate correct responses to works of art, commemoration, or literature. Here I follow James Young in his notion of collected memory as opposed to collective memory, noting that there is a range of responses to these works. See James Young, *Writing and Rewriting the Holocaust: Narrative and the Consequences of Interpretation* (Bloomington: Indiana University Press, 1988). For a fuller exploration of these questions, see chapter 1, where I offer a close reading of Hirsch's text in relation to a reading of the Tower of Faces in the USHMM.

19. In *Jews and Feminism: The Ambivalent Search for Home* (New York: Routledge, 1997), I began writing about both family pictures as well as family stories. The book is framed by an image of my maternal grandmother and in the first chapters I began writing about my father.

20. Ann Weiss, *The Last Album: Eyes from the Ashes of Auschwitz-Birkenau* (New York: W. W. Norton, 2001); Ann Weiss, *The Last Album: Eyes from the Ashes of Auschwitz-Birkenau, Updated and Expanded* (Philadelphia: Jewish Publication Society, 2005).

21. Kersten Brandt, Hanno Loewy, and Krystyna Olesky, eds., *Before They Perished . . . Photographs Found in Auschwitz* (Oświęcimiu: Państwowe Muzeum Auschwitz-Birkenau, 2001).

22. The museum mounted a permanent exhibit of these photographs on the walls of remembrance at Birkenau's sauna building in 2001. On these efforts by the museum, see Teresa Świebocka, "Archival Collections at the Auschwitz-Birkenau State Museum," www.rtrfoundation.org/webart/chappolteresa.pdf.

23. Jonathan Rosen, *The Talmud and the Internet: A Journey between Worlds* (New York: Farrar, Straus and Giroux, 2000); Daniel Mendelsohn, *The Elusive Embrace: Desire and the Riddle of Identity* (New York: Vintage Books, 2000).

NOTES TO CHAPTER 1

1. My efforts here to think about the legacies of ordinary and extraordinary loss together in relation to American Jews and the Holocaust have been greatly enhanced and inspired by the efforts of many queer scholars who hold together precisely these kinds of fraught and tense relationships between different kinds and different magnitudes of loss. See Ann Cvetkovich, *An Archive of Feelings: Trauma, Sexuality, and Lesbian Public Cultures* (Durham, NC: Duke University Press, 2003); Ann Cvetkovich and Ann Pellegrini, eds., "Public Sentiments," *The Scholar and the Feminist Online,* 2.1 (Summer 2003), www.barnard.edu/sfonline; David Eng and David Kazanjian, eds., *Loss: The Politics of Mourning* (Berkeley: University of California Press, 2003). In part, *Loss* is both closest and most removed from my project here. On the one hand, the editors attempt to displace the centrality of the Holocaust in scholarship on mourning and trauma to make room for considering all kinds of other losses; on the other hand, the Nazi Holocaust disappears. It is an absent presence in this powerful text. Although I am moved and persuaded by the editors' efforts to address other losses more fully, I also regret that in the process the text as a whole displaces the Holocaust. Decentering might have been a more instructive approach to shifting the focus of trauma studies away from an almost exclusive engagement with the Nazi Holocaust. As a Jewish Studies scholar writing about other less extraordinary Jewish losses, I cannot make this kind of move in my own work, nor do I find it productive. In the case of this book, such a move would do violence to the ways that the Holocaust has become a part of even the most ordinary tales of Jewish loss. I thank Ann Pellegrini for recommending that I look at many of these works.

2. This discussion also raised the question of humor in the face of the Holocaust. Who gets to play with this legacy? Why are some works funny while others are decidedly not? See the discussion of Holocaust humor in Tania Oldenhage, " 'Holocaust Laughter'? A German Response to *Punch Me in the Stomach,*" in William L. Blizek and Ronald R. Burke, eds., *Journal of Religion and Film* 1.2 (October 1997); Department of Philosophy and Religion: University of Nebraska at Omaha, http://www.unomaha.edu/jrf/holocaust.htm. See also the

heated discussion around the appropriateness of Bennini's *Life is Beautiful* and the contrast between the recent reception of Mel Brooks's *The Producers* on Broadway and the controversy over the show "Mirroring Evil" at the Jewish Museum. Norman Kleeblatt, ed., *Mirroring Evil: Nazi Imagery/Recent Art* (New Brunswick, NJ: Rutgers University Press, 2001); Laura Levitt, "Refracted Visions: A Critique of 'Mirroring Evil: Nazi Imagery/Recent Art,' " *Studies in Gender and Sexuality*, 6.2 (Spring 2005), 199–216.

3. Ordinary is defined as an adjective meaning commonly encountered, usual; of no exceptional ability, degree, or quality; average; of inferior quality; second-rate; having immediate rather than delegated jurisdiction, as a judge. As a noun, in ecclesiastical usage it refers to the part of the Mass that remains unchanged from day to day but is commonly used to mean the usual or normal condition or course of events. *The American Heritage Dictionary*, 4th edition, s.v. "ordinary." I use the notion of ordinary to describe the Jews I write about as both commonly encountered in the United States and seemingly not good enough, inferior, less worthy than others to claim their place in Jewish history and memory. This also echoes the dynamics of liberal inclusion that produce subjects, in this case American Jews, who try too hard, who never feel quite like they are worthy of claiming their Jewish and/or their American identities. See Laura Levitt, *Jews and Feminism: The Ambivalent Search for Home* (New York: Routledge, 1997), especially the introduction and chapter 1.

My focus on the ordinary is also influenced by the title of Christopher Browning's powerful study of everyday German soldiers and their role in the Holocaust. Christopher Browning, *Ordinary Men* (New York: Harper Perennial, 1992).

4. Peter Novak, *The Holocaust in American Life* (Boston: Houghton Mifflin, 1999).

5. Gary Weissman, *Fantasies of Witnessing: Postwar Efforts to Experience the Holocaust* (Ithaca, NY: Cornell University Press, 2004).

6. Ernst van Alphen, *Caught by History: Holocaust Effects in Contemporary Art, Literature, and Theory* (Stanford: Stanford University Press, 1997).

7. Susan Rubin Suleiman, *Risking Who One Is: Encounters with Contemporary Art and Literature* (Cambridge, MA: Harvard University Press, 1994). See especially Suleiman's introduction on the question of who are one's contemporaries, "The Risk of Being Contemporary," 1–12.

8. For my generation of American Jews, by and large, this was the role of Israel. It was, as my father always told me, our safety net. It was there just in case. It was the only place that would always be open to Jews no matter what.

9. See Laura Levitt, "Intimate Engagements: A Holocaust Lesson," *Nashim* 7 (Spring 2004), 190–205, and Shelley Hornstein, Laura Levitt, and Laurence

Silberstein, eds., *Impossible Images: Contemporary Art after the Holocaust* (New York: NYU Press, 2003).

10. On some of the shortfalls of van Alphen's work, especially his final chapter, see Susan Shapiro, "The Return(s) of the Uncanny in Post-Holocaust Discourse," in Marc Raphael, ed., *The Representation of the Holocaust in Literature and Film* (Williamsburg, VA: College of William and Mary Press, 2003), 113–138. For me, there is something too neat about what van Alphen does when he tries to "overcome the uncanny" at the conclusion of his text. Susan Shapiro systematically demonstrates why this is a problem, challenging the theoretical as well as the material foundations of his argument for overcoming the uncanny through the sublime. See van Alphen, "Sublimity in the Home, Overcoming Uncanniness," in *Caught by History*, 193–205.

11. It is not surprising, given this preoccupation, that van Alphen was a contributor to *Mirroring Evil*, the exhibition catalog to the show at the Jewish Museum. As I have suggested, in New York the furor was all about challenging taboos around the Holocaust and its representation. See *Impossible Images* for more on this question of challenging Holocaust taboos in visual culture.

12. The account I present here is intentionally schematic. It is not intended to be a thorough account of the exhibition but rather the impressions that have lingered. For a more careful and systematic account, see my reading of Marianne Hirsch's account of the Tower of Faces and how it functions within the Holocaust Memorial Museum later in this chapter.

13. This process is something that I have also experienced. In *Jews and Feminism*, I told the story of my father's uncle Shmuel. I told the story as my father had told it to me only to discover after the book was published that Shmuel had been a prisoner of war after being captured as a soldier in the Soviet army. This is what accounted for his diminished health. I am grateful to my second cousin Phil Pearl for offering me this other explanation and correcting what my father had told me.

14. This too is not a simple matter, as Daniel Mendelsohn made clear as he discussed his then book in process, a book about his relatives who died in the Holocaust. Even those with such relatives know very little, and trying to figure out what can be known is fraught. These are precisely the kinds of questions Mendelsohn addresses in this work. Daniel Mendelsohn, presentation, Temple University, May 2004. As I was completing this book, Mendelsohn published his book to great critical acclaim, Daniel Mendelsohn, *The Lost: A Search for Six of the Six Million* (New York: HarperCollins, 2006).

15. After describing my project to Peter Wissoker, an acquisitions editor at Temple University Press, he shared with me a story about his own family and their literal efforts to find their connections to the Holocaust. After extensive research they discovered a distant relative whose life had been lost in the Holo-

caust. This revelation was met with great joy and excitement. The family was somehow made more real. They were a part of 20th-century Jewish history in a way they had never been before this discovery. I am grateful to Peter for sharing this story with me. Phone conversation, May 2003.

16. This logic was also at the heart of the museum's use of "identity cards" to be carried throughout the museum. Initially these cards were to encourage visitors to literally identify with a single individual and see what happened to him or her at various points in his or her life that correspond to the temporal logic of the permanent exhibit. I thank Ruth Ost for reminding me of this connection. See Andrea Liss, "The Identity Card Project and the Tower of Faces at the United States Holocaust Memorial Museum," in *Trespassing through Shadows: Memory, Photography, and the Holocaust* (Minneapolis: University of Minnesota Press, 1998), 13–38. See also Susan Derwin's account of the plotting of the Wiesenthal Museum of Tolerance in Los Angeles: Susan Derwin, "Sense and/or Sensation: The Role of the Body in Holocaust Pedagogy," in *Impossible Images*, 245–259, as well as Wendy Brown's critical reading of the Museum of Tolerance: "Tolerance as Museum Object: The Simon Wiesenthal Center Museum of Tolerance," in *Regulating Aversion: Tolerance in the Age of Identity and Empire* (Princeton, NJ: Princeton University Press, 2006), 107–148.

17. In this project, I look specifically at this mythic narrative, but I also want to acknowledge that there is another and related narrative, and that is the story of the State of Israel and the re-creation of a Jewish homeland in Palestine. On these issues and especially the interrelationship between these stories, see Sidra Ezrahi, *Booking Passage: Exile and Homecoming in Modern Jewish Imagination* (Berkeley: University of California Press, 2000).

18. I am also interested in the various narratives, images, and stories that other non-eastern European Jews might bring to the museum, much less non-Jewish visitors. Here I would be especially curious about the kinds of Jewish family stories someone like the American Jewish artist Shimon Attie, whose family comes from Syria, might bring to this exhibit. This kind of identification across these Jewish legacies especially in relation to the Holocaust is not something that Attie has addressed thus far in his work, although he has done some work on American Jewish memory with his "Between Dreams and History," where he projected writing on the walls of the Lower East Side of Manhattan in 1998. See Michelle Friedman's discussion of this work in relation to his work on Holocaust memory in her essay, "Haunted by Memory: American Jewish Transformations," in *Impossible Images*, 31–50.

19. Marianne Hirsch, *Family Frames: Photography Narrative and Postmemory* (Cambridge, MA: Harvard University Press, 1997).

20. Laura Levitt, *Jews and Feminism: The Ambivalent Search for Home* (New York: Routledge, 1997).

21. Michelle Friedman and Tania Oldenhage accompanied me to Hirsch's

lecture. Tania Oldenhage's dissertation became the basis for her book, *Parables for Our Time: Rereading New Testament Scholarship after the Holocaust* (New York: Oxford University Press, 2000). Michelle Friedman completed her dissertation in 2001: Michelle Friedman, "Reckoning with Ghosts: Second Generation Holocaust Literature and the Labor of Remembrance," diss., Bryn Mawr College, 2001. See also Michelle Friedman, "The Labor of Remembrance," in Laurence Silberstein, ed., *Mapping Jewish Identities* (New York: NYU Press, 2000), 97–121, and Michelle Friedman, "Haunted by Memory," in *Impossible Images*, 31–50.

22. It was at this talk that I first heard about the conference Hirsch was organizing at Dartmouth and decided to attend. For more on that conference and the issues raised, see Marianne Hirsch, ed., *The Familial Gaze* (Hanover, NH: University of New England Press, 1999); see my afterword, "Blurring the Familial: An Afterword," 343–348. For a different take on issues raised at the conference and a specific engagement with how American Jews use family photographs to construct their American and Jewish identities, see Laura Levitt, ed., "Changing Focus: Family Photography and American Jewish Identity," *The Scholar and the Feminist Online* 1.3 (Winter 2003), www.barnard.edu/sfonline.

23. There would be many more to come. See Edward Linenthal, *Preserving Memory: The Struggle to Create America's Holocaust Museum* (New York: Columbia University Press, 2001); Oren Stier, *Committed to Memory: Cultural Mediation of the Holocaust* (Amherst: University of Massachusetts Press, 2003); Yaffa Eliach's *There Once was a World: A 900-Year Chronicle of the Shtetl of Eishyshok* (Boston: Back Bay Books, 1998).

24. This is similar to the placement/emplotment of the Klarsfeld photographs of the French children and their families who were deported as they are figured in the Jewish Heritage Museum in New York, at least as it was originally conceived. Although the museum has undergone a reconfiguration, this portion of the permanent collection remains in place.

25. I use Lori Lefkovitz's first name throughout this discussion because we are friends. It also needs to be noted that Lori was not the only child of survivors in the room, although she was the one person who positioned herself, helpfully troubling some of the operative assumptions that had shaped the discussion to that point. Others in attendance included Julia Epstein, the host for this lecture. See Julia Epstein and Lori Hope Lefkovitz, eds., *Shaping Losses: Cultural Memory and the Holocaust* (Urbana and Chicago: University of Illinois Press, 2001). Michelle Friedman was also one of the children of survivors in attendance.

26. After reading a draft of this introduction, Lori Lefkovitz wrote to me: "It's funny that I no longer even recall having shared that the Tower creeped me out (though I am sure that it did)—and am chastened that the comment had a dampening effect on your own response. . . . For me that fact alone deepens

your argument about entitlement, images, and subjectivity, adding the layer that in our own subjective response, we often cannot imagine how our reactions not only intersect with those of others but interfere with those of others." E-mail to Laura Levitt, June 2004.

27. Although some of this is also a part of Shimon Attie's work as Hirsch suggests, there are again important distinctions that need to be made. In "Sights Unseen," Attie very much locates his work solely in Europe. These installations do not bring together legacies from America and from Europe. In Attie's work are layers of European memory revisited there and in other work, the various layers of American pasts recollected here. The geographic distance between these works keeps these legacies apart, and I long to see what happens as they are brought together. What might it look like if the Lower East Side project "Between Dreams and History" were brought together with "Sights Unseen," if images or writings from the same moment in time but in these very distinct geographical locations were seen together? For Attie, geography continues to separate these similar engagements. The works share formal likeness but are not connected to each other. For a powerful reading of Attie's work in relation to another artist who brings these geographies and temporalities together through music, see Michelle Friedman's "Haunted by Memory." Friedman offers a reading of Stephen Reich's "Different Trains" in order to make a strong case for this kind of layering of different pasts and different memories. I am indebted to her for helping me appreciate this problem.

28. This impression was reinforced about a year later when I heard Hirsch present a version of what would become her essay, "Surviving Images: Holocaust Photographs and the Work of Postmemory," *Yale Journal of Criticism* 14.1 (Spring 2001), 5–38. At that presentation Hirsch was questioned about this issue of postmemory and its clear links to a single generation, the generation of children of survivors and exiled Jews. Barbie Zelizer and Liliane Weissberg were in the audience for that talk, as were many of their students, who were clearly a generation or two removed from those included in postmemory. Hirsch's essay "Surviving Images" is reprinted in Barbie Zelizer, ed., *Visual Culture and the Holocaust* (New Brunswick, NJ: Rutgers University Press, 2000), 215–246. Also included in this collection is an essay by Weissberg, "In Plain Sight," 13–27.

29. Again I want to reiterate the tensions Hirsch herself describes between some of the various writers and artists of this generation; see especially the opening sections of "Past Lives," the final chapter of *Family Frames,* especially 241–246.

30. On this question of ghosts, see Avery Gordon, *Ghostly Matters: Haunting and the Sociological Imagination* (Minneapolis: University of Minnesota Press, 1997).

31. For a clearer account of the ways Lori Lefkovitz's position differs from

Hirsch's, see Lori Lefkovitz, "Inherited Memory and the Ethics of Ventriloquism," in *Shaping Losses,* 220–230. In this essay, Lefkovitz offers what she describes as "an alternative to the concept of postmemory through a reading of ambiguity in a family photograph." As she goes on to explain, her notion of inherited memory is about ambivalence. For Lefkovitz, even as a child of survivors, what she experiences is her own "dynamic, confused, and mixed reaction to the 'entitlements' of proximity to the Holocaust." E-mail to Laura Levitt, June 2004. Again I am grateful to Lori for her help in clarifying and nuancing these distinctions even for children of survivors. This is something I conjecture, but I appreciate having this reference back to her essay to help substantiate the claim.

32. For more on this notion of Holocaust effects, see van Alphen, *Caught by History.*

33. This helps explain the differences among and between the various French Jewish writers and artists Hirsch discusses as well as the differences between Lori Lefkovitz's stance and Hirsch's. Some of these writers and artists include Christian Boltanski, Henri Raczymow, Alain Finkelkraut, and the psychotherapist Nadine Fresco. For her discussion of these artists and writers, see *Family Frames,* 241–246.

34. This interaction and critical engagement is something I will return to in my conclusion as I consider the broader implications of my telling my ordinary family story of loss to a broader audience. In that context I return to my relationship with these two women in the context of the writing of this book and what those interactions have enabled. Here I am especially interested in the way our work on the Holocaust is in our conversations, how we have inspired each other, and how we remain very much in conversation across the vast differences between us.

35. See Susan Shapiro's powerful critique of van Alphen's conclusion and her insistence on the power of haunting as depicted in the fiction of W. G. Sebald: Susan Shapiro, "The Return(s) of the Uncanny in Post-Holocaust Discourse."

NOTES TO CHAPTER 2

1. Of course this is not the only story to tell. Both on its own and in relation to the Holocaust, Zionism and the creation of the State of Israel has made space central to 20th-century Jewish identity. For a powerful account of this legacy in Jewish imagination, see Sidra Ezrahi, *Booking Passage: Exile and Homecoming in the Modern Jewish Imagination* (Berkeley: University of California Press, 2000). Ezrahi offers a compelling argument for the relation between exile and homecoming, especially in relation to the Holocaust and Israel, as well as why increasingly the rematerialization of Jewish imagination in Israel/Palestine is

fraught. See Laura Levitt, Review of *Booking Passage*, *Jewish Quarterly Review*, 42.1–2 (July–October 2001), 237–242. For a powerful critique of Zionist discourses, especially within the State of Israel, see Laurence Silberstein, *The Postzionist Debates* (New York: Routledge 1999).

2. See Jonathan Boyarin on this issue of Jews finding a place in time vs. physical space, in his essay, "Palestine and Jewish History," *Storm out of Paradise: The Politics of Jewish Memory* (Minneapolis: University of Minnesota Press, 1992), 116–129. See also Walter Benjamin, "Theses on the Philosophy of History," in *Illumination: Essays and Reflections* (New York: Schocken, 1968), 253–264.

3. In part, this disconnect is also a kind of evasion. We choose to evade the awkwardness of this in-between time between memory and history. In a somewhat different context, Carol Mavor describes this in terms of adolescence and its queerness. She writes, "With grave disappointment . . . we choose to evade the awkwardness of adolescence in favor of finding, rediscovering, reading our fantasy of the child." Citing the literary scholar Joseph Litvak, she continues, " 'But if the structural intermediacy of adolescence accounts for its reputation as that awkward age, what is the content of this awkwardness? In our eagerness to reclaim the child, inner or otherwise, do we seek to evade (or with greater cunning, indirectly to reach) her even more embarrassing, and even more exciting older sibling?' " Carol Mavor, *Becoming: The Photographs of Clementina, Viscountess Hawarden* (Durham, NC: Duke University Press, 1999), xxxii. I was struck while reading Mavor with the similarity between the adolescence that she writes about and the in-between, the awkward historical legacy of those closest to us in time. They are neither our ancestors, far way and thus made purer by distance, nor are they our contemporaries.

4. In the case of the Tower, the images are not individually labeled, they are identified together. For more on this question, see my final reading of the Tower in the conclusion.

5. As an example of this, I believe that the artist Judy Chicago traces her roots to the Vilna Gaon.

6. On this more contingent vision/version of home as a kind of identity, see Laura Levitt, *Jews and Feminism: The Ambivalent Search for Home* (New York: Routledge, 1997).

7. This incompleteness is part of what draws us in and what makes the engagement so alluring. We long for more. Mavor describes this insatiable desire in terms of a kind of flirtation and sees this desire animating even scholarly engagements with the past.

> All historical research, whether the objects of study are from a long time ago or yesterday, feeds on a desire to know, to come closer to the person or object under study. Though we go to great pains to cover up our desire, to make our voice objective, to see that our findings are grounded, to

dismiss our bodies, we flirt (some of us more overtly, others more secretly) with the past. Flirting, as a game of suspension without the finale of seduction, keeps our subjects alive, the more we fantasize about our subject, the more elusive and desirable it becomes. (*Becoming*, 16)

8. Michael Renov makes this point by discussing how in some of Ravett's earlier autobiographical films, this notion of being an only child plays out. See Michael Renov, "The Address of the Other: Ethical Discourse in *Everything's for You*," in *The Subject of Documentary* (Minneapolis: University of Minnesota Press, 2004), 159–167. For another powerful reading of *Everything's for You*, see Janet Walker, *Trauma Cinema: Documenting Incest and the Holocaust* (Berkeley: University of California Press, 2005), especially chapter 6, "Disremembering the Holocaust: *Everything's for You, Second Generation Video,* and *Mr. Death*," 158–193.

9. Hapic, in this context, has to do with touch as a sense and the way that film enables a strange approximation of this other sense. With this in mind, I use haptic to express how Ravett's film touches loss. In other words, I am arguing that he uses film to communicate, to represent, what it means not to be able to touch this loss, what it feels like to try to touch it. This is a notion I return to in my reading of the film, building on the work of film theorist Laura Marks, later in this chapter.

10. Shelley Hornstein, "Archiving an Architecture of the Heart," in Shelley Hornstein, Laura Levitt, and Laurence Silberstein, eds., *Impossible Images: Contemporary Art after the Holocaust* (New York: NYU Press, 2003), 14.

11. This uncle took my father and his siblings to visit Lena's grave when they were children.

12. I say this with all due respect and love. I have been especially grateful to both Frances and Phil for talking to me. I had never met Frances before embarking on this project, and I hardly knew Phil. Both have lived alone and kept a certain distance from most members of their extended families. I was moved that Phil and I got to know each other before his death in 2004. I remain in touch with Frances and cherish her presence. We keep in touch through phone calls and the mail. I met her for the first time in 1998 on the trip I took to Albany with my father where we found Lena's grave. At that time we also visited the grave of Frances's father, Louis Levitt.

13. Here I am thinking of Michael André Bernstein's notion of side shadowing. Michael André Bernstein, *Foregone Conclusions: Against Apocalyptic History* (Berkeley: University of California Press, 1994).

14. I am indebted to my dear cousin Frances Levitt for sharing many of her memories and family stories, often deeply painful and complicated tales, with me. She and I first met as I began this project in the late 1990s. I called her out of the blue, and since then we have come to know and cherish each other. This has been a gift for both of us.

15. I thank Michelle Friedman for pointing out how my text also enacts this slippage. As she explained to me, this slippage is even apparent in my writing. When I write about my family, my prose becomes less certain, less secure, and less clear. In this sense, I enact the "difficulty/impossibility of grasping an unfamiliar past." Personal correspondence, Michelle Friedman, May 2005.

16. For such anecdotal accounts, see, for example, Vivian Gornick, *Fierce Attachments: A Memoir* (New York: Farrar, Straus and Giroux, 2005). And for a powerful account of the history of illegal abortion in the United States, see Leslie J. Reagan, *When Abortion Was a Crime: Women, Medicine, and Law in the United States, 1867–1973* (Berkeley: University of California Press, 1997).

17. I am very grateful to Phil for telling me these things. I know from his sister that their mother, Sophie Pearl, had not wanted these issues ever discussed. I appreciate Sophie's position—something I imagine began as a desire to protect Lena's children—but I also appreciate knowing a bit more about how it might have been possible for a perfectly healthy thirty-six-year-old woman to die.

18. As an old man he enjoyed X-rated movies and burlesque shows. I read these activities in relation to the stories Phil told me. Before knowing all of this, my mother, the only one who said anything about this predilection, treated these forays as charming, the adventures of an old man; they were never presented to me as lurid. She thought he simply enjoyed seeing beautiful bodies on display. I think she discussed this with him in precisely these terms.

19. Although Ravett is not comfortable with this designation, I use it to signal that this film, like Ravett's other filmic work, is not commercial; it is not narrative or linear.

20. Up until July 2005, I had thought that the photograph was a picture of Abraham Ravett's mother and her daughter, Abraham Ravett's half sister. This is an assumption that haunts much of my reading of Ravett's film. Viewers who do not know better may, as I did, believe that this is a portrait of mother and daughter. I thank Abraham Ravett for clarifying this point after he read a draft of this chapter. Telephone conversation, July 2005.

21. I am grateful to Abraham Ravett for suggesting that I read Laura Marks's remarkable study, *The Skin of Film: Intercultural Cinema, Embodiment, and the Senses* (Durham, NC: Duke University Press, 2000). This study has given me some more critical terms to articulate how I have been engaging with Ravett's film. Rereading an early draft of my "reading" of Ravett's film—a manuscript I began writing almost four years ago—after reading Marks has been uncanny. Much of what I have to say echoes Marks's account of what intercultural cinema often does, although Ravett's work is not considered in Marks's study.

22. On the difficulty of analogies more generally, see Janet Jakobsen's important essay, "Queers Are Like Jews, Aren't They? Analogy and Alliance Politics," in Daniel Boyarin, Daniel Itzkovitz, and Ann Pellegrini, eds., *Queer The-*

ory and the Jewish Question (New York: Columbia University Press, 2003), 64–89. For more on the specific discomfort of making connections between ordinary Jewish lives and the extraordinary legacy of the Shoah, see Laura Levitt, "Intimate Engagements: A Holocaust Lesson," *Nashim: A Journal of Jewish Women's Studies and Gender Issues,* No.7 (Spring 2004), 190–205; and Laura Levitt, Introduction to "Changing Focus: Family Photography and American Jewish Identity," *The Scholar and Feminist Online,* 3.1 (Winter 2003), http://www.barnard.columbia.edu/sfonline/cf/index.htm.

23. I thank Michelle Friedman for pointing out the prevalence of this notion of the shadow of the Holocaust, a trope prominently figured in the title of Aaron Hass's book about children of survivors. Aaron Hass, *In the Shadow of the Holocaust: The Second Generation* (New York: Cornell University Press, 1990). In addition to this work there is also Constantin V. Ponomareff, *In the Shadow of the Holocaust and Other Essays* (Amsterdam and Atlanta: Rodopi Press, 1998), and Geoffrey Hartman, *The Longest Shadow: In the Aftermath of the Holocaust* (New York: Palgrave Macmillan, 1996).

24. "Film as a Medium for Memory and Mourning: A Critical Viewing of Two Films by Independent Film Maker Abraham Ravett," Association for Jewish Studies (AJS), Boston, December 1994.

25. "Film Screening and Discussion: Abraham Ravett's *Half-Sister,* facilitator, American Academy of Religion (AAR), Annual Meeting, San Francisco, November 1997.

26. In some ways I suspect that I found Ravett's not speaking, not explaining his film, familiar. It was not unlike my father's inability to speak. Here again I had to struggle with figuring out these things less directly, more on my own. I thank Ruth Ost for pointing out to me these connections. Conversation, February 2005.

27. Again, this process also echoes what Laura Marks calls "haptic cinema."

28. This notion of the power of the mimetic figures prominently in Andreas Huyssen's notion of mimetic approximation. See Andreas Huyssen, "Monuments and Holocaust Memory in a Media Age," in *Twilight Memories: Marking Time in a Culture of Amnesia* (New York: Routledge, 1995), 249–260.

There is much to be said for keeping Holocaust monuments and memorials site-specific, for having them reflect local histories, recalling local memories; this makes the Final Solution palpable, not just by focusing on the sites of extermination, but also by focusing on the lives of those murdered in the camps.

At some level, however, the question of the Holocaust as a whole, a totality, will reassert itself together with the problem of its unspeakability. After we have remembered, gone through the facts, mourned for the victims, we will still be haunted by that core of absolute humiliation, degradation, and horror suffered by the victims. How can we understand when even the witnesses had to say, "I could not believe what I saw with my own eyes." No matter how fractured by media, by geography, and by subject position representations of the Holocaust are, ultimately, it all comes down to this core: unimaginable, unspeakable, and unrepresentable horror. Post-Holocaust generations can only approach that core by mimetic approximation, a mnemonic strategy which recognizes the event in its otherness and as beyond identification or therapeutic empathy, but which physically innervates some of the horror and the pain in a slow and persistent labor of remembrance. Such mimetic approximation can only be achieved if we sustain the tension between the numbing totality of the Holocaust and the stories of the individual victims, families, and communities. Exclusive focus on the first may lead to the numbing abstraction of statistics and the repression of what these statistics mean; exclusive focus on the second may provide facile cathartic empathy and forget the frightening conclusion that the Holocaust as a historical event resulted, from, as Adi Ophir put it, from an exceptional combination of normal processes. The ultimate success of a Holocaust monument would be to trigger such a mimetic approximation, but it can achieve that goal only in conjunction with other related discourses operating in the mind of the spectator and in the public sphere. (259)

29. This process and the complicated dynamics I see in Ravett's film are also echoed in the words of novelist Jonathan Safran Foer, who describes some of his own preoccupations with a similar but more distant Holocaust legacy. In Foer's case he builds his fiction around the story of his grandfather. As Deborah Solomon explains, "It is easy to discern parallels between the fictive Thomas Schell and Foer's actual maternal grandfather, Louis Safran, a Polish Jew who lived through the Holocaust and the extermination of his first wife and young daughter. Safran immigrated to this country after the war, but Foer never met him; he died in 1954, more than two decades before his grandson was born." She then goes on to cite the novelist. As he explains:

I don't know how old I was when I learned of the life my grandfather had before the life that led to me. . . . There should be a name for those things that one feels one has always known without ever having learned. And a name for those things that are central to one's life without ever being thought about or felt.

He continues,

I suppose my mother told me. . . . Am I haunted by the story? Of course. The most haunting detail for me is that we don't know the name of the baby that was killed—my mother's half-sister. Maybe it goes back to Nietzsche's idea that everything we have words for is dead in our hearts. In this case, a dead, nameless child is more alive for me than many living things. (44)

Deborah Solomon, "The Rescue Artist," *New York Times Magazine*, February 27, 2005, 40–45. This essay and these particular insights resonate with not only Ravett's *Half-Sister*, but also with the urgency of my own project to engage with the legacy of my paternal grandmothers, especially the woman I never knew, the woman I am named for, Lena Levitt. I long to find words for precisely the things I have always known or felt around my father, things I could never know but that have been somehow central to my life.

30. On this notion of triggering memory, see James Young, *At Memory's Edge: After-Images of the Holocaust in Contemporary Art and Architecture* (New Haven, CT: Yale University Press, 2000); Barbie Zelizer, *Visual Culture and the Holocaust* (New Brunswick, NJ: Rutgers University Press, 2000); Yael Zerubavel, *Recovered Roots: Collective Memory and the Making of Israeli National Tradition* (Chicago: University of Chicago Press, 1995).

31. It is also true that my friend has always adored marine mammals.

32. In a sense, this also echoes my relationship with my father. Mother and child are at the center of Ravett's film, while I am interested in father and mother, my father and his mother, and ultimately my father and me, his child. I thank Ruth Ost for this insight. Conversation, February 2005.

33. The only sound sequence in the film is broken. There are two segments. For a very different engagement with this very act of witnessing, see Ravett's film *Toncia* (1986). In this film, Ravett offers the full take of his mother's telling of the story of his half sister's death. In the second film, Ravett offers only the narration as a single take, the same footage that he includes broken up and in a different order in *Half-Sister. Toncia* is a single 400-foot magazine of film. For more on his sister's name, I am grateful to Lori Lefkovitz for helping me appreciate the variations on this name. When I spoke to Abraham Ravett about seeing *Toncia*, we went back and forth over the phone with my mispronunciation of this name. Telephone conversation with Ravett, May 2004. Conversation with Lori Lefkovitz, Lehigh University, Bethlehem, PA, May 2004.

34. Here, unlike Ravett, I do not have any information to get from my family. There is no longer any envelope or letter to go along with the portrait of my grandparents. They no longer exist. I cannot look at them or touch them, as Ravett does in his film; and so it is only vicariously, through watching his camera do these things, that I imagine what this might feel like.

35. I am again grateful to Abraham Ravett for his close reading of an earlier draft of this chapter. In this instance, Ravett pointed out to me that, in fact, under optimal conditions, viewers do not hear the sound of the film projector. Given this, as Ravett explained to me, ideally viewers watching the film will not hear the projector. Telephone conversation with Abraham Ravett, July 2005. My engagement with the projector is not an intention of the filmmaker; it is part of my own experience of watching the film in small venues. This account is also indebted to many discussions about the film, and this issue in particular,

with Michelle Friedman who, like me, has seen the film on video and projected in venues where one hears the sound of the projector. For both of us, this was a salient issue that informed our readings of the film.

36. Roland Barthes, *Camera Lucida: Reflections on Photography* (New York: Hill and Wang, 1981), 82.

37. After reading a draft of this chapter, Ravett told me that I had mistakenly assumed that the photograph was of his mother and her daughter. Having learned this from Ravett, I had to go back and change my reading to make clear that this was not the case. Abraham Ravett, phone conversation, July 2005.

38. Although the image of the little girl's face never quite covers over the name and address of her half brother, there is something about this gesture that links it to the overshadowing presence of the Holocaust in this man's life. This link is quite specific in his case, but it also echoes some of the larger connections I have been drawing between different kinds of losses and how they are intertwined. This is also a motif in *Maus*, where the living child is always haunted by the legacy of the now idealized lost child, the one who died in the Shoah, although for Ravett and for Spiegelman, the Holocaust is an intimate family legacy. I thank Michelle Friedman for sharing these connections with me. These are notes from a discussion of this portion of the manuscript at the Annual Judaism Postmodernism Conference held at the Bermann Center for Jewish Studies at Lehigh University, Bethlehem, PA, June 2005.

39. On the limitation of cinema—especially in its ability to make present that which is no longer accessible, especially in the case of exile—see Laura Marks, *The Skin of Film*.

40. Barbara Johnson addresses this notion of animation in poetry. See Barbara Johnson, *The Feminist Difference: Literature, Psychoanalysis, Race and Gender* (Cambridge, MA: Harvard University Press, 1998). These particular dynamics are played out materially in Ravett's film.

41. *The American Heritage Dictionary of the English Language,* 4th edition, s.v. "animation."

42. The doll is also an uncanny figure, the automaton, the frightening figure of human construction, the gross attempt to re-create, to represent life in a mimetic form with only the semblance of life is spooky precisely as a playful substitution, a transitional object for the child, but also the figure of adult desires for mastery: Pygmalion, Eliza Doolittle, the man-made woman of Metropolis, a female golem? Not quite a golem, but spooky and all the more so as the projector, in its rhythmic pulsing, offers it a kind of animation on the screen, even as Ravett does not hide the fact that these and the other dolls he shoots are just that, dolls.

I write about the dolls precisely because I wanted to forget them and did so. I was so interested in making a narrative out of this film, a neat beginning that would explain all that follows, that I forgot that which preceded it as well as the dolls who came first and who come back again and again. Dolls are also cultural ideals, stereotypes; they are commodified versions of femininity that reproduce and help children rehearse dominant forms of normative femininity.

43. Here I want to thank Marian Ronan for calling my attention to another way of thinking about these images. As she explains, Catholics are often marked as identifiable Christians, often the only Christians with costumes, and as such are used in the media to stand in for Christians, especially when the situation is negative. Here Marian points to the proliferation of Catholic priests as demonic figures in the media, both in fictional representations and in the news. As Ronan explained to me, according to Keith Russell, "Catholicism is the only part of Christianity that is visually emphatic and so it becomes the symbol of Christianity in general, and perhaps this is the case for Christian evil, too." Private email, February 27, 2005.

44. In Irena Klepfisz's essay on the loss of secular Yiddish culture, she writes of Poland in similar terms. "In Poland I saw the shadows of Jewish Polish culture and was able to infer from them the magnitude of what had taken place. It was like stepping into a negative rather than a photograph." Irena Klepfisz, *Dreams of an Insomniac: Jewish Feminist Essays, Speeches and Diatribes* (Portland, OR: Eighth Mountain Press), 158.

45. In the film, Ravett does not formally identify this footage; there is no reference to where it came from even at the end of the film. I learned the origin of this footage in an article about the film, where it is identified as archival footage from the Warsaw Ghetto. See Michael D. Burke, "Making Contact with a Lost Sister: Hampshire College Filmmaker Reimagines a Child Lost to the Holocaust," *Daily Hampshire Gazette,* Northampton, MA, November 11, 1985.

46. In many ways this vision of the mother speaking and our inability to hear echoes not only how hard it is to hear her when her voice is actually heard on screen, but also how difficult it is to hear the story she has to tell, to witness and hear her testimony even in the intimacy of her son's home. This difficulty in telling and hearing is also echoed in the way the film must return to the mother's telling. Her story cannot be heard in just one take. This is an issue addressed otherwise in Ravett's later film, *Toncia* (1986), a thirteen-minute film. In *Toncia* Ravett presents the full text, the single take of his filming of his mother's telling without breaking it up. *Toncia* is a kind of meditation on that single take, a single 400-foot roll of film and the interaction, the conversation that it produced. In part, the brokenness of the telling in *Half-Sister* enacts the difficulty of listening, while in *Toncia,* the ability to appreciate the narrative demands multiple viewings of the same thing. For me, hearing the narrative in *Half-Sister* was in some ways easier to grasp because it is broken up.

47. Part of the difficulty of her name is its variations. Because these were not familiar to me as an English speaker, I found it difficult to discern her name and

how she is referred to in both of Ravett's films, *Toncia* and *Half-Sister*. Again, I thank Lori Lefkovitz for helping me understand the variations in this name.

48. Her break marks the break in the tellings in *Half-Sister*. Again this is in contrast to *Toncia* (1986), Ravett's later film. To reiterate, in that film, he offers the single take of his conversation with his mother, the raw footage he broke up into these two segments in *Half-Sister*.

49. I want to thank Marian Ronan for helping me appreciate how I seem to use this word as if its meaning is self-evident. Fraught, as Marian explained to me, is most commonly used to mean filled with, as in, "The situation was fraught with danger." My use of the term "fraught" is actually more archaic. I use it to mean "laden" or, according to my dictionary, "marked by or causing distress, emotional." I thank Marian for making me think more about this peculiar usage. Private email, February 27, 2005. See also *The American Heritage Dictionary of the English Language*, 4th edition, s.v. "fraught."

50. Recently, I have learned that this, too, was fraught. It turns out that my father's sister, the first to have a child, initially wanted to name her first child after Mary's father. She was to have been named "Dianne Linda," and it was only after the protests of Lena's brother that my cousin was named Linda. I now suspect that my great-uncle's protests were heard loudly and clearly by all of the Levitt siblings and that this led each of them to name their first children after our grandmother. I thank Jeanette Rosen, my second cousin, for telling me this story. Conversation, August 2004.

51. As Michelle Friedman pointed out to me, this is a bit like the various broken objects, the dolls, in Ravett's film. Personal correspondence, May 2005.

52. My mother's family was also complicated, like most. Here my mother had to deal with her own mother's discomfort and disappointments about my father and his family. For my maternal grandmother, it was hard to cope with my mother's marrying a man who had grown up poor, the son of immigrants, precisely the fate she and her husband had worked so hard to overcome. I read letters that my mother's mother sent her around the time she became engaged to my father, and I also read a few letters that Mary sent to my mother, welcoming her into the family. Again, the tensions here were great. A lot of these tensions stemmed from my maternal grandmother's class pretensions and wishes for her daughter. She wanted my mother to marry a doctor and not a poor Jewish man who, at the time, still did not even have a college degree. I was surprised by Mary's enthusiastic letter to my mother, given how cold my maternal grandparents were to both my father and his family. I also got a sense of Mary's energy that I had not fully remembered since my last encounters with her were when she was quite ill and frail. I thank my mother for sharing these letters with me. I am also grateful to both of my parents for telling me about this time.

53. The kind of childhood imaginary I imagine my father deployed might have looked something like that described by Kate Atkinson in her novel *Case*

Histories (New York: Little, Brown, 2005). Atkinson describes the childhood efforts of two young girls, Julia and Amelia, to deal with their younger sister Olivia's disappearance and presumed death.

> They had always found refuge in thinking of Olivia living a different life somewhere else, rather than being dead. For years and years the three of them had woven a story for Olivia—snatched in the night by a figure very like the Snow Queen, only kind and loving and coming from a more temperate kingdom. This empyreal creature had been desperate for a little girl of her own and had chosen Olivia because she was perfect in every way. The fictional Olivia was brought up in the most luxurious paradise their girlish imaginations could conceive of—wrapped in silks and furs, fed on cakes and sweets, surrounded by dogs and kittens and (for some reason) peacocks, bathing in golden baths and sleeping in silver beds. Although they knew Olivia was happy in her new life, they believed that one day she would be allowed to return home—which was always the unquestionable consummation of this wishful narrative.
>
> As they grew, so did Olivia, and it was only when Julia reached adolescence . . . that Olivia's other, fabulous life faded away. Yet it was so strongly embedded in Amelia's consciousness that even now she found it difficult to believe that Olivia might actually be dead and not a thirty-seven-year-old woman living in an Arcadian bower somewhere. (133)

Like Amelia, I do not think my father ever let go of the mythical narratives he and his siblings created around the loss of their mother. And I suspect that these narratives in my father's family were his creation.

54. I am grateful to Shelley Hornstein for this wonderful conception. See Shelley Hornstein, "Archiving Architecture of the Heart," in Shelley Hornstein, Laura Levitt, and Laurence Silberstein ed., *Impossible Images: Contemporary Art after the Holocaust* (New York: NYU Press, 2003), 13–30.

55. In the spring of 2004, I attended my cousin Linda's daughter's bat mitzvah and was reunited with all of my first cousins. Having begun this writing not long before attending this event, I came with these questions very much on my mind. For years I have considered the issue of resemblances, especially the ways my father and his brother looked alike and the ways my cousin Layne and I have always shared a certain resemblance. This time, as I looked again at Layne and her sisters and even as I looked at my aunt, their mother, I was struck by how much they reminded me of the image I now have of our long-lost grandmother. My cousins are all quite petite. And somehow, seeing them as still-young mothers with small children, not unlike my father's young mother, helped me again to imagine her. And here my cousin Layne especially struck me because, like me, she shares our grandmother's dark coloring. She also shares our grandmother's size, whereas Linda and I are both much taller, especially Linda.

56. "The House at Loon Lake," episode 199 of *This American Life*, WBEZ

Chicago, first aired November 16, 2001. Adam Beckman devoted the full fifty-five minutes of the show to this single story. I thank Deborah Hatcher for directing me to it. Her suggestion that I listen to this story has been amazingly fruitful. Dinner conversation with Ruth Ost and Deborah Hatcher, July 2004. As Catherine Staples reminded me, this is also the story at the heart of the 2001 French film *Amélie*, directed by Jean-Pierre Jeunet.

57. When I talked to Deb about the show the next day, she had forgotten the mother, and she had not noticed her accent. These were the things that I noticed.

58. I say this in the present, when the only living siblings are my father and his sister. His younger brother Aaron Levitt died in the early 1980s, although the questions I raise also affect Aaron's daughters and their children in the present.

59. As Shelley Hornstein explains, according to Walter Benjamin, in order to "approach one's buried past, one must conduct [oneself] . . . like a man digging. . . . [One] must not be afraid to return again and again to the same matter; to scatter it as one scatters earth, to turn it over as one turns over soil. For the matter itself is only a deposit, a stratum, which yields only to the most meticulous examination what constitutes the real treasure hidden with the earth: the images, severed from all earlier associations, that stand—like precious fragments or torsos in a collector's gallery—in the prosaic rooms of our later understanding" (14).

60. Mary Gordon, *The Shadow Man: A Daughter's Search for Her Father* (New York: Random House, 1996), 199–202.

61. Here I am also reminded of the final stanza of Adrienne Rich's poem, "Transcendental Etude," in *The Dream of a Common Language, Poems 1974–1977* (New York: W. W. Norton, 1978), 72–77. This final stanza, in many ways, echoes the promise of a kind of embodied feminism, but at the same time, it is very much about the pieces of a life, the messy disarray that most of us struggle to live with, that we can never fully master:

Vision begins to happen in such a life
as if a woman quietly walked away
from the argument and jargon in a room
and sitting down in the kitchen, began turning in her lap
bits of yarn, calico and velvet scraps,
laying them out absently on the scrubbed boards
in the lamplight, with small rainbow-colored shells
sent in cotton-wool from somewhere far away,
and skeins of milkweed from the nearest meadow—
original domestic silk, the finest findings—
and the darkblue petal of the petunia,
and the dry darkbrown lace of seaweed;

not forgotten either, the shed silver
whisker of the cat,
the spiral of paper-wasp-nest curling
beside the finch's yellow feather
Such a composition has nothing to do with eternity,
the striving for greatness, brilliance—
only with the musing of a mind
one with her body, experienced fingers quietly pushing
dark against bright, silk against roughness,
pulling the tenets of a life together
with no mere will to mastery,
only care for the many-lived, unending
forms in which she finds herself,
becoming now the sherd of broken glass
slicing light in a corner, dangerous
to flesh, now the plentiful, soft leaf
that wrapped round the throbbing finger, soothes the wound;
and now the stone foundation, rockshelf further
forming underneath everything that grows. (76–77)

62. This is an issue I address in my first book as well. On my engagement with my father's secrets, or all that I can never know about my father, see *Jews and Feminism: The Ambivalent Search for Home*, 22–25.

63. Hornstein, "Archiving Architecture," 14.

NOTES TO CHAPTER 3

1. Jane Lazarre, *Wet Earth and Dreams: A Narrative of Grief and Recovery* (Durham, NC: Duke University Press, 1998). All subsequent citations from this work will be noted in the text with page numbers.

2. Ann Weiss, *The Last Album: Eyes from the Ashes of Auschwitz-Birkenau* (New York: W. W. Norton, 2001); Ann Weiss, *The Last Album: Eyes from the Ashes of Auschwitz-Birkenau, Updated and Expand* (Philadelphia: Jewish Publication Society, 2005); Kersten Brandt, Hanno Loewy, and Krystyna Olesky, eds., *Before They Perished . . . Photographs Found in Auschwitz* (Oświęcimiu: Państwowe Muzeum Auschwitz-Birkenau, 2001).

3. *The American Heritage Dictionary*, 4th edition, s.v. "hide."

4. A *Tzeddakah* box is a "charity" box for collecting money. The blue and white boxes were specifically aimed at raising money for the creation and sustaining of Jewish settlement in Palestine and eventually for supporting the state of Israel. These boxes could be used for other Jewish causes as well.

5. This is something I have written about elsewhere in terms of a kind of gendered economy of artistic production and display I learned in my parents'

home. See Laura Levitt, "Gender and Generation," in "Changing Focus: Family Photography and American Jewish Identity," a special issue of *The Scholar and Feminist Online* 1.3 (Winter 2003). www.barnard.edu/sfonline.

6. Stephen Crane is one of my father's favorite writers, a writer my brother also loves.

7. When I first tried to write about this poem, having never actually read it, I missed the Trinitarian reference. I had two just men, and one was dead. When I finally found the poem, I was also a bit surprised. The version of the poem reproduced in Joseph Katz, ed., *The Complete Poems of Stephen Crane* (Ithaca, NY: Cornell University Press, 1966, 1972), scans the final two lines as follows "Listen! Listen! / And you will hear the third of his defeat." Needless to say, having always thought I knew the final line of the poem, I was taken aback by this rendition. In order to clarify this point, I placed a query to the Stephen Crane Society. According to Don Vanouse, who kindly answered my question, "The source of the troublesome word is clarified in the notes of the Virginia Edition of Stephen Crane's poetry (Vol X). The first publication of the poem in *War Is Kind* uses 'thud,' but there is a carbon copy of a typescript in which the word is 'third.' Fredson Bowers speculates that Crane corrected the primary copy of the typescript (now lost) in readying the poems for publication. Katz seems to have trusted the 'carbon' more than the published poem" (email February 19, 2005). I am grateful to Vanouse for clarifying this.

8. See Joseph Katz's introduction to *The Complete Poems of Stephen Crane*, xi. All quotations from the poems of Crane will be taken from this collection except for the emendation of "Have You Ever Made a Just Man?" that I have already described. When citing from the text, I will use the poem number and the page number from Katz's 1972 edition. I have subsequently consulted a few other versions of the poem and am most taken by the version found in the 1899 illustrated edition of *War Is Kind* arranged and printed by Will Bradley at University Press Cambridge. It was my pleasure to read through the pages of this beautiful edition in the Chapin Library of Rare Books at Williams College, Williamstown, MA, while I was a visiting professor in the religion department. In this edition, Bradley uses the work "thud" and not "third" in the final line of the poem. And like the more recent *Stephen Crane: Prose and Poetry* (New York: Library of America, 1984), a collection that also includes this poem and follows the University of Virginia edition, the poem includes quotation marks in each line. I thank Irving and Phyllis Levitt for sending me a copy of this version of the poem, which they found in the Dover Public Library in Dover, Delaware. In these versions the poem is arranged as follows:

"Have you ever made a just man?"

"Oh, I have made three," answered God,

"But two of them are dead,

"And the third—

"Listen! Listen!

"And you will hear the thud of his defeat."

In the Bradley rendition the second line is broken up into two parts,

"Oh, I have made three," answered

    God, (23)

Part of what makes this so striking in Bradley's 1899 edition is that the poem is set right after and facing another poem addressed to God, "What? You Define Me God with These Trinkets?" (22).

9. In part, this reading has been influenced by Wayne A. Meeks' first lecture in the Croghan Bicentennial Lecture Series on the Bible and Early Christianity, "A Story to Think With: From Crucifixion to Metaphor," Williams College, Williamstown, MA, February 21, 2005.

10. I stress the word "man" as a gendered term because the contrast between male and female is so stark throughout the poems in *War Is Kind*. Crane often contrasts mothers and fathers, maidens and sailors, and the optimism and life-affirming nature of women in contrast to the pessimism and destructiveness of men. The title poem, "Do Not Weep, Maiden, for War Is Kind," is addressed to such a young woman (Katz, poem 76, p. 81). Not long after this, Crane writes the following poem contrasting what the sea means for men and for women:

To the maiden

The sea was blue meadow

Alive with little froth-people

Singing.

To the sailor, wrecked,

The sea was dead grey walls

Superlative in vacancy

Upon which nevertheless at fateful time

Was written

The grim hatred of nature. (Katz, Poem 78, p. 84)

11. *The American Heritage Dictionary*, 4th edition, s.v. "just."

12. Here the "Listen" reminds me of the Hebrew pray, the Sh'ma, translated into English as "Hear oh Israel, the Lord Our God, the Lord is One." In this prayer the crucial command is for the people of Israel, the Jewish people, to hear their God's message, the message of God's oneness.

13. *The American Heritage Dictionary*, 4th edition, s.v. "thud."

14. Here I am referring to the injustice of random violence, sexual violence, and rape as I experienced it. I offer a rigorous critique of the American justice system and its rape laws in my first book. See Laura Levitt, *Jews and Feminism: The Ambivalent Search for Home* (New York: Routledge, 1997). There I challenge the happy version of public life my father gave me but do not begin to tap these darker, less overt legacies.

15. According to my father, they chose a particularly inexpensive brand of black-and-white 8mm film to do the film. They had to send away for it from a mail order company. It was the cheapest film they could find, and they needed to use it because their resources were profoundly limited. The actors were also not paid for their labor. The plural here refers to my father, my uncle (my father's brother-in-law), and cameraman Harold Wilson.

16. Although I write this now, as I have been reviewing the film and writing about it, my father reports that he has found a script he had forgotten he had written for the film. He is making me a copy of this handwritten document and will also send along the names of the two actors he hired to play the two characters in the film. Telephone conversation, March 6, 2005. I write this in process, knowing that it will shift some of what I have written. I want at least to record this sequence since it, too, echoes the way my father and I communicate. Somehow, my interest and writing trigger his memory, and once-hidden or unknown things emerge.

17. I will return to the setting shortly, for now I simply want to set the stage. The actual place where the film was shot, Albany, New York, is something I will return to as I consider another dimension of loss—lost spaces, radically altered landscapes, cityscapes.

18. "Bum" seems more like the word my father would have used, and perhaps did use, when describing the film, although it feels awkward in the present; it is not a term I would normally use. "Homeless" is my term. In my father's script—which, I discovered, is quite different from the actual film, with more fleshed-out characters and interactions between them—I notice that he refers to the first man as a derelict and the second as dejected. His script also names them. I will not use those names since they do not figure in the film that was made and my interest is in the film.

19. "Hire" is perhaps a misnomer, although it is the term my father uses. Nobody was paid for their labor on this film.

20. A large percentage of his classmates was black, and I think even the principal or some teachers were also black. In the script, it never says that the first man is black. What I found striking is that although it never says this, the dialect of the first man is presented as both southern and black. He speaks in a stereotyped version of that kind of speech. Linguists call this kind of speech African-American Vernacular English.

21. Even his cousin Phil Pearl, who eventually attended the New School for Social Research and earned a PhD in philosophy, was enrolled in Schuyler's vocational track. Despite being on the vocational track, when he graduated from Schuyler, Phil Pearl had the highest test scores and earned the key to the school at graduation. I thank Phil Pearl and his sister Jeanette Rosen for sharing this information with me. Phil never mentioned the key; this was something Jeanette shared with me after Phil died.

22. Here my father does play out a common stereotype, the black man as closer to nature. And this all matches up with the various contrasts he sets up throughout the film, black and white, life and death, happy and drunk, sad and sallow, etc. In his script my father describes the second man in precisely these terms. He is described in a side note as seemingly indifferent to nature and even sunshine. This is in contrast to the other fellow. Irving Levitt, handwritten script, page 8.

23. Here again I am eager to read the script although my father did not use it when he made the film because they had no sound equipment. Nevertheless, my father's brief retelling of the story to me over the phone suggests this motivation, and I now believe that it colored my expectations about what I would see as I returned to the film. It also explains, in part, why I had initially focused on the suitcase as a kind of disappointing treasure, something that had not been worth the effort. Telephone conversation, March 6, 2005. After I read the script, it seemed much clearer to me that my father was aiming for a much less ambiguous reading of the motivations of the first man. He suggests that the first man's motive for engaging with the second man is simply to get his hands on the suitcase.

24. There is a long sequence as the first man follows the second man through the streets of the city until they come to a bank. This building is presented in sharp contrast to the other, lesser buildings. This palace to capital is clearly presented in sharp contrast to all else. And here the first man longingly embraces the building's columns. This suggests the hopes and the fantasy of what he might find in the suitcase at the end of the film. In a phone conversation with my father, he recalled that the film moves through the various layers of the city, its most destitute and its most affluent neighborhoods. In this way, my father was attempting to capture something of the flavor of another Crane text, the short novel, *Maggie: A Girl of the Streets*. In that story, Crane presents the various classes who inhabit the city from the perspective of a poor destitute woman. The story follows Maggie's encounters with the various classes in progression, from the highest to the lowest. This is also a story that my father loves and has discussed with me at various times—also in relation to his film. I thank Catherine Staples for reminding me of the progressive movement of Maggie's journey.

25. This scene is not included in the script my father initially wrote. There are other characters who show up there, but there is no young man who happens to cross paths with either of these characters.

26. On this point, I thank Barbara Browning for helping me see this blind spot in my reading. I did not see the humor and playfulness in this scene. This discussion took place after my lecture, "Telling Stories Otherwise (or Revisiting My Father's Visual Archive)," Distinguished Lecture, Center for Religion and Media, New York University, New York, March 2006.

27. This is the dynamic that Kaja Silverman describes in her reading of Cindy Sherman's *The Untitled Film Stills*. See Kaja Silverman, *Threshold of the Visible World* (New York: Routledge, 1996), especially the final chapter of the book. I build on this insight to look at Larry Sultan's vision of his parents in *Pictures from Home* (New York: Harry N. Abrams, 1992) in Laura Levitt, "Seeing Jewishness in the Details: Excess/orizing American Jews: Another Look at Larry Sultan's *Pictures from Home*," unpublished conference paper, American Studies Association, Annual Meeting, Atlanta, November 2004.

28. Barbara Browning also pointed out to me that my father might, in fact, be the third man in the film. Here Browning offered a wonderful counter reading to my own informed by some of my father's other visual materials, which I offered as a part of that presentation. Browning saw in a doodle from the 1970s a rendition of Judge John Serica of Watergate fame with a caption saying "Here comes de Judge"—taken from the comedian, Flip Wilson. Browning suggested that my father's humor is clearly powerful, and given that his almost "thud" was not a defeat, but about his "feet." I am grateful to Browning for showing me this. He stumbles but does not fall. "Telling Stories Otherwise," NYU, March 2006.

29. In the script, this is not the final scene. But the sequence is there. My father writes in the script that this character opens the suitcase, throws the clothing all over the place, shakes out the emptied suitcase, and then kicks it. The scene ends with the character sitting down and brooding with his hands on his head; he stares into space. (Handwritten manuscript, p. 22.) There is no crucifixion pose.

30. I originally wrote that the third figure was missing.

31. In various ways this film echoes some of the feeling and tone of Samuel Beckett's *Waiting for Godot*, a play that was very much a part of my family's story. It was a play that my parents regularly taught in their Great Books course. It was also a play we all saw produced at various times. I took my father to see an amazing production at the Providence Repertory Theater in the early 1980s while I was still in college. I made special arrangements for my father to pick me up in time to see the production. I had already seen it and wanted to go back with him. I thank Ruth Ost for making this connection and reminding me of these resonances. Private exchange, September 2006.

32. The film offers a glimpse of this lost Jewish geography. It shows one of many places where Jews have lived in this country and which now no longer exists as it once did. What is striking about this example is that it is not what many think of as a lost Jewish home. It is not a site of great nostalgia and longing as is the Lower East Side of New York City. On that longing, see Beth Wenger's important essay, "Memory as Identity: The Invention of the Lower East Side," *American Jewish History* 85.1 (March 1997), 3–27; the edited volume, Hasia Diner, Jeffery Shandler, and Beth Wenger, eds., *Remembering The*

Lower East Side (Bloomington: Indiana University Press, 2001); and Hasia Diner, *Lower East Side Memories* (Princeton, NJ: Princeton University Press, 2000. In a different way, this place is similar to some of the kinds of abandoned spaces of the American Jewish past, especially the synagogues of small towns in the American South and Midwest. On these spaces in the South, see the picture book, Bill Aron, *Shalom Y'all: Images of Jewish Life in the American South* (Chapel Hill, NC: Algonquin Books, 2002). I thank my southern family in Alabama, especially Elise Watt, for my signed copy of this book. I am not making more of this point here for a number of reasons, including the fact that for my father, the lost home in Schenectady, the house his parents once owned, is more a site of longing than are these streets. These spaces came after that once-happy time. They were already bereft when my father lived here. And these are not and were never exclusively or especially Jewish streets. What is striking, as I go on to argue, is the larger loss of these streets and blocks for the larger community of lots of different folks for whom Albany has been home. See, for example, the work of the novelist William Kennedy. I thank the anonymous reader who suggested these connections.

33. This aspect of the film echoes a kind of archival impulse on the part of certain 20th-century photographers, although in this case, it was an unintentional aftereffect. In her reading of W. G. Sebald's *The Emigrants*, Stefanie Harris suggests a link between his use of photographs and "[Eugene] Atget's self-professed motivation behind the selection of his images, namely to create a photographic archive of precisely those elements of the old Paris that were disappearing under modernization. Indeed he was occasionally known to attach a note to his photographs stating, 'will disappear'" (385). Although my father did not consciously engage in such an effort, my reading does self-consciously build on the kinds of impulses Harris describes here. Stefanie Harris, "The Return of the Dead: Memory and Photography in W. G. Sebald's "Die Auswanderten," *German Quarterly Review* 74.4 (Fall 2001), 379–391.

34. Part of the confusion is that I do not do visual work. That labor, especially drawing and painting, was always configured as a masculine enactment in my family. It is what my father and my brother share. They are both artists, I am not. And yet I, too, do creative work. On the gendering of these activities in my immediate family, see Laura Levitt, "Gender and Generations."

35. As I move into the transition from this account of my father's film to the stash of snapshots at the heart of this chapter, I am struck by the way my father has affirmed my suspicions about how he indirectly makes these connections to me. One day, in the summer of 2005, I had just finished writing up my interpretation of his film in relation to my reading of the Crane poem when I talked to my parents. It was more or less one of our regular weekly conversations where my mother and I talk at great length and at some point my father gets on the phone briefly to add something to the conversation. That day, he picked up the

phone line in the basement of my parents' house and proceeded to tell my mother and me that he had just stumbled upon something he thought I would find interesting. He explained that he had been sitting at his desk, and there just happened to be an old box at his feet, and when he opened the box, he found a script for his 1952 film, the very film I had been writing about. He explained that he hadn't remembered that there was a script. My mother added her now common refrain to these conversations, these discoveries. She had not known that there was a script either—he had never told her. This was new to her! He went on to say that it wasn't quite a script because, in the end, they couldn't use it because they had no access to sound equipment. But still it seems to have been the basis of the film, something he used when they made it, anyway. He was going to make me a copy of this handwritten script and put it in the mail. My interest seems to spark something in my father, and in turn, this leads to his finding things, revealing once hidden or forgotten pieces of his past. This is very much the outline of what follows. In that instance, reading my book and my interest in my family's past led to my father's taking these pictures out from their hiding place. Telephone conversation, March 6, 2005.

The script arrived in the mail three days later. Reading a photocopy of this handwritten text, I appreciate my father's caution that this text was a preliminary treatment and not the actual script of the film. What he actually captured on film is a much starker vision. It is a pared-down version of the story, with no excess. In the film, there are no secondary characters, and the narrative is all gesture and angle. To me, the film works as well as it does because it is so stark. It does not feel dated. It feels more like a parable of the poem; it is more timeless. In this sense, my reading of the film echoes all of the ways in which my father and I communicate most powerfully, without words.

36. Perhaps not so strangely, as I edited this chapter in the summer of 2006, I asked my father for the actual pictures so that I could have them reproduced for this book. At that time, he again found himself unable to put his hands on the actual photographs. He now has copies and found various versions of them. I could not help but see this again as a kind of repetition of the initial emergence and disappearance of the photographs.

37. I called my father for more information about this book, and my information comes from him, including the fact Grosset and Dunlap did not include their publication dates in these reprinted volumes. As a part of this conversation, my father confirmed that not only were the pages the same as the first edition of *Blix* published by Doubleday, but the original cover was replicated as well. Here my father confirmed these facts with reference to an actual first edition of Blix. He purchased the first edition at a much later date. Telephone conversation, April 30, 2005.

38. I first remembered my father telling me that he also found a postcard in the book that is dated August 15, 1952, but the postcard is actually older. It is a

one-cent postage postcard from a gas station, a reminder that one's car needs service. The postcard is not filled out, but because it has an "NRA" symbol on it, my father dates it from around 1935–1936. In my latest conversation with him about these matters, he told me that he had put a few other things away in this book as well. He also included a series of postcards on courtship, six in all, with the following titles, "The Proposal," "The Trousseau," "The Wedding," "The Honeymoon" (this one apparently shows a European train), "The First Evening in Our Own Home," and "The New Love," a picture of a baby. First he wanted to date these to the time period that Norris was writing about, but as he looked them over to tell me about them, my father decided that they were of a later vintage, from the 1920s or possibly around the time of the First World War. To me, these postcards speak to my father's desires for a happy ending. They are a statement about his wish for the kind of love described in Norris's autobiographical novel about his courtship with his wife. I also think they are linked to the loss of the happy home he remembered, the time when his family owned their own home and were living out such a happily-ever-after scenario. Telephone conversation, April 30, 2005. In addition to all of this, I also want to note that my father hid these pictures in this book at around the same time that he was working on his film.

39. Here I am reminded of my father's interest in the quaint courtship post-cards and the middle-class norms they seem to represent. I think that for him these are an idealized version of a life just outside of his reach. They are also a reminder of the vision offered in Norris's novel, also the story of an idealized relationship. The class specificity of this ideal vision is especially evident in Norris's thick descriptions of the interior spaces of the Bessemer family home. For a careful study of these spaces in Norris's writing and their significance, see Don Graham, *The Fiction of Frank Norris: The Aesthetics Context* (Columbia: University of Missouri Press, 1978). Although Graham addresses even the internal critique of the aesthetics of these spaces within the novel, I do not think these accounts would have altered my father's reading of the novel's sentimentality, its idealized vision of an all-American middle-class courtship. Oddly, Norris's thick descriptions of these interiors are precisely the kinds of textured accounts I long for in attempting to reconstruct the home in which my father grew up.

40. In chapter 4, after a full day of adventure roaming the city of San Francisco, Condy Rivers and Travis Bessemer reflect on their relationship, the ways in which, although they do not love each other, at least not yet consciously, they do enjoy each other's company. They relish the unorthodox nature of their friendship. In response to Travis's reflections and her sense that he is not listening to her, the text reads as follows:

"Blix," he murmured staring at her vaguely. "Blix—you look that way; I don't know, look kind of blix. Don't you feel sort of blix?" he inquired anxiously.

"Blix?"

He smote the table with his palm. "Capital!" he cried; "sounds bully, and snappy, and crisp, and bright, and sort of sudden. Sounds—don't you know, *this* way?"—and he snapped his fingers. "Don't you see what I mean? Blix, that's who you are. You've always been Blix, and I've just found it out. Blix," he added, listening to the sound of the name. "Blix, Blix. Yes, yes; that's your name."

Frank Norris, *(I) Blix (II) Moran of the Lady Letty: A Story of Adventure off the California Coast*, Vol. 3 (New York: Doubleday, Doran, 1928), 44. *Blix* was originally published in 1899.

41. In her introduction to the 1928 edition of *Blix*, Kathleen Norris describes *Blix* as "gay, shining and laughing." This novel is the expression of a boy at twenty who believes in fairies, "the fairies that lurk along water-fronts, and behind practical jokes, and that dearest fairy of all—the fairy of platonic friendship" (vi–vii). She goes on to explain:

The dream of sending a manuscript to an Eastern publisher, and receiving the little slip of acceptance in reply—which of us did not know it? Frank knew it, and in *Blix* he gives Condy his own fears and doubts and joys over a first story. He gives Blix herself the qualities he found in his first love—and his last!—in the woman to whom that little first promise of literary success was as important as it was to Frank, and who was to share the brief years that remained to him, as his wife. (viii)

For more on these autobiographical connections, see Franklin Walker, *Frank Norris: A Biography* (New York: Doubleday, Doran, 1932), and Ernest Marchand, *Frank Norris: A Study* (New York: Octagon Books, 1981).

42. Norris died very young in 1902. He was born in 1870.

43. Here I am moved by the powerful analysis of this problem in Michael André Bernstein, *Foregone Conclusions: Against Apocalyptic History* (Berkeley: University of California Press, 1994).

44. Bernstein's *Forgone Conclusions* haunts these readings. In this case, I take him up on his notion of the power of the prosaic to consider how, even in these less monumental circumstances, it is difficult to resist the allures of back-shadowing, and it is difficult to appreciate what could never be known before it happened. For my father and his siblings, this meant, of course, not knowing that their mother would die.

45. The pictures of Lena are now framed and displayed in my parents' home and in my home. They are also on display in my aunt's and my cousins' homes. And most recently, my father placed a Yortzeit plaque in the Synagogue in Dover for Lena. This was done during the summer of 2005.

46. Ann Weiss, *The Last Album: Eyes from the Ashes of Auschwitz-Birkenau* (2001, 2005), and *Before They Perished . . .* (2001). All subsequent refer-

ences to these volumes and editions will be included in the body of the text with page and volume, and edition references.

47. I am grateful to references to both of these volumes in Janina Struk, *Photographing the Holocaust: Interpretations of the Evidence* (London: I. B. Tauris, 2005). Struk writes about the collection in relation to the Tower of Faces (see my conclusion and chapter 1 for more on the Tower) and in relation to the albums that were found and the inclusion of Nazi photographs in the collection and the controversy around whether to include them in subsequent circulations of the images. Neither Weiss nor the State Museum chose to include these images in their books or in their displays of the photographs. Following up leads in Struk's notes, I contacted the Photo Archive at the USHMM. There I was fortunate to have been in contact with Teresa Pollin and Judith Cohen in the Collections Division. Teresa Pollin was kind enough to exchange a series of emails and to send me a copy of her essay, "Photographs from Auschwitz," *History of Photography* 23.4 (Winter 1999), 350–356. In her emails she also mentioned the Nazi photographs and the discomfort they caused. Personal emails to the author, July 2006.

48. I emailed Weiss using the contact information provided on her Web site. I tried a couple of times, including one time when I tried to purchase her video, and I never received a response from her. I also emailed the museum and asked them about this. In answer to my July 6, 2006, email, I received the following reply from Krystyna Oleksy, deputy director of the museum: "I would like to inform you that Ann Weiss's work on her book and our work on the publication 'Before They Perished' and the exhibition in the so-called Sauna Building in Birkenau were conducted independently of each other." Email, July 12, 2006.

49. Both the museum and Weiss have books as well as ongoing efforts to identify the photographs. The museum, in conjunction with the USHMM, continues to seek information through their research branches and archives. Weiss has set up a nonprofit organization and Web site devoted to these photographs as well as a video. The video, *Eyes from the Ashes,* which came out before the book, is available for purchase from Ann Weiss on the Web site that is devoted to the project, www.thelastalbum.org. The Web site lists her ongoing work as a lecturer and teacher of this material. She also makes images available for a photography exhibit of the Last Album images. Weiss continues to lecture and mount these exhibitions to raise awareness and, whenever possible, to learn more about the photographs. As of January 2007 the site was down.

50. For more information, see the Web site www.thelastalbum.org. Under the tab "Updates," the site has a listing of upcoming events as well as an extensive archive of past events by Weiss. Under the tab "Media," the site includes links from radio and television appearances by the author, and under the tab "Talk" there is a simple link for visitors to the site enabling them to add their voices and send the author more information they might have about particular

images. This link offers some sample entries as well. A Google search also locates publicity about some of these exhibitions and talks, which take place primarily at universities and colleges across the United States. The Web site offers a more extensive account of these venues, Holocaust museums, and research centers, including Yad Vashem in Jerusalem and the USHMM in Washington, D.C. Other venues include synagogues, community centers, and secondary schools.

51. For more on this, again a simple Google search produces various programs around the book's publication in Europe. One such example is a program sponsored by the Leo Baeck Institute, www.leobaeck.co.uk/lectures/perished.htm. One of the contributors to this project, Marek Pelc, also worked collaboratively on a film about the gathering of survivors from the Fürstenberg High School in Będzin which took place in Israel in 1997. The film was done as the contributors gathered information about those depicted in the photographs in the collection. . . . *Verzeihung, ich lebe* (2000) (. . . Pardon, I Live), a film by Andrzej Klamt and Marek Pelc, distributed by Basis-Film-Verleih GmbH.

52. These efforts are similar to the Tower of Faces at the USHMM in Washington, D.C., and the work undertaken by the State Museum at Auschwitz-Birkenau. See my earlier chapter on the Tower of Faces. Also note that Young makes explicit reference to this connection in his introduction. He writes, "Like Yaffa Eliach's tower of photographs from the shtetl Ejszyski on display at the U.S. Holocaust Memorial Museum, Ann Weiss's collection of photographs recovered from the transports of victims to Auschwitz show us what was lost" (18). Other works that engage in ongoing efforts to identify and name those lost include the new Hall of Names at Yad Vashem. See http://www1.yadvashem .org/new_museum/Galleries/gal10Hall.html, and "I Still See Their Faces: Images of Polish Jews." Hanno Loewy explains the origins of the latter in his essay in the supplement in this way: in 1994, Golda Tencer "launched an appeal in Poland asking people to send her photographic memories of Jewish people and of life before the Shoa, a world before her time" (*Before They Perished . . .* , Supplement, 14). This project, which began as a book of selected images and an exhibition, is now housed at the Wiesenthal Center in Los Angeles, and it is available online at http://motlc.wiesenthal.com/site/pp.aspx?c=jmKYJeNVJrF&b =478527. In a different context, see www.akakurdistan.com. For an interesting reading of both Weiss's project and the Kurdistan project in the context of museum exhibitions and the changing status of snapshots, see Joel Smith, "Roll Over—Analysis of Snapshot Photography, Photos of Everyday Life Not Initially Produced as Art," *Afterimage* 29.2 (September/October 2001), 8–11.

53. On this profoundly difficult problem, see Michael André Bernstein, *Foregone Conclusions*.

54. For a different reading and response to these kinds of works, see Ruth-Ellen Boetcher Joeres and Marjorie Gelus, eds., *Women in German Yearbook*

2003: Feminist Studies in German Literature and Culture, Vol. 19 (Lincoln: University of Nebraska Press, 2004); Pascale Bos, "Positionality and Postmemory in Scholarship on the Holocaust," 50–74; Karyn Ball, "Unspeakable Differences, Obscene Pleasures: The Holocaust as an Object of Desire," 20–49; Elizabeth R. Baer and Hester Baer, "Postmemory Envy?" 75–99; Lisa Disch and Leslie Morris, "Departures: New Feminist Perspectives on the Holocaust," 9–19.

55. In his account of these pictures, I read Young as building on not only his own powerful work on writing and rewriting the Holocaust, but also on Bernstein's critique of backshadowing in *Foregone Conclusions*. James E. Young, *Writing and Rewriting the Holocaust: Narrative and the Consequences of Interpretation* (Bloomington: Indiana University Press, 1988).

56. For a strong critique of this aspect of Weiss's book, its beauty, and its odd coffee-table format, see Pascale Bos, "Positionality and Postmemory in Scholarship on the Holocaust." Bos writes, "This book presents an odd disjunction, for not only does one not expect such photographs in the format of a coffee-table book, it is also highly unusual to see such a book introduced by prominent intellectuals, suggesting that the book belongs to a different (scholarly) genre" (62). She goes on to highlight the beauty of the book as an invitation to overly identify and fetishize those depicted, especially for those readers who have no familial connections to the Holocaust. Bos writes: "My problem with the book is that it seems packaged to do precisely that. The book's layout is beautiful, many of the men, women, and children in the photos are attractive and the images are presented without much context. All of this invites fetishization. It is a pleasure to look at these pictures, just as it would be if they had been in a regular family album, and this pleasure is possible precisely through a process of identification" (64).

57. These texts include Yaffa Eliach, *There Once Was a World: A 900-Year Chronicle of the Shtetl of Eishyshok* (Boston: Back Bay Books, Little, Brown, 1988); Serge Klarsfeld, *French Children of the Holocaust* (New York: NYU Press, 1995); and James E. Young, *The Texture of Memory: Holocaust Memorials and Meaning* (New Haven, CT: Yale University Press, 1993). According to NYU Press, publisher of Klarsfeld's almost 2,000-page book, which includes over 2,500 pictures and sells for $95, the initial print run was for 1,500 books. "[H]elped enormously by the *New York Times* review of December 5, 1996," the press immediately printed another 2,000 copies (Private correspondence from Jennifer Hammer, associate editor, August 20, 1997). This fascination is part of what I describe in chapter 1, and it is also something I discuss in my essay, "Photographing American Jews: Identifying American Jewish Life," in Laurence Silberstein, ed., *Mapping Jewish Identities* (New York: NYU Press, 2000), 65–96. In this essay I describe what the purchasing of these huge books of photographs masks, some of the more ordinary losses they cover up.

58. Leon Wieseltier, *Kaddish* (New York: Vintage, 1998).

59. Weiss does not identify the man in this photograph even in the 2005 edition of her book. I looked for the image in *Before They Perished* . . . , which identifies it as a picture of a soldier. More striking is the difference between the renditions of the photograph in these two books. In *Before They Perished* . . . , the photograph is considerably smaller (p. 39, image 2, identified as 3-0231). It is described in the second narrative volume that includes a guide to what the museum has come to learn about each photograph as such (p. 34). The photograph does not take up an entire page or bleed to its edges. It is a sepia-toned portrait done on a postcard, and the photograph is configured in a stylized oval frame that marks the photograph within the larger postcard, a standard framing device. In Weiss's text, there is no indication of the oval frame. And of course, given that her book is printed in black and white, the sepia is not evident.

60. This passage from Elie Wiesel, "Let Us Tell Tales," Opening Address at International Symposium on the Holocaust, Cathedral of St. John the Divine, New York, June 3, 1974.

61. Gary Weissman, *Fantasies of Witnessing: Postwar Efforts to Experience the Holocaust* (Ithaca, NY: Cornell University Press, 2004). Weissman offers a challenging argument for all who come after, asking what our desires are all about. He also presents a provocative reading of Wiesel. See especially chapter 1, "Reading Wiesel," 28–88.

62. See, for example, James E. Young, *Writing and Rewriting the Holocaust.*

63. For more on Cukierman, see p. 120ff in the 2005 edition of *The Last Album.* In *Before They Perished* . . . , there is also a full section devoted to "Beniamin Cukierman." See pp. 277–306 and pp. 93–99 in the supplement. Zvi Cukierman is identified as one of the sources for the narrative provided in this work as well. Although the spelling is different, Cukierman is one of the survivors who spoke to both Weiss and to those from the State Museum.

64. This distinction is crucial. It is what distinguishes Weiss's project most profoundly from my own. And the dangers involved in blurring these differences between what is Weiss's family story and the stories she depicts in this book of other Jewish lives destroyed by the Nazis is part of a broader discussion of the dangers of sentimentality discussed in Ruth-Ellen Boetcher Joeres and Marjorie Gelus, eds., *Women in German Yearbook 2003: Feminist Studies in German Literature and Culture.*

65. See my discussion of this issue in chapter 1.

66. Later in the first edition of the book, we learn the name and some of the story of the man in this photograph, although he is not identified at this point. He is Arthur Huppert and the photograph was apparently taken in 1933. For more on Huppert and his family, see Weiss, *The Last Album* (2001, 2005), 144–155. The mirror image is described on p. 148 along with other stylized images. Weiss's label reads, "A selection of stylized, choreographed photos taken

before Arthur Huppert became a father, at which time his focus became the baby" (148). Tragically, like so many of those depicted throughout this book, Huppert and his wife and young child were all murdered by the Nazis. This section is not altered in the 2005 edition.

As in Weiss's text, there is an extended discussion of the Huppert family and the various images of Arthur Huppert and his wife and child in the second volume of *Before They Perished* . . . (62–67). The complete set of these photographs is included in the first photographic volume of the text as well (159–176). This particular image is photograph 1 on p. 162. It is identified as "One of the Huppert brothers (presumably). Czechoslovakia, 1930s, 3-0226."

In this case, Weiss offers a more extensive account of this particular member of the Huppert family. There is some information on "Artur Huppert" on p. 62 of the supplement to *Before They Perished* . . . , but some of the images Weiss clearly identifies as Arthur are not labeled as such here.

67. My reading of Wieseltier is indebted to the work of both James E. Young and Michael André Bernstein. In *Foregone Conclusions,* Bernstein identifies this double reading as common in works on the Holocaust and explains how it operates on a number of different levels. He writes:

> In the corpus of work on the Shoah, I think there is a powerful but largely unrecognized connection that links together a set of contradictions which are so persistent that they have become constitutive of the discourse. On a historical level, there is the contradiction between conceiving of the Shoah as simultaneously unimaginable *and* inevitable. On an ethical level, the contradiction is between saying no one could have foreseen the triumph of genocidal anti-Semitism, while also claiming that those who stayed in Europe are in part responsible for their fate because they failed to anticipate the danger. On a narrative level, the contradiction is between insisting on the unprecedented and singular nature of the Shoah as an event and yet still using the most lurid formal tropes and common-place literary conventions to narrate it." (23)

68. In this way, he addresses a common and important fear raised by many commentators about sentimentality. The concern is that we forget that these Holocaust victims are not our relatives and in so doing confuse their pasts with our own, forgetting the difference between us and them. My work, like Marianne Hirsch's notion of postmemory, opens up this space as a way of better recognizing these differences so as not to tell viewers what they should see. On the problem of sentimentality, see Boetcher Joeres and Gelus, eds., *Women in German Yearbook 2003.* For more on Hirsch and postmemory, see chapter 1; and for more on my position, see my conclusion.

69. Bernstein, *Foregone Conclusions,* 120–121.

70. This image is not identified in either edition of Weiss's text, and it is difficult to find in *Before They Perished* . . . According to Judith Cohen at the

USHMM, the photograph has not been identified by either the museum at Auschwitz or in the collection at the USHMM. There is no marking on the back of the photograph. It is identified as image 1–0656 in the State Museum collection and 53399 at the USHMM. I thank Cohen for her help in identifying this picture. Email, July 2006.

71. As I have noted, whenever possible, the pagination in both editions of Weiss's text has been maintained. In some cases, like this one, the narrative text is condensed but the layout of the page is otherwise the same. I note a number of these changes and their import at various places in my reading of Weiss's original edition of her book.

72. In the original edition, Weiss's note about this photograph reads, "Auschwitz I entrance gate in morning light, taken on the author's first visit to Poland, 1986. The famous slogan 'ARBEIT MACHT FREI' translating to 'WORK MAKES YOU FREE,' taunted prisoners with false hope." In the second edition, Weiss adds an additional clause and another sentence. The clause reads as follows: "yet the inverted 'B' of the sign, tried to alert new prisoners that life here in Auschwitz-Birkenau, like the 'B' was inverted, insane and upside down." The additional sentence follows, "The Jewish prisoner, forced to produce the sign, ingeniously found a way to give warning" (23). There is no reference for this additional statement. On this image as iconic, see Oren Stier, unpublished manuscript, "Thresholds of Holocaust Memory: Arbeit Macht Frei," paper presented at the Judaism and Postmodern Conference, Bethlehem, PA, Lehigh University, June 2004; and Marianne Hirsch, "Surviving Images: Holocaust Photographs and the Work of Postmemory," *Yale Journal of Criticism* 14.1 (2001), 3–37.

73. I thank Ruth Ost for pointing out to me the importance of this image. The other important thing about this photograph of the author is that she is depicted copying these photographs while they were still in the albums in which they had been found. The narrative offered about the images and their identification in *Before They Perished . . .* describes what it meant to take the images out of these albums and when the albums themselves were put together.

74. As Weiss tells it, "I was in the company of prominent and philanthropic leaders, having been offered one of the coveted places because of my investigative reporting a few years earlier during 'Operation Moses,' Israel's daring rescue of Eritrean Jews, who had walked out of a primitive, persecuted life in Ethiopia to the Sudan where they were airlifted into Israel" (23).

75. This account echoes the kind of affective engagement with photographs described by Roland Barthes in *Camera Lucida: Reflections on Photography* (New York: Hill and Wang, 1981).

76. The issue of the notes on the backs of many of the photographs is an issue raised in more detail in *Before They Perished . . .* It is also something discussed by Teresa Pollin in her essay, "Photographs from Auschwitz."

77. Weiss, *The Last Album*, 2d edition, 26. Weiss does not describe how she

learned of the inscription. This image is found in *Before They Perished . . .* as image 1 on p. 357. It constitutes an entire section devoted to this family (357–364). Underneath the photograph on p. 357 is an image of the back of the postcard with the inscription Weiss translates into English. In *Before They Perished . . .*, the family name is "Laudon" not "Landon," and looking at the German inscription it is not clear if the letter is a "u" or "n" in the writer's cursive. Also on this page are two images of Abraham Laudon. In the supplement to *Before They Perished . . .*, the photograph of Adolf is labeled as Adolf Laudon on his first day at school, 1928." There is also a translation of the German inscription. It is identified as photograph 3-0348. *Before They Perished . . .*, Supplement, 110.

78. Some illustrations of this strategy include many of the longer narratives that accompany some of the images. Here is just one example from the first edition:

> At a Detroit exhibition of Eyes from the Ashes (October 1996), an attractive woman pointed to a photo of a man in an elegant hat and asked me, "Do you know who he is?"
>
> "Yes, the son of Gayleh Rifkeleh." In frustration I added, "So many people have identified him, but I've never met anyone from the family itself."
>
> Helen Pergament a survivor from Bendin, beamed and explained, "That's because there is only one person left in the world." Triumphantly she added, "And he's my friend! I'll call him. He lives in Israel." (120)

Although it seems that Weiss has used the photo archive at the USHMM in Washington, D.C., that now includes the information on the backs of the pictures and other research done by the museum in collaboration with the State Museum in Poland and others, it is also clear that there has been no direct collaboration between Weiss and the State Museum and its researchers. This is clear in the acknowledgments of both works. It is also unfortunate, given the shared aims of both of these efforts.

79. And, as of August 2006, these changes were not found on her Web site in the update section. For an example of this, see note 87 below on the Desnos section, which has been deleted from the 2005 edition. As of April 2007, the newly updated Web site has no information posted about these changes.

80. In the second edition, the statement is condensed. She continues to insist on privileging the accounts of survivors but does not elaborate as extensively as she does in the first edition. She shortens her statement and concludes this time with a quote that makes a distinction between truth and truthfulness from Charlotte Delbo, the French survivor of Auschwitz. "Today I am not sure that what I wrote is true. I am certain that it is truthful." This sums up Weiss's own stance. She seems to have condensed this discussion in order to make room on the bottom of the page for an update and for more information on the photo-

graph on the facing page. The story is about a woman who identified the man in the photo as her father after seeing it in a newspaper article about a talk Weiss was going to give. The story, told by this man's postwar American daughter, explains that the child depicted was murdered by the Nazis along with another sibling and their mother. The man, Leibl Henesh, survived. His story is told on p. 38 and continued on p. 113. See also note 86 below.

81. Here I am thinking about such dramatic changes as the removal of the two pages on the poet Desnos after she learned that the photograph she thought was Desnos was confirmed to be of someone else. See my discussion of this change below.

82. On this point, it was sad to see that no reference is made to the museum and its work; the efforts to take the photographs out of the albums in which they were found and to note what was written on their backs, discussed at length later in this chapter, is not acknowledged.

83. Although she says this most emphatically, having discovered that there is another volume devoted to these images not addressed by Weiss even in her second edition, I wonder about this claim. See my discussion of *Before They Perished . . .*, below.

84. On the two volumes and this process, see Janina Struk, *Photographing the Holocaust*, 198.

85. This talk, presented on the 45th Anniversary of the Warsaw Ghetto Uprising, on April 19, 1988, is included in Irena Klepfisz, "*Yom Hashoah, Yom Yerushalayim:* A Meditation," in Rita Falbel, Irena Klepfisz, and Donna Nevel, eds., *Jewish Women's Call for Peace: A Handbook for Jewish Women on the Israeli/Palestinian Conflict* (Ithaca, NY: Firebrand Books, 1990), 39–45. All subsequent references will be noted in the text with page numbers. A longer version of this essay, also entitled "*Yom Hashoah, Yom Yerushalayim:* A Meditation," is included in Irena Klepfisz, *Dreams of an Insomniac: Jewish Feminist Essays, Speeches, and Diatribes* (Portland, OR: Eighth Mountain Press, 1990), 115–140.

86. In the second edition, Weiss identifies the man and child in this photograph in an additional note on the bottom of this page. She writes, "Leibl Henesh, with child from his first family in Poland, identified by child from his second family in America. Stella Photo Studio, Zawiercie, Poland, a town in Silesia, near the German border, not far from Bedzin" (39). This same photograph is not identified in *Before They Perished . . .*; it is included on p. 210 as image number 4. The supplement copy reads, "Unknown people 1930s," and also includes the information about the photo studio. It is identified as image 3-0351. What is striking in comparing the two versions of this image is the way that Weiss has enhanced it. Instead of a small postcard portrait, the image is enlarged to bleed to the edges of an entire page. Because *Before They Perished . . .* reproduces the images in color, we see the sepia tone of the original. What is

most striking is how Weiss has cropped the image, taking out the oval frame and most of the discoloration in the original. Seeing this image, I was struck by both Weiss's aesthetic and her skill as a photographer, and I was also struck by the problems involved in changing the pictures, their size, framing, and condition in the process of copying them.

87. There is no discussion of this change in the second edition, nor any of the other changes, included on Weiss's Web site link devoted to updates. The man in the photograph, now not identified by Weiss as Desnos, is presented as unknown. There is, as in the original edition, a reference to the name on its back, "Leon" (Weiss, 2d edition, 75). This same photograph is identified more fully in *Before They Perished . . .* and its supplement. The photograph is included on p. 336 as image 2. The man in the picture is identified as Józef England. "Sosnowiec, 1930s Photo: Photo Apollo, Sosnowiec. Inscription on the back: Leon (. . .)." The photograph is number 3-0446 (Supplement, 106). It is accompanied on the facing page by another image of this same man with another man, and these are all part of a section devoted to "Machela and Josef England, Basia and Hersz Kugelman," one of the family groups. In the text this section runs from p. 329 to p. 342. The narrative about this section, and the information on all of the photographs identified as from this family, are on pp. 104–107 of the supplement. In the original 2001 edition of Weiss's book, the explanation for identifying the man in this photograph as Desnos reads as follows in a note on page 112: "Desnos's photograph was identified by Chattanooga poet Kemmer Anderson and his honors poetry class at the McCallie School, while on exhibition at the Hunter Museum of American Art, Chattanooga, Tennessee. Primary source material from Louis Simpson and Josef Stuna contributed greatly to the Desnos story, as did further research from journalist Michele Baum of the *Chattanooga Times,* who located a photograph of Desnos wearing the same overcoat."

88. This photograph is not further identified in the second edition. In *Before They Perished . . . ,* this photograph is presented in its actual postcard size and includes the identification of the photo studio at the bottom of the picture (p. 205, photograph 3). The explanation given on p. 71 of the supplement reads as follows: "Unknown People / Kudowa Zdrój / Photo: Arthur Giebel Bad Kudowa / Inscription on the front (German) Arthur Giebel Kudowa / Zdrój Honorary Gold Medal Prize. / Inscription on the back (German) Photograph: Arthur Giebel Atelier, Kudowa Zdój, the Merkury Villa. The first and oldest store on the square. Honorary gold medal prize, the plate awaits the next orders." The photograph is identified as 2-0739. The label on the front of the photograph is cropped out of Weiss's enlarged version of the picture and there is no reference to what is written on the back.

89. See pp. 216–221 of the second edition of Weiss's text.

90. Actually, all of the images of Jewish prisoners are reproduced. There

were other images included in the original collection, as both Weiss and the editors of this text acknowledge. The tensions around whether or not to include the Nazi photographs in the museum's publication was at issue as the various collaborators did the research that led to this publication. Email, Teresa Pollin, July 2006.

As Struk notes, neither volume includes these other photographs: see *Photographing the Holocaust,* 198.

91. Weiss, *The Last Album* (both editions), 25.

92. Although Weiss does talk about some of what is written on the backs of some of these pictures, she does not explain how she eventually gained access to the loose photographs. Readers do not learn when or where Weiss encountered the pictures finally, outside of the albums.

93. "To speed work on collecting information on those in the photographs, the Museum initiated cooperation with the Fritz Bauer Institute in Frankfurt am Main and the US Holocaust Memorial Museum in Washington (Genya Markon, Sharon Muller, Teresa Pollin)"; *Before They Perished . . . ,* Supplement, 4.

94. For full German references, see footnote 1, *Before They Perished . . . ,* Supplement, 6.

95. These sections play with the notion that photography captures a singular moment in time. Some of these section titles include: "1. Family Portrait, Będzin, 20.8.1996, 10 a.m."; "3. The Cemetery: Będzin, 20.8.1996, 11 a.m."; and "5. A View from the Castle, Będzin 1996, midday."

96. This reading is similar, in part, to the objections to Weiss's book and larger project raised by Pascale Bos. It is also somewhat different. Like me, Bos argues that Weiss's project is redemptive and, as such, problematic. Bos writes, "I find her [Weiss's] lecture presentation problematic because the story of the photos' (re-) 'discovery' and 'rescue' by Weiss, the child of survivors, who grew up without any photos of her own murdered relatives, becomes so central" (62). Despite this, in her reading of Weiss's book, Bos suggests that Weiss's overidentification as a child of survivors, albeit not from these towns, does have some merit: "Weiss presents her work as a personal mission, and the act of painstakingly reproducing and archiving these photos may well have served an important personal function for her, a daughter of survivors who grew up with few family pictures. This perhaps constitutes important 'postmemory work,' since, for Weiss, the photos can represent the loss of her family and of Eastern European Jewish culture, and allow for a process of mourning and 'working through'" (64).

Bos contrasts this position with how a general reader without familial connections to the Holocaust might approach this book. This is where I strongly take issue with Bos's reading. Although I appreciate how urgent these efforts may be for Weiss as a personal mission, I want to insist on knowing the difference, not only between general readers and our experiences but also between Weiss's own family album, however sparse it might be, and this collection of family photographs that once belonged to other victims and survivors of the Holocaust. Even children of survivors can, with all the best of intentions, engage in acts of "idiopathic narcissism," looking at and appropriating other people's suffering. For more on the problems involved in these kinds of appropriation in general, see both Bos and Hirsch on postmemory and the complexities of identification. Marianne Hirsch, *Family Frames: Photography, Narrative, and Postmemory* (Cambridge, MA: Harvard University Press, 1997); "Surviving Images: Holocaust Photographs and the Work of Postmemory," *Yale Journal of Criticism* 14.1 (Spring 2001), 5–37.

97. Weiss has information about some images that they do not. And the editors of *Before They Perished . . .* , in their narrative about the work of identifying the pictures, do not mention or give Weiss any credit for the work she did in recovering the photographs. The time period overlaps. Weiss began rephotographing the pictures in the late 1980s and early 1990s and began identifying those depicted while the collection was still pasted in the ledger books.

98. Salvage is itself a tricky notion. I cannot write the word without thinking about James Clifford's critique of "salvage ethnography." As Clifford explains, "The salvage paradigm reflect(s) a desire to rescue 'authenticity' out of destructive historical change" (121) and is tied to some of the deepest colonial assumptions at the heart of early 20th-century anthropology. See James Clifford, Virginia Dominguez, and Trinh T. Minh-H, "The Politics of Representation: Of Other Peoples: Beyond the 'Salvage Paradigm,' " in Hal Foster, ed., *DIA Foundation Discussions in Contemporary Culture* (Seattle: Bay Press, 1987), 121–150.

99. Bernstein, *Foregone Conclusions*; James E. Young, *Memory's Edge: After-Images of the Holocaust in Contemporary Art and Architecture* (New Haven, CT: Yale University Press, 2000).

100. Again, I am indebted to Bernstein for making this argument so persuasively in *Foregone Conclusions*.

101. Bernstein, *Foregone Conclusions*.

NOTES TO CHAPTER 4

1. Here I am referring to the notion of contemporaries described by Susan Suleiman in *Risking Who One Is: Encounters with Contemporary Art and Literature* (Cambridge, MA: Harvard University Press, 1994). See also my discussion in chapter 1 about my identification with the Dutch cultural critic Ernst van Alphen as my contemporary following Suleiman. For more on my engagement with van Alphen's work, see chapter 1.

2. Jonathan Rosen, *The Talmud and the Internet* (New York: Farrar, Straus

and Giroux, 2000); Daniel Mendelsohn, *The Elusive Embrace: Desire and the Riddle of Identity* (New York: Vintage Books, 1999).

3. As I first wrote these words, Mendelsohn was about to publish a book about his European family, the part of his family that did not survive the Holocaust. A portion of this book project was published in the *New York Times Magazine* cover story. Daniel Mendelsohn, "What Happened to Uncle Shmiel?" *New York Times Magazine*, July 14, 2002, 24–29, 38, 49, 52, 55. Since I wrote this chapter, Mendelsohn's book has been published and widely acclaimed. Daniel Mendelsohn, *The Lost: A Search for Six of the Six Million* (New York: HarperCollins, 2006).

4. Adrienne Rich, "Split at the Root," is included in her collection of essays, *Blood, Bread and Poetry: Selected Prose 1979–1985* (New York: W. W. Norton, 1986), 100–123. For Rich, the split is between her parents—her Jewish father and her Protestant mother.

5. This is also a predicament that Michelle Friedman and I have discussed on various occasions. Reading my work, she has always been struck by the ways the difficulties I describe also in part mark her experience. Like Rosen, Michelle is not only the child of a child survivor; but she is also, on her father's side, the child of immigrant American Jews.

6. I thank the students in my seminar on gendered Jewish narratives during the spring semester of 2005 at Williams College—Meg Bossong, Emily Gorin, and Deborah Hemel—for their insights into Mendelsohn's text. I am especially grateful to them for their insights into how Mendelsohn uses the classical tradition to build his contemporary notion of identity. This reading of Mendelsohn is indebted to those discussions.

7. Terrence Des Pres, *The Survivor: Anatomy of Life in the Death Camps* (New York: Oxford University Press, 1976, 1980).

8. This phrase comes from Irena Klepfisz's poem *Bashert*, "3. Brooklyn, 1971: I am almost equidistant from two continents." Irena Klepfisz, *Keeper of Accounts* (Watertown, MA: Persephone Press, 1982), 82–84.

9. The *Kindertransports* brought Jewish children from Austria and Germany to the British Isles during the war. They were separated from their parents and families. These transports ended up saving the lives of these children.

10. As Rosen explains a bit earlier in his narrative, "It is the side-by-side culture of the Talmud I like so much. 'On the one hand' and 'on the other hand' is frustrating for people seeking absolute faith, but for me it gives religion an ambidextrous quality that suits my temperament" (85). I was curious after reading this passage about what "ambidextrous" means. According to the various dictionary entries listed at www.dictionary.com, ambidextrous, as an adjective, means to be able to use both hands with equal facility. It also suggests that one is unusually skillful or adroit. And finally, as a third definition, it means to be deceptive or hypocritical. This third definition seems to come from Middle Eng-

lish, where *ambidexter* meant double-dealing. I do not see Rosen as double-dealing or deceptive, but I am struck by the notion that ambidextrous suggests only two sides, on the one hand and on the other, that there clearly are no other hands.

11. This phrase comes from Michelle Friedman. I am grateful to her for it. See Michelle Friedman, "The Labor of Remembrance," in Laurence Silberstein, ed., *Mapping Jewish Identities* (New York: NYU Press, 2000), 97–121, and Michelle Friedman, "Reckoning with Ghosts: Second Generation Holocaust Literature and the Labor of Remembrance," diss., Bryn Mawr College, 2001.

12. This is a familiar trope. Another example of this is Leo Spitzer's understated and powerful account of his aunt Ella and her marriage. See Leo Spitzer, *Hotel Bolivia: The Culture of Memory in a Refuge from Nazism* (New York: Hill and Wang, 1998), chapter 1, "Desperate Departures," 35–44.

13. "The Bride's Registry provides the full maiden name of every woman married in New York City between 1847 and 1937; beside her name, the number of the marriage certificate is listed, and using this number you can find the certificate, and, if you like, view it on a large, unwieldy, gunmetal-gray projector" (186).

14. The story is more complicated in Mendelsohn's beautiful narration. In fact, this man, the cousin/brother-in-law, ended up marrying yet another sister after Ray's death. For more on this more complete tale, see Mendelsohn's chapter 4, "Mythologies," 156–202.

15. Especially when children are still quite small, mothering is a more than full-time endeavor.

16. Here I am reminded of all of the haunting images of little girls and dolls in Abraham Ravett's film *Half-Sister*.

17. Here I want to be clear that I am *not* denigrating the role of mothering. I appreciate how difficult it is to mother and all of the structural obstacles that make mothering increasingly difficult. On these issues, see Miriam Peskowitz, *The Truth behind the Mommy Wars: Who Decides What Makes a Good Mother* (Seattle: Seal Press, 2005). I am trying to get at the difficulties and taboos around what it means for women to choose not to have children and how this decision remains unacceptable. I appreciate Miriam Peskowitz's asking me to discuss these issues as a part of her larger argument in *The Truth behind the Mommy Wars*.

18. I am somewhat embarrassed to admit this, but feel that I need to say this somewhere in this discussion; this doll is still with me. A number of years ago my mother brought boxes of my childhood possessions to Philadelphia. She insisted that they live at my house. Included among these things were many of my dolls. There were boxes of Barbie dolls, Tiny Tears, Thumbelina, and Chatty Cathy (I don't know what happened to her brother, Chatty Brother, whom I also owned). There was also the doll with the pink hair, as well as a few less-

cherished dolls. For a few years, the dolls sat in my basement. I couldn't open the boxes and sort through them. In the summer of 2004, I finally felt inspired, and I suspect that this had something to do with writing about Ravett's film. I cleared out many of the boxes and donated some of the contents to charity, but I kept most of the dolls. Not only did I keep them, but I also felt compelled to clean them up and find other places to store them. Among these was the doll with the pink hair. I washed her dress and cleaned her up as well. Her hair is a bit more unruly, and it has faded from the pink I once knew. I could not get rid of her even now. She is still among the dolls I most adored, those named above. And now they reside together in an antique trunk that includes all of my Barbie dolls and their clothes. There was a part of me that wanted to get rid of this doll even in the present, but I could not do it. The complicated embarrassment and shame that this doll invoked in me as a child persist. Somehow I cannot let myself hold on to only the name-brand dolls who were once gifts from my middle-class grandmother without also keeping the doll that Mary gave me.

19. Toni Morrison, *The Bluest Eye* (New York: Pocket Books, 1970).

20. Fortunately, these papers are still in trunks at my parents' house. They have not yet been shipped off to Philadelphia. In part, I insisted that they remain in their house as the last trace of my presence in this home. After my childhood bedroom was dismantled in the late 1980s at my request, my parents added the boxes of toys and dolls to these papers, which were already boxed up and in the basement.

21. In this I am reminded of Melissa Klapper's book on Jewish adolescent girls and her combing various American Jewish archives for the diaries of these middle-class Jewish girls, and what the diaries told Klapper about their lives. See Melissa Klapper, *Jewish Girls Coming of Age in America, 1860–1920* (New York: NYU Press, 2005). See also Rachel Kranson's review of this book. "Early 20th Century Jewish Girls," *Lilith* 30.2 (Summer 2005), 43–45.

22. Irena Klepfisz, "Women without Children/Women without Families/ Women Alone," in *Dreams of an Insomniac: Jewish Feminist Essays, Speeches and Diatribes* (Portland, OR: Eighth Mountain Press, 1990), 3–14.

23. For more information on object relations theory, see the various works of D. W. Winnicott. For a good introduction and various links to this work, go to http://www.mythosandlogos.com/Winnicott.html. For a classic feminist reading of object relations theory, see Jessica Benjamin, *The Bonds of Love: Psychoanalysis, Feminism, and the Problem of Domination* (New York: Pantheon Books, 1988).

24. Barbara Hahn, *The Jewess Pallas Athena: This Too a Theory of Modernity* (Princeton, NJ: Princeton University Press, 2005).

25. As I reflected on this section title, I was reminded of the words to the Beatles song "Let It Be." The lines that keep running through my head, however overdetermined they might be, are, "When I find myself in times of trouble,

Mother Mary comes to me, speaking words of wisdom, let it be." I understand that is a profoundly Christian reference, but given my grandmother Mary's role in my father's family, these words seem apt. And although I suspect that her name was in Yiddish or Hebrew "Miriam," part of her proud American identity was signified by this very American name. This was true for her and for my father. Even now when I tell people that my grandmother's name was "Mary," they are puzzled, not understanding why this Jewish woman was named Mary. In my extended family, there are in this same generation a number of other Marys, including the wife of one of my maternal grandfather's brothers, Mary Bialow.

26. Irena Klepfisz, *Keeper of Accounts* (Watertown, MA: Persephone Press, 1982).

27. Here I am struck by how much my discussion of what it means for me not to have children, in the account described in Miriam Peskowitz' book *The Truth behind the Mommy Wars*, echoes precisely the kinds of arguments Klepfisz made in 1977. See Peskowitz, *The Truth behind the Mommy Wars,* chapter 3.

28. This decision was also connected to the fact that Klepfisz is a lesbian feminist. And for her generation of lesbian feminists, the kinds of reproductive technologies now available were not yet available. On the issue of what it means to be a woman with children and even a lesbian with children, see Christie Balka, "Lesbian Parenting and Jewish Communities," *Bridges* 3.2 (Spring 1993), 57–65.

29. Some of the irony in all of this is that despite the longing for more Jewish babies, those in Jewish studies and in the larger world of Jewish communal and religious service—those most committed to Jewish continuity—have not figured out how to support the women in their ranks who do have children and want to both mother and run Jewish agencies or minister to Jewish religious congregations as rabbis. The statistics on the status of Jewish women professionals, much less the structures that are clearly not in place to support these women as mothers, especially the lack of high-quality child care in these various environments, all point to the fallacy in this argument. Despite insisting that Jewish women have babies, various and diverse Jewish communities, at least in the United States, have not made this a viable option or a communal priority. They have placed the burden of making this happen, the burden of parenting, solely on the backs of individual Jewish women who must make private arrangements for child care and spend precious individual resources in order to make all of this work. An exception to this pervasive problem is the work of the Center for Cultural Judaism. This secular Jewish organization has not only subsidized child care at the Association for Jewish Studies annual meetings since 2005, but it has also worked to provide child care for its staff and for scholars who attend its own academic conferences. See "Grant Enables Full Professional

Childcare at AJS Conference," *Reflections: Newsletter of The Center for Cultural Judaism,* Issue One (Fall 2006), 8. See also Megan Pincus Kajitani, "Finding a Parent-Friendly Place," *Chronicle of Higher Education,* July 26, 2006, http://chronicle.com/jobs/news/2006/07/2006072601c/careers.html.

In Israel, these issues are dealt with quite differently. Pronatal policies and child-care support in Israel contrast sharply with some of the obstacles faced by women in the United States; however, Israel poses its own complicated gender dynamics and problems. On pronatal politics and policies in Israel, see Susan Kahn's important book, *Reproducing Jews: A Cultural Account of Assisted Conception in Israel* (Durham, NC: Duke University Press, 2000).

30. For more on this problem, see the powerful, groundbreaking study of women in Jewish federations spearheaded by Shifra Bronznick and the similar finding of the recent report on the status of women rabbis in the Conservative movement. For a powerful analysis of the structural problems around parenting and especially mothering in the United States more broadly conceived, see Peskowitz, *The Truth behind the Mommy Wars.*

31. For this full discussion and the various women Klepfisz names, see "Jewish Lesbians, the Jewish Community, Jewish Survival," in *Dreams of an Insomniac,* 71–89, especially 77–78.

32. My mother retired in 1992 just as I begin teaching at Temple in my first academic position.

33. This former student is a published poet who ran an arts center. Not long after my first book was published, my mother sent him a copy of it. And in the strange way my family works, this man ended up writing a poem in response to my book. In truth, the poem is less about my book and more about what the subject matter triggered in him. Nevertheless, the poem was occasioned by my book and was published as such. It was a lovely and powerful gesture. At the time, we were in touch over email and I wrote to him about sharing my mother with all of her children, about the way I saw him as one of my other siblings. As I will explain, my understanding of this sharing has shifted since then. Kenneth Salzmann, "Psalm for Laura Levitt," in *Small, Round Words: Poems by Kenneth Salzmann* (2003). On the title page of this collection, Salzmann writes "for the Levitts." The poem, "Psalm for Laura Levitt," reads following its title, "*upon reading her book, Jews and Feminism: The Ambivalent Search for Home.*"

34. I thank Deborah Lamb for helping me to appreciate this aspect of my fascination. I didn't realize how fascinated I was with my mother, watching her in this role and not simply with her students. This is not an "either/or" situation, but I stress this fascination with my mother because it is only in this recent visit that I have been able to identify this aspect of my engagement and love of these visits.

35. Laura Levitt, review, "The Jewess Pallas Athena" in *Jewish Quarterly Review,* forthcoming.

36. See also Miriam Peskowitz and Laura Levitt, eds., *Judaism since Gender* (New York: Routledge, 1997).

37. Miriam Peskowitz has talked about writing a book about contemporary intellectual Jewish women, a book we often refer to as "the Smart Girls book." As I read Hahn's book, I could not help but think that this work is a brilliant prequel to that imagined volume.

38. In this I am keenly aware again of the difficulties all around, the ways that Miriam and I have continued to write as women with and without children.

39. I am grateful to Susan Shapiro for bringing this dictum to my attention. Telephone conversation, July 2005.

40. Here I think about some of the issues at the heart of my first book about multiple and shifting Jewish feminist identities; see Laura Levitt, *Jews and Feminism: The Ambivalent Search for Home,* as well as a quite specific discussion of this dilemma recounted in Teresa de Lauretis's "Feminist Studies/Critical Studies: Issues, Terms, and Contexts," her introduction to *Feminist Studies/Critical Studies* (Bloomington: Indiana University Press, 1986), 1–19. In this introduction, de Lauretis writes: "What is emerging in feminist writing is, instead, the concept of a multiple, shifting, and often self-contradictory identity, a subject that is not divided in, but rather at odds with, language; an identity made up of heterogeneous and heteronomous representations of gender, race, and class, and often indeed across languages and cultures; an identity that one decides to reclaim from a history of multiple assimilations, and that one insists on as a strategy: 'I think,' writes Elly Bulkin, 'of all the women [of mixed heritage] who, told to choose between or among identities, insist on selecting all' " (9). The Bulkin quote comes from Elly Bulkin, "Hard Ground: Jewish Identity, Racism, and Anti-Semitism," in Elly Bulkin, Minnie Bruce Pratt, and Barbara Smith, *Yours in Struggle: Three Feminist Perspectives on Anti-Semitism and Racism* (Brooklyn: Long Haul Press, 1984), 106.

41. I am grateful to one of the thoughtful anonymous readers of this manuscript for suggesting the link to *Kaddish* in all of this. For me, this ritual has been less salient, but I suspect that as my parents continue to age, it will become increasingly poignant. I am reminded not only of Wieseltier's book, but also of the powerful and painful feminist accounts of women who struggled to say *Kaddish* for their parents—Letty Pogrebin, Susannah Heschel, and Rachel Adler, among others. In a conversion with Catherine Staples, my former student, a woman who is older than I am, we laughed thinking about her saying *Kaddish* for me. As we continued to consider who might do this, she suggested her younger sister. Cathy's sister is a rocket scientist, otherwise known as a mechan-

ical and aerospace engineer. At the time, she was in the process of becoming an Orthodox Jew, and, as I pointed out to Cathy, as such could not be a viable candidate. She would find our creative considerations of this problem not particularly compelling, at least not now. And, as I told Cathy, I am not sure I want to burden anyone with this obligation. I would rather hope that someone might decide it is theirs to do, perhaps many years after I am gone, after reading these words. This conversation led me to think about Irena Klepfisz and who will say *Kaddish* for her. I wondered what it might mean to take on this kind of obligation for a writer I love. These are very difficult questions, and despite our levity, the conversation was not an easy one. The humor was utterly serious. Conversation with Catherine Staples, July 2006. I thank Cathy for understanding these things.

NOTES TO THE CONCLUSION

1. For an excellent account of this process, see Susannah Radstone's discussion of "memory work" in her edited volume, *Memory and Methodology* (Oxford, UK: Berg, 2000).

2. This title echoes the title of my essay, "Intimate Engagements: A Holocaust Lesson," *Nashim: A Journal of Jewish Women's Studies and Gender Studies,* no. 7 (Spring 5764/2004), 190–205.

3. This notion of the intersection of different legacies as they overlap with one another is part of what Michelle Friedman addresses in her reading of, among other texts, Steven Reich's "Different Trains." This musical composition brings together the composer's childhood memories of traveling by train across the United States, exciting journeys taken with his African-American nanny between New York and California. The composition includes the various voices that animated those trips in 1940, '41, '42, '43 . . . and other trains, the European trains that traversed Europe carrying other Jews to ghettos and concentration camps. Friedman argues that Reich is able to allow these different trains to be heard next to one another, to intersect and overlap, in some of the same ways photographer Shimon Attie does with his projections. Michelle Friedman, "Haunted by Memory: American Jewish Transformations," in Shelley Hornstein, Laura Levitt and Laurence Silberstein, eds., *Impossible Images: Contemporary Art after the Holocaust* (New York: NYU Press, 2003), 31–50.

4. I am indebted to Tania Oldenhage for this section. The text I am citing here is from an email Tania sent me June 2000. She wrote it from Ohio, where she and Markus were living at the time. Subsequent discussions have been via email between the United States and Switzerland, where Tania and Markus have been living since 2003.

5. Email to Laura Levitt from Tania Oldenhage, June 11, 2000.

6. Email to Laura Levitt from Tania Oldenhage, June 11, 2000.

7. For a dramatic example of this problem, see the critiques of German accounts of the rape of German women by Russian soldiers as they entered Berlin in 1945. "Berlin 1945: War and Rape, 'Liberators Take Liberties,'" special issue, *October 72* (Spring 1995). I thank Dagmar Hertzog for helping me remember this citation. I also thank Jay Lockenour for discussing these issues with me in relation to his work on German soldiers and their memories of victimization at the end of the war.

8. Tania Oldenhage, "Walking the Way of the Cross: German Places, Church Traditions, and Holocaust Memories," in Oren Stier and J. S. Landres, eds., *Recovering Memory: Exposing Religion, Violence, and the Remembrance of Place* (Bloomington: Indiana University Press, 2006), 89–99; Tania Oldenhage, "Reading the Cross at Auschwitz: Holocaust Memories und Passion Narratives," in Tod Linafelt, ed., *A Shadow of Glory: Reading the New Testament after the Holocaust* (New York: Routledge, 2002), 140–154; Tania Oldenhage, "Jüdische Dichtung und christliches Unbehagen. Zum Umgang mit jüdischen Texten in christlichen Kontexten," in K. v. Kellenbach, B. Krondorfer, N. Reck eds., *Von Gott reden im Land der Täter. Theologische Stimmen der dritten Generation seit der Shoah* (Darmstadt: Wissenschaftliche Buchgesellschaft, 2001), 257–268. What differentiates Tania Oldenhage's work from earlier efforts to see the Holocaust through Christian tropes and figures, and especially the Cross, is her insistence on the power of this trope for Christians and that the Cross cannot be seen as either the same or as an explanation of what the Holocaust means, even for Christians. She insists on the differences without denying the ways that Christian tropes and figures do inform how Christians engage with this historical trauma.

9. Toward the end of her memoir, Jane Lazarre writes, "How did I get to this place after so long a time, to be able to retrieve my mother's photograph from the bottom of a hutch drawer, frame it, and hang it on the wall?" (103). Jane Lazarre, *Wet Earth and Dreams: A Narrative of Grief and Recovery* (Durham, NC: Duke University Press, 1998).

10. Marian Ronan shared these stories with me in an email. All subsequent quotations come from this email. Email to Laura Levitt from Marian Ronan, February 26, 2005.

11. See Yaffa Eliach, *There Once Was a World: A 900-Year Chronicle of the Shtetl of Eishyshok* (New York: Little, Brown, 1998), for the book that is a companion to the exhibit. See also Kersten Brandt, Hanno Loewy, and Krystyna Olesky, eds., *Before They Perished . . . Photographs Found in Auschwitz* (Oświęcimiu: Państwowe Muzeum Auschwitz-Birkenau, 2001); Ann Weiss, *The Last Album: Eyes from the Ashes of Auschwitz-Birkenau* (New York: W. W. Norton, 2001); Ann Weiss, *The Last Album: Eyes from the Ashes of Auschwitz-Birkenau, Updated and Expanded* (Philadelphia: Jewish Publication Society, 2005).

12. I seem to have forgotten that there is something important about just being there. On this point see, Laura Levitt, "Refracted Visions: A Critique of 'Mirroring Evil: Nazi Imagery/Recent Art,'" *Studies in Gender and Sexuality* 6.2 (Spring 2005), 199–216.

13. Given the ongoing popularity of the museum, I was concerned that I would get there midweek confronted by busloads of school groups and that I would not be able to get in. As it turned out, I arrived early and was able to walk right in, but I do not think I was wrong to worry. It was a Tuesday morning in early October 2005. After having spent three hours in the museum, I overheard a regular visitor talking on his cell phone in the cafeteria telling whomever he was talking to how lucky he was to have been able to go right in. This was an unusual experience for him, a regular visitor to the museum.

14. On museums as sacred spaces that require certain ritualized behaviors, see Carol Duncan, *Civilizing Rituals: Inside Public Art Museums* (London, New York: Routledge, 1995).

15. I did not recall seeing this, but I was later told that this is the only room in the museum that has a mezuzah on its doorframe marking it as a Jewish space. I thank Oren Stier for telling me about this. Conversation, Fall 2006.

16. These images are included in Roman Vishniac, *A Vanished World* (New York: Farrar, Straus and Giroux, 1983).

17. And yet, it was only after I returned to Philadelphia and reread Marianne Hirsch's description of the permanent exhibit in *Family Frames,* which included a reference to this room, that I understood that it had been there all along. Marianne Hirsch, *Family Frames: Photography Narrative and Postmemory* (Cambridge, MA: Harvard University Press, 1997). I was so taken aback by this seemingly new discovery that I even wrote to my friend and colleague Oren Stier, who had recently been a fellow at the museum to ask if the room was a new addition. Email, October 2005. For a powerful and critical reading of the Vishniac photographs, see Carol Zemel, "Z'chor! Roman Vishniac's Photo-Eulogy of Eastern European Jews," in Julia Epstein and Lori Lefkovitz, eds., *Shaping Losses: Cultural Memory and the Holocaust* (Urbana: University of Illinois Press, 2001), 75–86.

18. As Marianne Hirsch explains, "Most of the photographs remain anonymous, but some have names and dates inscribed on them; some have arrows leading from a name to a face. Even these names, however, serve less to individualize then to generalize: in the photographs' multiplicity, the names become anonymous and generic"; *Family Frames,* 254.

19. I think that this is where a series of abstract paintings once hung. I recall that these paintings were criticized and later removed. In part, I remembered them because I had heard a paper about them at a small conference. Eric Zakim, Judaism Postmodernism Conference, Lehigh University, Bethlehem, PA.

20. This reading of the contrast between the Tower of Faces and the Ausch-

witz photographs is actually in sharp contrast to the reading of Weiss's book and the Tower offered by Pascale Bos. Although in many ways Bos and I share a commitment to a more rigorous interrogation of the allures of identification, especially in works of art and commemoration that use prewar family photographs, we come to somewhat different conclusions about the contextualization of the Tower of Faces in the USHMM. In part, I suspect that these differences are related to our different backgrounds. Bos is the child of survivors and, like Lori Lefkovitz, sees the photographs in the Tower and in books like Weiss's as especially close to home. For Bos, the distance between viewer/visitors and the images in the Tower is helpful. It offers a way of maintaining crucial distinctions between those depicted and viewers with no familial connections to the Holocaust. Pascale Bos, "Positionality and Postmemory in Scholarship on the Holocaust," in Ruth-Ellen Boetcher Joeres and Marjorie Gelus, eds., *Women in German Yearbook 2003: Feminist Studies in German Literature & Culture* (Lincoln: University of Nebraska Press, 2004), 50–74. Writing about what it is like to view the images in the Tower, Bos writes, "As the spectator is confined to different bridges each time, suspended in the air between the walls of the photos, the photo collection prevents the satisfying sense of completeness from taking hold that Weiss's collection elicits. In fact, as spectators we seem to 'miss' the encounter with many of the people in the portraits because they are too far away from us clearly to see them, and we are thereby confronted both with the fact that we literally 'missed' knowing these people while they were alive, and the realization that a complete presentation of the millions of people murdered by the Nazis, or even of the people of just one village, is not possible" (67). I cite Bos on this point because it is a powerful reading and I see it as the flip side of my own second reading of the Tower, in which I want more information as a way of making this same point. I think that both strategies perform a similar function. This is also echoed in Bos's reading of what she describes as the second part of Weiss's book, where the narratives of those depicted are very much a part of the text, again preventing readers and viewers from too facile an identification with the photographs Weiss has collected. "Through the in-depth interviews the photographs come to life and do justice to the victims, and a more appropriate distance between them, the Holocaust experience, and the viewer/reader is reinforced" (65). This is how I believe, at their best, both *Before They Perished . . .* and *The Last Album* may be read, given the extensive efforts of the editors to learn as much as possible about each photograph in the collection. This is part of what I want from the Tower. For another reading of the Tower that challenges Hirsch's notion of postmemory from the perspective of a child of survivors, see Adrienne Kertzer, "Circular Journeys and Glass Bridges: The Geography of Postmemory," in Marlene Kadar, Linda Warley, Jeanne Perreault, and Susanna Egan, eds., *Tracing the Autobiographical* (Waterloo, Ontario: Wilfrid Laurier University Press, 2005), 205–221.

21. The opening display includes the clear plastic man, the idealized model of the regime's eugenic vision for the future. Oddly, this model reminded me of an exhibit that had just opened in Philadelphia at the time of my trip to Washington: "Body Worlds: The Anatomical Exhibition of Real Human Bodies," the Franklin Institute, Philadelphia, October 7, 2005–April 23, 2006. This exhibit shows plasticized versions of actual human bodies. It is the work of Gunther von Hagen, a contemporary German artist. I thank David Watt for reminding me of this creepy connection.

22. This title is taken with liberty from Mary Gordon's *Shadow Man*; it is the title of the section of that book where she tries to explain to her long dead father what it has been like to try to discover who he had been. See my reading of this portion of Gordon's text in "Postmarked Pictures."

23. Klepfisz, *Dreams of an Insomniac*, 133.

24. In a discussion with some of the photography curators at the USHMM, I learned that there is a great deal of information on each of the individual photographs that make up the Tower. They are collected in the archive around family groupings and other themes. In addition to this, I learned that there have been some discussions about how to make identification of individual images easier to access in relation to the Tower. There was some discussion about a computer database that would follow the outline of the Tower and enable viewers to click on individual images and learn more about them. Right now, it remains difficult to easily identify any individual images because this mapping has not been done. This is a project I wish I had the skills to do, and I hope that others will take up the task. I thank Nancy J. Hartman, Museum Specialist in the Photo Reference Collection, for all of her help with this and many other matters. The staff at the USHMM photography archive and research center is extraordinary; it was a pleasure working with them. These conversations took place during a visit to the Photo Reference Collection, November 2006.

Bibliography

Aron, Bill. *Shalom Y'all: Images of Jewish Life in the American South*. Chapel Hill, NC: Algonquin Books, 2002.

Atkinson, Kate. *Case Histories*. New York and Boston: Little, Brown, 2004.

Azoulay, Ariella. "The [Blind] Gesture: Hiroshima." In *Death's Showcase: The Power of Image in Contemporary Democracy*, 76–88. Cambridge, MA: MIT Press, 2001.

Balka, Christie. "Lesbian Parenting and Jewish Communities." *Bridges*, 3.2 (Spring 1993): 57–65.

Bammer, Angelika. "Hamburg Memories." *German Quarterly Review*, 74.4 (Fall 2001): 355–367.

Barthes, Roland. *Camera Lucida: Reflections on Photography*. New York: Hill and Wang, 1981.

Benjamin, Walter. *Illumination: Essays and Reflections*. New York: Schocken, 1968.

"Berlin 1945: War and Rape, 'Liberators Take Liberties.'" Special issue, *October*, 72 (Spring 1995).

Bernstein, Michael André. *Foregone Conclusions: Against Apocalyptic History*. Berkeley: University of California Press, 1994.

Boetcher Joeres, Ruth-Ellen, and Marjorie Gelus, eds. *Women in German Yearbook 2003: Feminist Studies in German Literature and Culture*. Vol. 19. Lincoln: University of Nebraska Press, 2004.

Boyarin, Daniel, Daniel Itzkovitz, and Ann Pellegrini, eds. *Queer Theory and the Jewish Question*. New York: Columbia University Press, 2003.

Boyarin, Jonathan. *Storm out of Paradise: The Politics of Jewish Memory*. Minneapolis: University of Minnesota Press, 1992.

Brandt, Kersten, Hanno Loewy, and Krystyna Olesky, eds. *Before They Perished . . . Photographs Found in Auschwitz*. Os'wie,cimiu: Pan'stwowe Muzeum Auschwitz-Birkenau, 2001.

Browning, Christopher. *Ordinary Men*. New York: Harper Perennial, 1992.

Bulkin, Elly, Minnie Bruce Pratt, and Barbara Smith. *Yours in Struggle: Three Feminist Perspectives on Anti-Semitism and Racism*. Brooklyn, NY: Long Haul Press, 1984.

Burke, Michael D. "Making Contact with a Lost Sister, Hampshire College Filmmaker Reimagines a Child Lost to the Holocaust." *Daily Hampshire Gazette,* Northampton, MA, November 11, 1985, 10.

Clifford, James, Virginia Dominguez, and Trinh T. Minh-H. "The Politics of Representation: Of Other Peoples: Beyond the 'Salvage Paradigm.'" In Hal Foster, ed., *DIA Foundation Discussions in Contemporary Culture,* 121–150. Seattle: Bay Press, 1987.

Crane, Stephen. *War Is Kind.* Cambridge: University Press, 1899.

Cvetkovich, Ann. *An Archive of Feelings: Trauma, Sexuality, and Lesbian Public Cultures.* Durham, NC: Duke University Press, 2003.

Cvetkovich Ann, and Ann Pellegrini, eds. "Public Sentiments." *The Scholar and the Feminist Online,* 2.1 (Summer 2003), www.barnard.edu/sfonline.

De Lauretis, Teresa, ed. *Feminist Studies/Critical Studies.* Bloomington: Indiana University Press, 1986.

Des Pres, Terrence. *The Survivor: Anatomy of Life in the Death Camps.* New York: Oxford University Press, 1976, 1980.

Diner, Hasia, Jeffery Shandler, and Beth Wenger, eds. *Remembering The Lower East Side.* Bloomington: Indiana University Press, 2001.

Duncan, Carol. *Civilizing Rituals: Inside Public Art Museum.* New York: Routledge, 1995.

Eliach, Yaffa. *There Once Was a World: A 900-Year Chronicle of the Shtetl of Eishyshok.* New York: Little, Brown, 1998.

Eng, David, and David Kazanjian, eds. *Loss: The Politics of Mourning.* Berkeley: University of California Press, 2003.

Epstein, Julia, and Lori Hope Lefkovitz, eds. *Shaping Losses: Cultural Memory and the Holocaust.* Urbana and Chicago: University of Illinois Press, 2001.

Ezrahi, Sidra. *Booking Passage: Exile and Homecoming in Modern Jewish Imagination.* Berkeley: University of California Press, 2000.

Friedman, Michelle. "Reckoning with Ghosts: Second-Generation Holocaust Literature and the Labor of Remembrance." Diss., Bryn Mawr College, 2001.

Gordon, Avery. *Ghostly Matters: Haunting and the Sociological Imagination.* Minneapolis: University of Minnesota Press, 1997.

Gordon, Mary. *The Shadow Man: A Daughter's Search for Her Father.* New York: Random House, 1996.

Gornick, Vivian. *Fierce Attachments: A Memoir.* New York: Farrar, Straus and Giroux, 2005.

Graham, Don. *The Fiction of Frank Norris: The Aesthetics Context.* Columbia: University of Missouri Press, 1978.

Hahn, Barbara. *The Jewess Pallas Athena: This Too a Theory of Modernity.* Princeton, NJ: Princeton University Press, 2005.

Harris, Stefanie. "The Return of the Dead: Memory and Photography in W. G.

Sebald's *Die Auswanderten.*" *German Quarterly Review,* 74.4 (Fall 2001): 379–391.

Hartman, Geoffrey. *The Longest Shadow: In the Aftermath of the Holocaust.* New York: Palgrave Macmillan, 1996.

Hass, Aaron. *In the Shadow of the Holocaust: The Second Generation.* Ithaca, NY: Cornell University Press, 1990.

Hirsch, Marianne. "What's Wrong with These Terms? A Conversation with Barbara Kirshenblatt-Gimblett and Diana Taylor." *PMLA,* 120.5 (October 2005): 1497–1508.

———. *Family Frames: Photography, Narrative and Postmemory.* Cambridge: Harvard University Press, 1996.

———. "Surviving Images: Holocaust Photographs and the Work of Postmemory." *Yale Journal of Criticism,* 14.1 (Spring 2001): 5–38.

Hirsch, Marianne, ed., *The Familial Gaze.* Hanover, NH: University of New England Press, 1999.

Hornstein, Shelley. "Archiving Architecture of the Heart." In Shelley Hornstein, Laura Levitt, and Laurence Silberstein, eds., *Impossible Images: Contemporary Art after the Holocaust,* 13–30. New York: NYU Press, 2003.

Hornstein, Shelley, Laura Levitt, and Laurence Silberstein, eds. *Impossible Images: Contemporary Art after the Holocaust.* New York: NYU Press, 2003.

Huyssen, Andreas. "Monuments and Holocaust Memory in a Media Age." In *Twilight Memories: Marking Time in a Culture of Amnesia,* 249–260. New York: Routledge, 1995.

Jakobsen, Janet. "Queers Are Like Jews, Aren't They? Analogy and Alliance Politics." In Daniel Boyarin, Daniel Itzkovitz, and Ann Pellegrini, eds., *Queer Theory and the Jewish Question,* 64–89. New York: Columbia University Press, 2003.

Johnson, Barbara. *The Feminist Difference: Literature, Psychoanalysis, Race, and Gender.* Cambridge, MA: Harvard University Press, 1998.

Kadar, Marlene, Linda Warley, Jeanne Perreault, and Susanna Egan, eds. *Tracing the Autobiographical.* Waterloo, Ontario: Wilfrid Laurier University Press, 2005.

Kahn, Susan M. *Reproducing Jews: A Cultural Account of Assisted Conception in Israel.* Durham, NC: Duke University Press, 2000.

Katz, Joseph, ed. *The Complete Poems of Stephen Crane.* Ithaca, NY: Cornell University Press, 1966, 1972.

Kertzer, Adrienne. "Circular Journeys and Glass Bridges: The Geography of Postmemory." In Marlene Kadar, Linda Warley, Jeanne Perreault, and Susanna Egan, eds., *Tracing the Autobiographical,* 205–221. Waterloo, Ontario: Wilfrid Laurier University Press, 2005.

Klapper, Melissa. *Jewish Girls Coming of Age in America, 1860–1920.* New York: NYU Press, 2005.

Klarsfeld, Serge. *French Children of the Holocaust.* New York: NYU Press, 1995.

Kleeblatt, Norman, ed. *Mirroring Evil: Nazi Imagery/Recent Art.* New Brunswick, NJ: Rutgers University Press, 2001.

Klepfisz, Irena. *A Few Words in the Mother Tongue: Poems Selected and New (1971–1990).* Portland, OR: Eighth Mountain Press, 1990.

———. *Dreams of an Insomniac: Jewish Feminist Essays, Speeches, and Diatribes.* Portland, OR: Eighth Mountain Press, 1990.

———. *Keeper of Accounts.* Watertown, MA: Persephone Press, 1982.

Kranson, Rachel. Review of Melissa Klapper, *Jewish Girls Coming of Age in America, 1860–1920.* "Early 20th-Century Jewish Girls." *Lilith,* 30.2 (Summer 2005): 43–45.

Lazarre, Jane. *Wet Earth and Dreams: A Narrative of Grief and Recovery.* Durham, NC: Duke University Press, 1998.

Lefkovitz, Lori. "Inherited Memory and the Ethics of Ventriloquism." In Julia Epstein and Lori Hope Lefkovitz, eds., *Shaping Losses: Cultural Memory and the Holocaust,* 220–230. Urbana and Chicago: University of Illinois Press, 2001.

Levitt, Laura. "Intimate Engagements: A Holocaust Lesson." *Nashim: A Journal of Jewish Women's Studies and Gender Studies,* no. 7 (Spring 5764/2004): 190–205.

———. *Jews and Feminism: The Ambivalent Search for Home.* New York: Routledge, 1997.

———. "Photographing American Jews: Identifying American Jewish Life." In Laurence Silberstein, ed. *Mapping Jewish Identities,* 65–96. New York: NYU Press, 2000.

———. "Refracted Visions: A Critique of 'Mirroring Evil: Nazi Imagery/Recent Art.'" *Studies in Gender and Sexuality,* 6.2 (Spring 2005): 199–216.

———. Review of *Booking Passage. Jewish Quarterly Review,* 42.1–2 (July–October 2001): 237–242.

Levitt, Laura, ed. "Changing Focus: Family Photography and American Jewish Identity." *The Scholar and Feminist Online* 1.3 (Winter 2003), www.barnard .edu/sfonline.

Linenthal, Edward. *Preserving Memory: The Struggle to Create America's Holocaust Museum.* New York: Columbia University Press, 2001.

Liss, Andrea. *Trespassing through Shadows: Memory, Photography, and the Holocaust.* Minneapolis: University of Minnesota Press, 1998.

Marchand, Ernest. *Frank Norris: A Study.* New York: Octagon Books, 1981.

Marks, Laura. *The Skin of Film: Intercultural Cinema, Embodiment, and the Senses.* Durham, NC: Duke University Press, 2000.

Mavor, Carol. *Becoming: The Photographs of Clementina, Viscountess Hawarden.* Durham, NC: Duke University Press, 1999.

Mendelsohn, Daniel. *The Elusive Embrace: Desire and the Riddle of Identity.* New York: Vintage Books, 2000.

——. *The Lost: A Search for Six of the Six Million.* New York: HarperCollins, 2006.

——. "What Happened to Uncle Shmiel?" *New York Times Magazine,* July 14, 2002, 24–29, 38, 49, 52, 55.

Morrison, Toni. *The Bluest Eye.* New York: Pocket Books, 1970.

Norris, Frank. *Blix.* New York: Grosset and Dunlap.

Norris, Frank. *(I) Blix (II) Moran of the Lady Letty: A Story of Adventure off the California Coast.* Vol. 3. New York: Doubleday, Doran, 1928.

Novak, Peter. *The Holocaust in American Life.* Boston: Houghton Mifflin, 1999.

Oldenhage, Tania. *Parables for Our Time: Rereading New Testament Scholarship after the Holocaust.* New York: Oxford University Press, 2000.

——. "Reading the Cross at Auschwitz: Holocaust Memories and Passion Narratives." In Tod Linafelt, ed., *A Shadow of Glory: Reading the New Testament after the Holocaust,* 140–154. New York: Routledge, 2002.

——. "Walking the Way of the Cross: German Places, Church Traditions, and Holocaust Memories." In Oren Stier and J. S. Landres, eds., *Recovering Memory: Exposing Religion, Violence, and the Remembrance of Place,* 89–99. Bloomington: Indiana University Press, 2006.

Peskowitz, Miriam. *Spinning Fantasies: Rabbis, Gender, and History.* Berkeley: University of California Press, 1997.

——. *The Truth behind the Mommy Wars: Who Decides What Makes a Good Mother.* Seattle: Seal Press, 2005.

Peskowitz, Miriam, and Laura Levitt, eds. *Judaism since Gender.* New York: Routledge, 1997.

Pollin, Teresa. "Photographs from Auschwitz." *History of Photography,* 23.4 (Winter 1999): 350–356.

Ponomareff, Constantin V. *In the Shadow of the Holocaust and Other Essays.* Amsterdam and Atlanta: Rodopi Press, 1998.

Radstone, Susannah, ed. *Memory and Methodology.* Oxford, UK: Berg, 2000.

Reagan, Leslie J. *When Abortion Was a Crime: Women, Medicine, and Law in the United States, 1867–1973.* Berkeley: University of California Press, 1997.

Renov, Michael. "The Address of the Other: Ethical Discourse in *Everything's for You.*" In *The Subject of Documentary,* 159–167. Minneapolis: University of Minnesota Press, 2004.

Rich Adrienne. *Blood, Bread and Poetry: Selected Prose 1979–1985.* New York: W. W. Norton, 1986.

——. *The Dream of a Common Language: Poems 1974–1977.* New York: W. W. Norton, 1978.

Rosen, Jonathan. *The Talmud and the Internet: A Journey between Worlds.* New York: Farrar, Straus and Giroux, 2000.

Rosenstone, Robert A., ed. *Reinventing History: Film and the Construction of a New Past.* Princeton, NJ: Princeton University Press, 1995.

Roth, Michael S. "*Hiroshima Mon Amour,* You Must Remember This." In Robert A. Rosenstone, ed., *Reinventing History: Film and the Construction of a New Past,* 91–101. Princeton, NJ: Princeton University Press, 1995.

Schlant, Ernestine. *The Language of Silence: West German Literature and the Holocaust.* New York: Routledge, 1999.

Shapiro, Susan. "The Return(s) of the Uncanny in Post-Holocaust Discourse." In Marc Raphael, ed., *The Representation of the Holocaust in Literature and Film,* 113–138. Williamsburg, VA: College of William and Mary Press, 2003.

Silberstein, Laurence, ed. *Mapping Jewish Identities.* New York: NYU Press, 2000.

———. *The Postzionist Debates.* New York: Routledge, 1999.

Silverman, Kaja. *Threshold of the Visible World.* New York: Routledge, 1996.

Smith, Joel. "Roll Over—Analysis of Snapshot Photography, Photos of Everyday Life Not Initially Produced as Art." *Afterimage,* 29.1 (September/October 2001): 8–11.

Solomon, Deborah. "The Rescue Artist." *New York Times Magazine,* February 27, 2005, 40–45.

Spitzer, Leo. *Hotel Bolivia: The Culture of Memory in a Refuge from Nazism.* New York: Hill and Wang, 1998.

Stier, Oren. *Committed to Memory: Cultural Mediation of the Holocaust.* Amherst: University of Massachusetts Press, 2003.

Struk, Janina. *Photographing the Holocaust: Interpretations of the Evidence.* London: I. B. Tauris, 2005.

Suleiman, Susan Rubin. *Risking Who One Is: Encounters with Contemporary Art and Literature.* Cambridge, MA: Harvard University Press, 1994.

Sultan, Larry. *Pictures from Home.* New York: Harry N. Abrams, 1992.

Torgovnick, Marianna. "The Politics of the 'We.' " In Marianna Torgovnick, ed., *Eloquent Obsessions: Writing Cultural Criticism,* 260–277. Durham, NC: Duke University Press, 1994.

van Alphen, Ernst. *Caught by History: Holocaust Effects in Contemporary Art, Literature, and Theory.* Stanford, CA: Stanford University Press, 1997.

Vishniac, Roman. *A Vanished World.* New York: Farrar, Straus and Giroux, 1983.

Walker, Franklin. *Frank Norris: A Biography.* New York: Doubleday, Doran, 1932.

Walker, Janet. *Trauma Cinema: Documenting Incest and the Holocaust.* Berkeley: University of California Press, 2005.

Weiss, Ann. *The Last Album: Eyes from the Ashes of Auschwitz-Birkenau.* New York: W. W. Norton, 2001.

———. *The Last Album: Eyes from the Ashes of Auschwitz-Birkenau, Updated and Expanded.* Philadelphia: Jewish Publication Society, 2005.

Weissman, Gary. *Fantasies of Witnessing: Postwar Efforts to Experience the Holocaust.* Ithaca, NY: Cornell University Press, 2004.

Wenger, Beth. "Memory as Identity: The Invention of the Lower East Side." *American Jewish History,* 85.1 (March 1997): 3–27.

Wieseltier, Leon. *Kaddish.* New York: Vintage, 1998.

Young, James E. *At Memory's Edge: After-Images of the Holocaust in Contemporary Art and Architecture.* New Haven, CT: Yale University Press, 2000.

———. "The Biography of a Memorial Icon: Nathan Rapoport's Warsaw Ghetto Monument." *Representations,* 26 (Spring 1989): 69–106.

———. *Writing and Rewriting the Holocaust: Narrative and the Consequences of Interpretation.* Bloomington: Indiana University Press, 1988.

Zelizer, Barbie, ed. *Visual Culture and the Holocaust.* New Brunswick, NJ: Rutgers University Press, 2000.

Zemel, Carol. "Z'chor! Roman Vishniac's Photo-Eulogy of Eastern European Jews." In Julia Epstein and Lori Lefkovitz, eds., *Shaping Losses: Cultural Memory and the Holocaust,* 75–86. Urbana: University of Illinois Press, 2001.

Zerubavel, Yael. *Recovered Roots: Collective Memory and the Making of Israeli National Tradition.* Chicago: University of Chicago Press, 1995.

Index

About the Author

Laura Levitt is the director of Jewish Studies and an Associate Professor of Religion at Temple University. She is the author of *Jews and Feminism: The Ambivalent Search for Home* (1997), and with Shelley Hornstein and Laurence Silberstein, an editor of *Impossible Images: Contemporary Art after the Holocaust* (2003) and co-editor with Miriam Peskowitz of *Judaism since Gender* (1997).